Don Shaw

CLOUGH'S
WAR

EBURY
PRESS

1 3 5 7 9 10 8 6 4 2

Published in 2010 by Ebury Press, an imprint of Ebury Publishing
A Random House Group company

First published in the UK by Ebury Publishing in 2009
This edition published in 2010

The Random House Group Limited Reg. No. 954009

Addresses for companies within the Random House Group
can be found at www.randomhouse.co.uk

A CIP catalogue record for this book is available from the British Library

The Random House Group Limited supports The Forest Stewardship
Council (FSC), the leading international forest certification organisation.
All our titles that are printed on Greenpeace approved FSC certified paper
carry the FSC logo. Our paper procurement policy can be found at
www.rbooks.co.uk/environment

Mixed Sources
Product group from well-managed
forests and other controlled sources
www.fsc.org Cert no. TT-COC-2139
© 1996 Forest Stewardship Council
FSC

Printed in the UK by CPI Cox & Wyman, Reading, RG1 8EX

ISBN 9780091928643

To buy books by your favourite authors and register for offers visit
www.rbooks.co.uk

contents

Dramatis Personae v
Author's Note vii

1: Overthrown 1
2: Uprising 13
3: Mutiny 31
4: Attack 42
5: Counter Attack 53
6: In the Trenches 66
7: Over the Top 81
8: Open Warfare 91
9: Entrapped 101
10: Raiding Party 109
11: Espionage 123
12: Strike 131
13: Bloody Sunday 147
14: Operation Clough 163
15: Operation Snowball 180
16: Cloak and Dagger 191
17: Downfall 197
18: Traitor 208
19: Ambushed 218
20: Never Say Die 229
21: Requiem 237

Acknowledgements 247

To my grandson Zak, already courted at the age of six years and one month by two premiership clubs.

I just hope he plays for Derby, in whichever league they may reside.

Except Third Division North.

dramatis personae

THE BOARD
SAM LONGSON – Chairman
SYDNEY BRADLEY – Director
GEORGE HARDY – Director
BOB INNES – Director
MIKE KEELING – Director
BOB KIRKLAND – Director
JACK KIRKLAND – Director
HARRY PAINE – Director
KEN TURNER – Director

INSIDE DERBY COUNTY
SIR ROBERSTON KING – President
BRIAN CLOUGH – Manager
PETER TAYLOR – Assistant manager
STUART WEBB – Club Secretary
JIMMY GORDON – Trainer

PLAYERS
COLIN BOULTON
WILLIE CARLIN
ARCHIE GEMMILL
KEVIN HECTOR
ALAN HINTON
DAVE MACKAY
ROY McFARLAND
JOHN McGOVERN
HENRY NEWTON

DAVID NISH
JOHN O'HARE
JOHN ROBSON
COLIN TODD
RONNIE WEBSTER
TOMMY MASON (a reserve)

JOURNALISTS
MIKE CAREY – Local and national newspapers
GEORGE EDWARDS – *Derby Evening Telegraph*
JOHN HALL – Radio Derby
NEIL HALLAM – Local and national newspapers
MIKE INGHAM – Radio Derby commentator
GERALD MORTIMER – *Derby Evening Telegraph*
GARY NEWBON – ATV Sport presenter.

PROTEST MOVEMENT
DON SHAW – Writer
BILL HOLMES – Brewery Manager
JOHN McGUINNESS – Health-club owner

OUTSIDE DERBY COUNTY
BARBARA CLOUGH – Wife of Brian
DERRICK ROBINS – Chairman of Coventry City FC
LOUIS EDWARDS – Chairman of Manchester United FC

MEMBERS OF PARLIAMENT
PHILIP WHITEHEAD – MP Derby North
DENIS HOWELL – Minister for Sport

author's note

IN THE PREPARATION and writing of *Clough's War* the diaries I kept proved invaluable. Exploring by Internet revealed many Clough-orientated newspaper reports and articles which were extremely productive. I also owe a debt to the *Derby Evening Telegraph*'s website for its wonderfully nostalgic 'Bygone Derbyshire'. The Derby County website also added to the research material, as well as introducing me to an enthusiastic fan, Kalwinder Singh Dhindsa. Kal collected photographs and other memorabilia of the Protest Movement's activities, all of them helping to establish dates and details of meetings as well as stirring my recollection of its sense of urgency and commitment.

The players involved, Kevin Hector and Roy McFarland in particular, threw up fascinating stories and gave me snippets of information that occasionally contradicted opinions and views on Clough written by sports writers and others since his death in 2004.

Libby Clough helped with domestic detail and assisted in trying to track down the owners of photographic copyright.

Sam Longson's autobiographical account in his *Memoirs* was proof enough that he had found an ally in Stuart Webb, whose part in bringing about Clough's departure from Derby County has long been a subject of passionate argument. At a Baseball Ground meeting I had with him in 1984 he gave me an account of the legendary wastepaper baskets incident and its link in the chain of events leading to Clough's resignation. It proved most useful. His own version of events in his book *Stuart Webb: My Derby County Years* also helped give an all-round perspective.

However, of all the books and many articles written about Clough, it was Tony Francis's *Clough* which was most productive, ironical in that I had assisted him in the researching of it in 1984–5.

Duncan Hamilton's *Provided You Don't Kiss Me*, an account of his association with Clough in his time at Nottingham Forest, helped confirm details of Clough's life after Derby County.

The Real Mackay, by Dave Mackay, *Cloughie: Walking On Water*, by Clough himself, *Derby County: The Complete Record* by Gerald Mortimer, *Toddy: The Colin Todd Story* by Colin Todd and *Right Place Right Time*, the latter by my friend George Edwards, were all useful.

The official *Clough: The Autobiography* was illuminating, helping me to understand how the influence of a strong and proud mother helped fashion Clough into the image of a working-class hero, as well as football icon.

It is not normal for writers to criticise each other, but I had no choice when, in November 2007, Barbara Clough having heard of my feelings about my own depiction in *The Damned United*, asked me to express publicly her abhorrence of the way Brian had been treated in the book.

I obliged. Clough never used the 'F' word with me or any player and had given up smoking long before he came to Derby. *The Damned United* features me as a character called 'John Shaw' and embellishes some anecdotes and dialogue I gave to Tony Francis for his book. This is my attempt to set the record straight and draw the man as I knew him.

Fans and friends from the Protest Movement furnished me with their own memories of events as well as a number of Rams fans who emailed me with their personal memories of the most exciting and dramatic years in the history of Derby County.

THE USE OF dialogue in situations beyond my personal knowledge, or from the recollection of individuals involved, I justify on the grounds of dramatic licence. It is deployed at pivotal moments in the story, hoping to give a better understanding and explanation as to why events occurred than would be provided by the use of pure narrative. I hasten to add that the 'invented' dialogue in scenes in which I was not involved, are in the minority.

1

OVERTHROWN

Sunday, 21 October 1973

BRIAN CLOUGH, wearing slippers and smartly dressed in white shirt, tie and dark trousers, stood in his front doorway giving furtive glances up and down the road. At the same time he made paddling gestures with his hand, quickly bidding Liz and I to enter, with our small son, Martin.

Clough closed the door. 'Snappers. Can't be too careful.' Facing Liz, he gave a stiff bow of the head as if to royalty, stuck out his hand and smiled charmingly. 'You're Liz. You're lovely.'

Liz, smiling, shook his hand. 'Hello.'

He turned to me. 'And you're Don and your hair needs cutting.'

We all laughed. Clough grinned at Liz, while nodding sideways at me. 'Are you my saviour, or him? I'd rather have you. Far more pretty.' He led us into the lounge, a solid, well-furnished room. A budgie cheeped in a cage by the window.

'Nigel? Guests here!'

Seven-year-old Nigel walked in, neatly dressed in pullover and short trousers. He stood, feet together dutifully, awaiting orders.

'Nigel. Take Martin to feed the rabbits then upstairs to play with your *trains*.' It came out as 'trayearns' – the familiar Clough twang, the rising inflection and stress on the last syllable.

Nigel obediently led Martin out of the room.

Clough offered Liz an armchair. 'Don, you sit over there. So I can take a good look at *yoou*.' He went to the sideboard. 'In your honour, Liz, champagne. Breakfast's as good a time for champagne as any, eh?'

We laughed politely as he deftly screwed and unplugged the cork. The foam was caught in the glass, topped up and handed to Liz. 'Full English breakfast, madam? He adopted the pose of a waiter.

'Pardon?' Liz hesitated. 'Oh...no. We're just toast and coffee. Thanks.'

'Continental. Easily done. Barbara, this is Liz and Don. My best half.'

His wife had entered the room, dark, petite, attractively round-faced and smiling. The pleasant introductions over, she went back into the kitchen.

Clough sat down to face me, chin lowered and peering at me with the expression of a headmaster scrutinising a wayward school-boy, the look veering on the edge of disapproval, but receptive in case my excuse sounded reasonable. I squirmed inwardly but tried not to look nervous.

Finally Clough spoke. 'George said you've just come back from Israel.'

George Edwards, who had arranged the meeting, was the sports editor at the *Derby Evening Telegraph*.

'Yes,' I said. 'It was a Hollywood film. About Wingate. I was there when the war broke out.'

'Wingate,' said Clough. 'There was a man. All of us scared of the Japs. We can beat them, he said. All it needs is belief. Did you see *Patton: Lust for Glory*? He'd have gone to Berlin if they'd given him diesel for his tanks. Men behind the front lines. Makes you sick.' He paused. 'Israel. We've got fans there.'

'Yes,' I said. 'They take *Star Soccer* from ATV. Derby's on prac-tically every week.'

Clough's finger was pointed at me, the rest of the hand immo-bile. 'So what are you going to do for me?'

I was thrown by the suddenness of the sharp question. 'Well, try and get you back.' It sounded pathetic.

'No'. Clough leaned forward, intently. 'What are you going *to do* to get me back? I'm not crawling on my hands and knees. They've got to ask me back. Where do you sit?'

'Sorry?'

'Sit. At the ground?'

'Oh. The Ley Stand.'

'I got that built. The chairman told me we couldn't afford it. A Division One team? Couldn't afford it?' He shook his head in contempt. 'All we needed was a bit of land off a dirty great factory next door. I said I'll make them an offer they can't refuse. I went round to the factory, dragged out the boss and I measured the area we needed. I did that. Every bit of progress in that club is down to me.' Clough took a sip from his glass. 'Every bit.'

In his bitterness I sensed a vulnerability, which was surprising. 'There's nobody in Derby who isn't against the board,' I said, in a lame attempt to offer him support. I felt totally inadequate. This was the god I regularly worshipped at the Baseball Ground, the home of Derby County Football Club. An imperious god, unapproachable, unbeatable, someone who had metamorphosed soccer management into the cult of the personality. I struggled to find what to say next. But Clough, as if suspecting a chink had shown in his armour, was at me in a flash.

'Okay. You've got a movement,' he said briskly. 'You're having a march next Saturday. From where to where?'

'From the Market Place to the ground.'

Clough shook his head peremptorily. 'Won't do a thing. Won't shift them. Not Longson and Webb.' Longson was chairman, Webb the secretary.

'Okay.' I took a breath. 'We think you should go to the match. The crowd will demand you back.'

'They won't let me in. The ground staff have orders. How do I get through the turnstiles?'

'Wear a cap, scarf high up, coat collar tucked up. And glasses. Big horned ones.'

'And do what?'

'Walk around the track perimeter. It's bound to get the crowd going.'

'I'm not walking round the pitch. I'm not being carted off by

3

stewards. Me, dragged out of my own ground on *The Nine O'Clock News*?' The headmaster's frown intensified as Clough took a larger sip of champagne. Suddenly he stood up, giving me a 'wait, got something to show you' gesture and went out of the room, leaving Liz and I to lift eyebrows at each other. I could hear boyish laughter and scuffling sounds as Martin and Nigel scrambled upstairs.

Somewhere a clock chimed the hour, ten o'clock. For the past five days I'd hardly noticed the time, working sixteen hours a day in meetings and phone calls. It was difficult to believe that it was only five days since I had come across the news placard at the corner of St James Street and Victoria Street in the middle of town.

3 p.m., Tuesday, 16 October 1973, Raining

LIKE THE GRIM REAPER that bloke, standing pale and drawn, selling the *Derby Evening Telegraph* since I was at school, his placard proclaiming every world shaking news event. 1948: 'Gandi Murdered'; 1958: 'Man Utd Crash. Many dead'; 1961: 'Russian in Space'; 1963: 'Cuba. Atomic threat'; …and now, 1973: 'Clough Quits'.

Shocked, I bought a paper, scanned the front-page story and then broke into a run, bound for Northcliffe House opposite the fish market, the home of the *Derby Evening Telegraph*. I managed to speak to George Edwards. He told me that Clough had resigned in a fit of temper at the way he'd been treated by the directors, especially Longson, the chairman. He hadn't expected it to be accepted and so it had come as a shock. Edwards thought that Longson had set a trap into which Clough had fallen. He had no more information. But he was pleased to report my concern.

The late edition of the *Derby Evening Telegraph* led the front page with the headline 'Clough Resigns'. The story was careful to avoid any controversy, stating that the board of directors 'felt it unable to work with the manager…the feeling was mutual and in the interest of both parties Clough had tendered his resignation, which had been accepted.' A side column reported that 'Don Shaw, the well-known local playwright' was seeking to form an action group.

Within less than an hour of publication I was called into Radio Derby for a 'live special', debating the crisis at Derby County. I expressed my shock, along with three football reporters from newspapers and radio. Such was the unanimous pro-Clough view that the station manager switched off the red light and brought the broadcast to a temporary halt, calling for a balanced argument. Appeals were made to the public in general. But there were no 'fans' prepared to support Clough's virtual dismissal. The community, to a man, wanted not a balanced discussion, but Clough's immediate reinstatement. Unsurprisingly, no one was 'available for comment' at the Baseball Ground.

The following morning the national tabloids seized on the story, some splashing it on the front page. Clough was a national celebrity, a favourite on chat shows and constantly in the news for his unpredictable and sometimes outrageous comments. News of his 'sacking' was not just a local drama but resonated around Britain, even reaching foreign newspapers.

George Edwards rang me with the telephone numbers of fans anxious to help start up an action group. I contacted as many as I could, each one in turn promising to bring along a fellow fan or two.

That night we assembled in the lounge bar of the Crest Hotel, a crowd that was so large, we had to adjourn to the wedding reception room.

Questions were immediately asked, some in anger, about the absence of Mike Keeling, a club director who had resigned in sympathy with Clough. I had hoped that he would have led the campaign. In his absence, I was elected leader of the Derby County Protest Movement. Then votes were taken to elect two men to serve alongside me. We wanted someone who had experience of public relations and could act as general adviser on strategy, plus someone who had the time and contacts to get involved with the day to day running of the Movement.

Bill Holmes volunteered himself to act as chief adviser. He was a smooth speaking, delicately featured and slightly built man in his late forties, exhibiting a genteel charm, a manager of one of the major breweries in Burton upon Trent.

John McGuinness, well known in Derby as a health-club owner, put himself forward as the 'hands on' activist. He was a dead ringer for Popeye, the cartoon character, an Irishman of diminutive stature with a withered leg. His handicap, however, was compensated with him having a barrel-like chest and bulging muscles in his upper body, the product of many hours spent in his gymnasium.

The meeting ended with a decision to hold a public meeting at the Grand Theatre, Babington Lane. The campaign to save Brian Clough for Derby County had begun. I had no idea of the trauma that lay ahead.

I'D SUPPORTED THE Rams since that day during the Second World War when, as a ten-year-old, wearing a brand-new black-and-white rosette and waving a wooden rattle, I had watched Derby beat Leicester in the Midlands Cup. Two years later, in 1946, my post-man dad won the lottery prize of a ticket for Wembley where we beat Charlton in the FA Cup Final. I had listened to the match, ear pressed to an Ultra wireless, its faint crackly reception as if coming from a hut in the Antarctic.

And only forty-odd hours after the victory, as I walked to school with other lads, we spotted the hero of the Final sitting in his furni-ture van munching a bun and drinking from a flask of tea. 'Riddell & Stamps Removals' it said on the front. Jack Stamps never earned more than eight pounds a week as a footballer.

In those austere years, when an apple core was worth begging for and when central heating, pyjamas and a bathroom were mostly absent in the homes of the working classes, professional football provided a wage equal to that of a manual worker and no more. The players were worshipped by the fans much as they are today, but it was the expression of that high regard that was different. Respect for adults and their privacy over-rode any temptation on our part to rush to the cab and ask for his autograph.

What did we Bemrose Grammar School kids do, that distant time ago, to acknowledge our hero's triumph in the greatest of all foot-ball competitions? A shy grin, or a wave, was all we could muster.

Days after our Wembley victory I stood outside Derby Police Station to applaud the players as they ended their victory procession through the streets. Out they came one by one on the balcony. Woodley, Howe, Leuty, Bullions, Musson, Nicholas, Harrison, Stamps, Carter, Docherty, Duncan.

'Thanks' each said, brief and matter-of-fact, and what do you expect from men who earned less than many of their fans, a large percentage of whom were Rolls-Royce workers in the town, part of a twenty eight thousand strong work force? And what was each player's reward for winning the Cup? Thirty quid a man, plus the medal. Carter, inside forward and pride of England, lived in a semi-detached house close to where I lived in the working-class district of Chaddes-den. He would walk his dog down the road towards where we kicked a ball on the green. How we strived to show off our skills as 'Raich' watched us from its edge. But approach – let alone speak to him?

Even when he sat with us on the number 66 trolley bus wending its way to the Saturday afternoon match we dare not address him. Shout at him, yes, but on the pitch. Everything had its place in those days when the main source of entertainment for the working man was football. But football on a pitch, not on a TV set as the latter was unknown. And, because travel to away games was often too expensive the fortnightly wait aroused lip-smacking sensations. Heroes like Jack Stamps were only seen in action about fourteen times a year. Thus, in him and his teammates resided all our dreams and hopes.

And, in such reverie, we made them gods, deserving of space and dignity. As a child I kept scrapbooks of Derby County, cutting out and pasting in newspaper photographs of the players in action. I paid my sixpence to enter the boys' enclosure at the Baseball Ground for each game. I was captivated, hooked, a Rams fan until I died.

Once, for an important cup-tie, the 'boys' entrance had the 'full' notice pinned to it, so I managed to nip under a turnstile and quickly get lost in the adult, Osmaston end of the ground. Knowing I had no chance of actually seeing the match, I was content with the smell of Woodbine cigarettes mingling with the musky odour of damp clothing. And, unable to reach the brick open lavatory block, peed between a forest of black shoes. Stuffing my willy back inside my pants, I suddenly found myself elevated by a pair of strong hands and passed over a carpet of cloth-capped heads.

'Lad coming over, in front!' Heads turned. Disciplined heads. Men who'd served in the Sherwood Foresters, been captured at Singapore and tortured by the Japanese. Men who worked from 8 a.m. till 5 p.m. every day of the week and for whom sick notes meant they really were sick.

I ended up placed behind the goal netting to stare at the immense hands of Frank Swift, the visiting goalkeeper. At that moment, sitting in majesty with an unimpeded view of the game, I would not have exchanged it for anything on earth.

There was no choral chanting or singing – and no pushing. They were to be invented by Liverpool fans in the early Beatle days. The 40,000 crowd 'ooh'ed and 'aah'ed as the shots came and missed, as if one giant instrument.

Sixty-four years on I still remember that game, which we won, as Wordsworth did of nature: 'Felt in the blood and felt along the heart, and passing even into my purer mind with tranquil restoration.'

As I grew older and taller and able to peer over shoulders I, too, became an element in the electricity that flows through a crowd as the teams run out from the tunnel. If the game was really important the starting whistle tripped a thrill through the body that changed to delirium if we scored a goal, all workaday worries forgotten.

In 1948 Arsenal had gone eighteen games without losing. As a dispensation my mam and dad allowed me to queue all night for a ticket in the hope we'd put an end to the 'Brylcreem Boys' record.

For hours I joined other lads in a makeshift game with a bald tennis ball and then lay curled up on the blue tiled pavement. At 5 p.m. the next day, tired but exuberant, I went home with a neat 1–0 victory shouting in my head.

Later, in my twenties, I watched Derby take on Middlesborough at the Baseball Ground. I was impressed by their centre forward, his hair in a shaved crew cut, leading the line, shouting, leaping and diving. He scored a goal and made another. Number 9: Brian Clough.

CLOUGH RETURNED TO the living room, clutching a bunch of tickets. 'Right,' he said. 'These are for the Leicester game on Saturday. Give them out free to anybody who'll shout up for me.'

'So you're going,' I said.

He paused, irritated slightly. 'Don. I've a lot to think about.'

We had breakfast with the family, Elizabeth in her carrycot. The brothers, Simon and Nigel, were calm and quiet, a perfect example of well-brought-up children. It struck me then that the public perception of Clough – loud mouthed, boorish and rude – was not in evidence that morning. Yes, wives and children were present, but in all our subsequent meetings I never heard him utter swear words of four letters, nor had he a reputation in the town for incivility. On the contrary, he was well known for being a gentleman, easily angered by anti-social behaviour and unfairness of any kind, ever courteous to strangers and the elderly. My dignified mother-in-law adored him. He was difficult to assess, never a man for all seasons.

His haircut remark, though made in jest, stemmed from an aversion to long hair. Clough, an ex-National Serviceman, believed, as did the military, that the image and feel of a squad on the parade ground had to be that of a single unit. For 'squad' read 'team' and for 'parade ground' read 'pitch'. None of the players today seen sporting dyed hair, Mohawk crops or wearing Alice bands would have had a place in Clough's Derby side, regardless of talent.

After breakfast, we said our goodbyes. 'Will you give it a go on Saturday?' I asked at the doorway, tensing myself for a sharp retort.

'Hope to,' he said abruptly, checking to ensure there were no photographers lurking.

We crossed the road to where a small, estate-type house of yellow brick stood. Number 11, Ferrers Way, was the Cloughs' first house in Derby, the mortgage paid out of his £100 per week wage. As his income grew, he had bought number 28, a more substantial house with a bigger garden, the kind of move a careful, conventional Rolls-Royce engineer would have made after a wage rise.

I'd imagined Cloughie to have lived in something more flamboyant, not what you might expect from a TV celebrity, image self-fashioned by wild and extravagant outbursts. 'Old Big 'ead' was, in matters of lifestyle, very ordinary. It was just one of the contradictions I would come across in the life of Brian Clough.

'Eh.'

I turned. He stood in his doorway, arm outstretched. 'You look after her, your missus. I don't want you spending all your time on me. Or else...' He left the threat lingering and went back into the house. That was the players' Clough, atavistic, striding at you finger pointed, eyes unblinking, brutal, unafraid, leaving you not knowing whether he came to shake your hand or give you a good clout.

Liz gave a short laugh, but she was seeing the other Clough, charismatic, charming and graceful. 'My mother will be so jealous! What a lovely man. What style. Champagne, at breakfast. In our honour. Oh my.' She clutched her chest in pleasure.

It was many years before I discovered he drank it every morning.

UNTIL THE ARRIVAL of Brian Clough – and as long as I could remember – The Baseball Ground shed on the 'Pop Side' had sported the advertisement 'Offilers Ales' displayed in large white painted letters on its tin roof.

On his first entry to the ground as manager Clough plonked himself down in the dug-out and glared at it from across the pitch. 'The first thing I'm gonna do is sack the entire team. That's for starters. Then I'm gonna get rid of that name on there. Offilers Ales doesn't exist any longer and it's bloody depressing. That's a Third Division ad and we're in Division Two.'

We had to thank that retired football legend, Len Shackleton, for the Coming of Brian, six years earlier in 1967. 'He's a young bugger, Sam,' he told Longson. 'But by God he gets things done. You want to see his players at Hartlepool. They're so scared of him. But he puffs 'em up as well. They all think they're world beaters. Any road, who else could have got Hartlepool, think of it – *Hartlepool* – up to the Third Division? They've never been that high up. They'll go dizzy and fall off.'

Longson remembered a Rams match against Sunderland two seasons earlier. The outstanding player on the pitch that day had been Clough, pointing here, pointing there, giving orders. 'They call him arrogant,' Longson declared. 'So what? It's leadership. He's a born leader.' He put down his cigar to clasp his hands tightly together. 'Is there anybody else after him, Shack?'

'Yeah. West Brom. Get your skates on.'

'Shack', as go-between, got Longson to call Clough. But, for the utmost secrecy, the call would be made to a Hartlepool phone box that night at eight o'clock.

'This is Sam Longson. Is that Brian Clough?'

'It is. But I had to pay somebody a quid to go away.'

'Put it down to expenses. I won't beat about the bush. Can you get down here for interview?'

'No. Too busy. You'll have to come up here. I'm not anxious to leave Hartlepool, you know. Love the place, love the club. It would take a lot to get me away.'

A side of Clough's character, at odds with his impetuosity, was his skill in manipulating people, often done by telling bold white lies, even bold black lies, if he felt the cause was just.

'Bloody hell, lad. You want me to bring my entire boardroom up to you? That's the North Pole, Hartlepool!'

'I'll meet you halfway at Scotch Corner.'

'Eh? That's not halfway! It's not even quarter way! I've run a haulage business. I know distances. Let's meet at The Old Swan at Harrogate. That's halfway.'

'No. Impossible. It's the kids, you see. And the wife. Lot going on.'

'I've got a lot going on an' all,' Longson said in defeat.

That Sunday, he packed the protesting directors into his Rolls-Royce: Sydney Bradley, Harry Paine and Bob Kirkland. Kirkland, the most vociferous, shook his head. 'What are we doing? The lad's thirty-two and he's a Division Four manager!'

Sam grinned. 'Was. Division Three now.'

The precocious Clough was waiting for them, with a cheery

grin, at the designated car park. 'Never mind,' he said, registering the tired faces. 'All in a good cause.'

Longson, the directors and Clough had lunch together. As soon as they sat down Clough laid into them. 'You've won nothing since Third Division North. You finished seventeenth in Division Two. What you want is me. I'll sort it out. This time next year you'll want to double my wages.'

Amidst the laughter Longson gave Clough a second, careful, look of close scrutiny.

He spoke about it on the return journey. As an employer of a large labour force he reckoned to be able to accurately judge any man given half an hour in his company.

'That lad – and he is a lad. Thirty-two? He looks twenty-two. That lad *believes*. I tell you. He's our man. By God, doesn't he inspire you, eh?'

Kirkland was a shade sceptical. 'Yeah, I know, Sam, but let's step back a bit and think about it. Let's sleep on it.'

'Look,' said Longson. 'He's got some ambition he has. He never stopped talking. What he'd achieved at Hartlepool. What he could do with a club like ours. It's all about belief in your own talents,' he said. 'An' he's got it in bucketfuls, the lad has. He bloody well has.'

Longson continued to talk about Clough in bewilderment and delight. Even in The Midland, the next day, he was marvelling into his beer. 'I can't believe it. He bloody well hypnotised me. He must have done. He wanted five thousand pounds a year. And I agreed! He said he wanted a hundred grand for players. I told him fifty. He got me up to seventy grand! We gave it him. Nobody's screwed owt like that out of me like that since I was playing marbles!' He shook his head. 'I can't get over it. He got me to take my boardroom up to him. Up to *him*. It was more like him interviewing us. More like he was the bloody boss!'

He should have known. As it started, so it would continue. You can't bottle genius.

And Shackleton's reward for a golden capture? A tin of biscuits and a box of chocolates.

He never spoke to Longson again.

2

UPRISING

THE WORLD PREMIERE of the stage version of *Count Dracula* was performed at the Grand Theatre, Derby, on 15 May 1924. It is said that some of the patrons left in terror before the final curtain. On 18 October 1973 an audience of a different kind were packed inside, eager to express their horror at events taking place in the real world. The Protest Movement staged its first public meeting.

The stage, as McGuinness, Holmes and I climbed on to it, was decorated with huge red-and-white placards of Clough's face. The chanting grew louder. 'WHO DO WE WANT, BRIAN CLOUGH, WHEN DO WE WANT HIM – NOW!

Fury was quickly channelled into heated calls for action. A whip round with a bucket produced a fighting fund of £150.53. I calmed the crowd sufficiently to make my speech. 'Brian told me he hopes to be at the game on Saturday.' My voice, over-amplified by the auditorium system, echoed beyond the packed mass into the high roof and walls of the theatre and looped back again. 'We've got to make an impact inside the ground as well as outside. We've got to let those directors know what they've unleashed.'

'Where's Mike Keeling?' A group of fans shouted out the question.

It was McGuinness who answered. 'He's not joining us. He doesn't think it's any use.' Boos and jeers greeted the announcement. Someone cried out, 'Why did he resign from the board then?'

No one could answer. As a movement we were left with only the blunt weapons of marching and demonstration. And it would require media coverage on a big scale and for that we had no guarantee. It was years before the ubiquitous coverage of satellite channels dedicated to twenty-four-hour sports reporting.

The theatre lighting, for purposes of economy, was concentrated on the stage and the front stalls, leaving the rear of the theatre in relative darkness. The back row was vacant, apart from a man sitting in an aisle seat, wearing a rattin' cap and raincoat with the collar turned up. A man with a pock-marked face came to the stage apron.

'That fella at the back. I think he's a club spy,' he hissed, staring up at me. He jerked his head eagerly towards the rear seating.

'I'll sort him out,' said McGuinness. Putting hand to mouth he slipped out a dental plate and jumped down from the stage into the aisle. At this point the 'spy', seeing McGuinness stride determinedly for him, upped and nipped quickly out of the theatre.

LATER THAT EVENING, I arrived in Etwall, a village a few miles west of Derby, paying little attention to the Mercedes parked close to where I lived at the head of a cul-de-sac. As I walked towards my front door, key in hand, I could hear the ten o'clock ITN news jingle from inside the house.

'Don.'

I turned to see Clough's head stuck out of the driver's side window of the Mercedes, beckoning me. I quickly joined him, inside the car. 'I've just come from the meeting,' I said.

'I was there,' Clough said tautly. 'I was at the back. That fella McGuinness was after me. Let's talk. Not here.' He drove out of the cul-de-sac and headed up a lane into open countryside. After a short distance he parked in a gateway. He answered my query as to the missing club director, Mike Keeling. 'Mike?' Clough was contemptuous. 'He resigned without telling me. I'd have stopped him if I'd known he'd do that. Nobody to speak up for me on that board now.' I learnt that Keeling was a man smitten by Clough's fame and spent most of his time as his helper and gofer, content as reward to trail in the wake of his glory. His resignation had been simply a reflex action.

Clough continued his diatribe. 'Directors. They flaunt their money, but when do they put their hands in their pockets to buy players? They borrow it from the bank, that's what they do. There's Sydney Bradley, got businesses in town. How much money's he put in the club? Nowt. Longson – he's the chairman. Flogged off his transport business for millions and boasts he's only got twenty-five quid in shares. They don't give a damn about the fans. Oh they want promotion, oh yes, so they can wine and dine with their clubmates at Arsenal and Manchester United.'

Clough came out of his dudgeon. 'Don, if you have a chance go for Bradley. He's a little man with a little mind. Scare him and it might spread.' As he stared into the darkness of the field I wondered why he'd followed me home. Surely not just to moan about club directors. He answered my silent query by what he said next, speaking casually. 'There's a rumour that Don Shaw's only doing this to write a film about me.' He looked at me quizzically.

'Do you think that?' I looked back at him.

He made a mild gesture with his hand. 'I wouldn't blame you. You've got bairns to feed, like we all have.'

I became emotional. 'Brian, I've supported Derby since I was ten. I've queued up all night to get a ticket. I've—' I stopped myself. Clough was studying me, with a hint of a smile.

'That's okay,' he said. 'I believe you.'

So that was the reason he'd collared me, to test my integrity.

He added, 'George Edwards at the *Telegraph* told me you were all right. Just wanted to confirm it.' With that security clearance he reversed the car out of the gateway.

'Mind,' he added as he drove me home, 'not certain about that bloke McGuinness. Not the way he took his false teeth out.' He gave a laugh.

I noticed a tape cassette hand-labelled 'My Way' lying by the gear stick.

Clough stopped the car outside my house. 'Okay, let me tell you. I'll lay you a pound to a penny that rumour about you only being in it to write about me – I'll guarantee it came from the board. And they'll try other tricks if they think you're winning. They're cowardly rattlesnakes. So watch it.'

I hesitated, then leaned forward into the car. 'Brian. We need to know. Will you be at the game on Saturday?'

'Yeah, I'm going to try and get the crowd behind me, raise hell. Night, Don.'

I watched him drive away. That was my first encounter with Clough in action. He was going to carry out my idea and yet he claimed it as his own. Getting upset by Clough, I would learn, was a hazard for anyone who worked or associated with him. My irritation vanished when I remembered my self-imposed task and why I had undertaken it.

Clough had created another world into which I could slip. He lifted my spirits, not just on match day but the whole week long. Through him the Rams played the 'beautiful game'. Like orchestral music, the wave out of defence would flow smoothly, rippling through midfield with precision to reach target man O'Hare, who would pivot and slip the ball forward of a running striker, climaxing as the ball found the net. Or, Hinton, on the wing, would make inch perfect crosses to the strikers against a back-pedalling opposition with the same result. McFarland dominated the midfield with a wide-legged stance, head up, always reading the game. Simplicity in passing the ball was the keynote. Clough never tired of telling people: 'If God had meant the ball to be kicked in the air he wouldn't have invented grass.'

Looking forward to a Saturday afternoon at the Baseball Ground was a treat in itself. Rarely did we lose and even then the sight of Hector running at goal, with Todd, Carlin and Gemmill spraying accurate passes, or Hinton unleashing a thunderbolt shot at goal, was reward enough.

I let myself into the house and phoned George Edwards at the *Derby Evening Telegraph*, then Neil Hallam, sports reporter. My message was brief. 'Clough will be at the match on Saturday. He'll take over the ground. He'll be back.' Then I rang Raymonds News Agency to leave a similar message for the nationals.

Before I could fall asleep a troubling thought crossed my mind. Clough's secretive attendance at the meeting was inexplicable. It would have been far better had he taken the stage. What an uproar there would have been, what inspiration for the faithful. I made a mental note to ask him about it when the opportunity arose. I was dozing off when another thought woke me. I didn't like what he'd said about the board's 'tricks'. At the first opportunity I would try to find out the source of the rumour about me.

CLOUGH RANG THE following morning. 'Doing anything this afternoon? Come for a walk. Bring Liz and your Martin. Two o'clock?'

'Thanks, Brian. We'll do that.' I told Liz that her hero wanted to take her for a walk. She needed no more inviting.

Clough was ready when we arrived at Ferrers Way on the dot of two o'clock. We immediately set off for nearby Allestree Park, Nigel and Martin kicking a ball around as we went. In these relaxed moments he began to talk about the team and their achievements. The players could only turn on a superb performance, he said in a matter-of-fact voice, when he 'turned the switch on'.

'Do you do that in the dressing room?' I asked.

'No. I do it all the week before.' He tapped his forehead. 'I tell them how brilliant they are. I tell them I'm watching every move, even if the ball's at the other end of the pitch. Then I make them laugh.' He gave a slight chuckle.

I could see the pleasure it gave him. It wasn't boasting, more like someone expressing their enthusiasm for a special skill as in flying or rock climbing.

He took me into a fascinating world, in which he played God. Apart from using his natural powers to scare, humour and motivate the team into playing at the top of their game, he said he took great pains to get to know the players individually through the trivia of their non-playing lives. He even kept a record of the birthday of each player's wife. The team could be in Rome, Moscow or Leipzig when the celebratory day occurred and Clough would despatch flowers to the wife, but in her husband's name. The delighted wife would call her husband at the hotel. 'You are lovely. And it's your big game tonight. I wouldn't have minded if you'd forgotten.'

The player, mind working feverishly, would say, 'Glad you got them.'

Later, Clough would casually ask: 'Oh, it was your wife's birthday today. Did you send her flowers?'

And the player, covered in confusion, would stammer, 'Yes, she got them, thanks boss,' and race on to the pitch that night, determined to pay him back by playing a blinder.

As the military took raw recruits to knock them down, only to rebuild them into parts of an efficient machine, so Clough assembled a unique battery of reinforcing techniques designed to meld his players into a winning unit. Thus, he stimulated, fed and inspired their ambitions.

He chose players not only for their playing skill, but also for their natural obedience to authority. In conditioning them to regard him with respect, any statement of his had a better chance of being believed. With this relationship he only had to tell a player that he was highly talented for 'self-belief' to become the order of every match day. The players might fear him, but they never feared the opposition.

Clough took pains to ensure that each player was easy and relaxed in the company of his teammates. If a potential player showed any doubt about how he would fit in with the team Clough would tell him to 'Go for an hour or two with Archie and Roy. See if you like them.' Clough's criteria in choosing such likeable and innocent lads who were vulnerable to pressures outside the game, gave him the opportunity to act as their adviser and counsellor on all manner of domestic problems and even marital difficulties. They were only too happy to play a subservient role, having been given in return the joy of victory, fame, status and a higher standard of living.

Wives' birthdays were just a small part of a large mental dossier that Clough kept. Any item could be used in motivating a player at his choosing. Shock tactics were also used, such as telephoning a player at 11 p.m. to ensure he was on the straight and narrow. Not only did it serve to keep him on his toes, it also maintained the 'awe' factor. Uncertainty, allied to self-belief, Clough told me, was a powerful motivating force.

His habit of suddenly taking the team to a park or wood to show his appreciation of nature may have seemed peculiar, but odd though his eccentricities were, each and every act built up a respect for him which kept the players in a state of wrapt uncertainty, which was always his intention.

'That's been growing for over two hundred years, maybe more.' He stopped walking in the park to show me a gnarled oak tree in wonder. 'Fantastic.' He caressed the bark sensuously.

It kept me in uncertainty.

I completely forgot to ask why he hadn't made himself known to the meeting at the Grand Theatre, captivated as I was in his presence.

WHEN CLOUGH FIRST stepped into the Baseball Ground in 1967 Longson was there to shepherd him towards the trophy cabinets, showing him first a photograph of the 1946 FA Cup winning team.

'Great players they were, Brian. That's Reg Harrison, winger. Still lives in Derby. Wonderful chap. That's Jackie Stamps. Comes every Saturday, you know, to watch the games. He's blind now. A pal gives him a commentary.' As Longson pointed out the rest of the team, Clough's coiled impatience struggled within him. He had work to do. Sacking the first team and getting rid of the 'Offilers Ales' advert were top of the list. But Longson wasn't done yet, keen to impress his protégé. Photographs, minor cups, there seemed no end to it. 'That team there, Brian, nearly all local lads. That's what we want here, don't we? A team of decent lads. Lads who've supported us as boys. You can't beat club loyalty, can you?'

Clough twisted his mouth, about to say something sharp but relented. It was his first day at the lathe as he liked to say – he'd been an apprentice fitter at ICI – and actions would speak louder than words. 'Yes, Mr Chairman. But...'

'Sam. Call me Sam out of the boardroom,' Longson cut in, patting him on the shoulder.

'Yes, Sam, but quality comes first. I'm not here to sign on local lads if they're not up to it.'

'Oh, of course not, Brian.' Longson was quick to reassure

him. 'You've got your money. You do what you like with it. That's your job.'

'Yes,' said Clough. 'And it's going to be a big job.' He gestured at the trophy cabinet. 'You've been going nearly a hundred years and you've won the FA Cup. Twenty-two years ago. What's the last thing you won?'

'Third Division North championship.'

Clough laughed. 'I wouldn't mention it, Sam. Keep it quiet.'

'Well, you asked and don't forget the fans were proud of it.'

'Look. What's Derby famous for? Rolls-Royce and a painter called Joseph Wright. But it's not famous for its football team, is it?'

'Oh, come on Brian, we're one of the founders of the Football League.'

'Aye, back in the stone age.' He could see it hurt Longson, but Clough pressed on. 'I'm going to fill that cabinet. Forget the past. Let's bury it. Now, I must get on. Got to earn my corn.'

Longson, although miffed, told the story in the boardroom, mellowing over a gin and tonic with Kirkland. 'He's a right cocky devil. But that's what he said. "I'm going to fill that cabinet." Where else, Bob, would you find somebody like him?'

Kirkland was pleasantly bucolic. 'You were right, Sam. He's going places.'

'And we're going with him,' said Longson. 'To Derby County.'

'To Derby County.' They touched glasses.

Clough hit the club like a tornado. Five players were shown the door after a few practice sessions. The exodus became a rush. Next went the groundsman, two secretaries and two tea ladies who had the misfortune to express their dislike of Clough within his earshot. He strode through the offices asking pointed questions, unearthing backsliders and clock watchers. In his first week Clough spent twelve hours a day judging this and measuring that, noting the decay in the stands and wondering what to do about the Pop Side shed.

Sammy Crooks, an old Derby star and now chief scout, was an early casualty, causing Longson some concern. He almost intervened and would have brought up – again – the virtue of club loyalty, but thought better of it.

The new manager was considerably helped by his assistant Peter Taylor. He first met Clough in 1956 when the two of them played for Middlesbrough, Taylor as goalkeeper. After the match he praised Clough as the best centre forward he'd ever seen. The relationship blossomed. Taylor talked openly about their chances as talent scouts, even in management, when they came to hang up their boots. It felt right and proper that, when Clough became manager of Hartlepool, he immediately gave Taylor the job as his assistant. Curiously, as though tempting fate, he kept it secret from the chairman of the board.

When Ernest Ord, the rumbustious chairman, discovered Taylor on the premises and asked him what he was doing there, he was so incredulous at the reply that he found himself laughing out loud. 'It's bad enough having to shell out forty pounds a week for Cloughie without having to give twenty-four pounds for some other bloke. No club's got two managers,' he complained. 'Not even Manchester United or Spurs.'

Clough treated Longson in the same manner. He, too, happened to come across a stranger in his ground. To his bewilderment and no little resentment, Longson found he was talking to the assistant manager. He managed to keep his temper. After all, hadn't Shack warned him that Clough was a young bugger? Hah, well, Longson could forgive one mistake. Even so, he couldn't help but give Clough a warning. 'You should have told me, Brian, when we first met.'

In the event he did ring Shackleton who, fortunately, was still giving Longson time in which to repay him properly for recommending Clough. Politely, he advised Longson that Clough 'worked better with familiar faces around him'.

It was true. Under the ambitious duo, Hartlepool could not have been better managed. They had worked instinctively, Clough exploiting his talents in press and public relations, Taylor, the streetwise and shrewd footslogger, searching for talent. They had lived side by side in a couple of small semis facing the sea, paying a modest rent, the scene set for a French film comedy.

Clough took a public service vehicle licence in order to drive the team coach. One day, en route to Darlington, it broke down. He later appeared in the away dug-out, covered in oil and dirty grease. Nothing was beneath or beyond him. Sweeping out the dressing room, rushing on to the pitch as trainer with bucket and sponge and getting his wife to knit football socks, were all part and parcel of his job as manager. Dietary considerations were settled by using the chip shop just off the A1 at Wetherby for a cheap and nourishing meal on their return from away games.

Together Clough and Taylor performed trick after trick even to the extent of cheating the FA rule that every match had to kick off with a new ball.

Not having the funds to buy more than one, Clough would keep the referee talking while Taylor snatched the new ball off the centre spot to substitute it with the old re-polished ball from a fort-night ago. But Clough never penny pinched when it came to keeping up the players' morale. He always put them in decent hotels if the away game was played at too far a distance for a return journey on the same day. And knowing that factions and cliques could threaten team unity he ensured that no two players shared a hotel room in successive matches.

The players were allowed to play cards downstairs until 11 p.m., during which they would sip their permitted half pint of beer. On the stroke of the hour Clough would make his announcement. 'Time, gentlemen.' Ten minutes later he and Taylor patrolled the corridor on the lookout for any miscreants.

During the early sixties the permissive age had not yet begun. The working family was still founded on solid virtues. The wearing of Sunday Best, the proud housewife scrubbing the front doorstep white each week, the sending of young pregnant girls away to give birth and – running through the whole of society – respect for all kinds of authority from park keeper to police officer was imbued in the psyches of most of the working class. Clough and his family lived by this code and he carried these values into the world of soccer. Taylor shared them too. Although they were opposites temperamentally they complemented each other. Clough had not been lying when he told Longson that he loved Hartlepool. Even following his meeting at Scotch Corner he had had no intention of joining Derby County. It was the first of his little games with club directors, probing here, delving there, enjoying the moment. He was a home bird by nature and felt insecure at the thought of leaving, moving on. Longson, confident in his new signing, would have been shocked to know that Clough was telling Taylor he was happy with his wife and children settled nearby and that the challenge of taking little Hartlepool up through the divisions was something he relished.

Taylor stressed that Derby had a proud tradition, that the fans were 'fantastic', that together they could work wonders. 'You've got the gift of the gab. You can charm sparrows off trees. You can make players tick. I can do the back-room scouting, setting up, planning. We're the best management team in the whole country! Deny it!'

Clough smiled ironically. 'You're right. Because there aren't any management teams except you and me.' Discussing it with Barbara, he was forced to admit that Taylor's stories of Derby County and its legion of loyal fans was attractive. The children were not yet of secondary school age and so the move would not be too traumatic for them. In a rare moment of disclosure he told me that he was the sixth of nine children and that money meant a lot, not for its own sake but for the feeling of comfort that it gave him. The increase in income by joining Derby County, therefore, was tempting. Clinching it was the warm partnership with Taylor, whom he trusted and relied on – his other marriage. It was Taylor who told me that Clough was not an insufferable 'big head' driven by vanity, but a manager whose fierce need to win matches stemmed from a deep, underlying insecurity.

Longson, in those early days of Clough's reign, continued blissfully to regale anyone who strayed into his path with stories about his wonder boy, poking fun at himself in the process. 'This is the lad,' he'd say, drawing a photograph of Clough from his wallet. 'Smart isn't he, eh? He outsmarted me. He could sell ice to Eskimos.'

While Clough cleansed the Baseball Ground of 'hangers on' and time servers, Sam luxuriated in his retirement from 'Sam Longson (Buxton) Ltd, Town End Garage, Chapel-en-le-Frith, Derbyshire'. Much of his time was now spent at the ground to be close to the 'lad' he now regarded as his son. Longson was a proud man, a farmer's boy who had built up a large haulage business. This he had recently sold and with some of the proceeds acquired a hire purchase company, two farms with a pedigree herd and a fruit growing business in the High Peak. He showed how much he liked Clough by offering him and his family the use of his holiday bungalow in west Wales.

One of Longson's stories, told at his own expense, was that Clough had 'mesmerised' him into paying him a salary above his budget. Such talk inflated Clough's self-confidence beyond that already generously afforded him by nature. At Hartlepool he had motivated players by first scaring them, confronting them eyeball to eyeball like a drill sergeant. This gained him their respect. From this position of authority he could then relax, tell jokes and by such methods 'fine tune' his players the week before a match. Taylor, with his humorous anecdotes, was also adept in this regard.

Now, at Derby, Clough was beginning to take himself seriously. He saw his unusual personality as a gift. It would soon be tested in the art of player recruitment. His first signing, naturally, was that of John McGovern, his favourite player from Hartlepool. McGovern needed no persuasion, knowing he had hitched himself to a rising star. Clough and Taylor then targeted as the keystone of their Derby team, a centre half and a centre forward. John O'Hare, centre forward from Sunderland, was captured for a tidy sum of £21,000. He would have to drop down a division but had made his own enquiries as to the worth of Clough and Taylor. Like McGovern, he saw in them his pathway to success.

Their next target, though, required a full deployment of Clough's personal weaponry. Taylor had spotted a player bound for Liverpool, but still playing for a minnows club, Tranmere Rovers. 'An uncut diamond,' said Taylor. 'Let's get him before Liverpool scouts wake up.'

Roy McFarland would not be easy to snatch. It required thought and cunning. The plan began with Clough approaching Longson. 'Sam, we're having a look at a lad at Tranmere Rovers tomorrow night. It's a big job, this, and we'd be glad of your experience and company.' The chairman's face lit up. Never had he expected Clough to defer to his own, special talents.

Taylor then made an anonymous phone call to Tranmere to say that an important scout (no names or clubs mentioned) would be attending the game the next evening, his target Roy McFarland. Clough called it 'geeing up', the intention being to motivate McFarland into giving of his best. At the same time he asked Longson a favour. 'Love your Rolls, Sam. Any chance of going up to Tranmere in it?'

Longson, still warm with pride at being invited to act as adviser, was only too eager, quick to boast to Bob Kirkland 'Brian sees I've got spotting talent. I've always said so,' he said smugly. 'Pity the last manager didn't see it.' He sighed in pleasure. 'If he had we'd never have had Clough, though, would we.'

Shortly before departure he took his protégé into the empty boardroom to toast their mission, not knowing that Clough had been trying to kick the habit. He also had no inkling that Clough's introduction to the seductive joy of champagne would not just give him a taste of it, but a taste *for* it.

And so they set off chatting and joking for Tranmere, rather like Ratty, Toad and Mole venturing into the wide world, the wicker basket in the Rolls-Royce boot containing bubbly and other delicacies. Any fear that McFarland hadn't got the message vanished with him playing the game of his life. 'Well, Sam. What do you think of him?' Clough asked, as the final whistle blew.

'What do I think of him? Get him,' ordered Longson. 'By God, Brian. If you value my advice, you get him.'

Now came the vital phase in the operation. Longson, as part of Clough's devious plan but not privy to it, was urged to engage the Tranmere chairman in small talk while Clough buttonholed his manager, Dave Russell, in the small club lounge.

Talking non-stop Clough came finally to make an offer of

£15,000. Russell, already bemused by the verbal onslaught, managed to pull himself together. 'Oh no. That's not enough. Nowhere near.'

'Well, what do you want to go up to?' said Clough. 'Look...' He dropped his gaze for the first time in apparent submission. 'Pete?' He addressed Taylor in a plaintive voice. 'Ask our chairman if we can stretch it to twenty grand.'

'Twenty?' exclaimed Russell. 'He's worth far more than—'

'I know it's a lot,' interjected Clough, leaving Russell with his mouth wide open. 'Hang on.' He turned back to Taylor. 'Make it twenty-four grand. Push the boat out.'

Before Russell could speak Taylor had gone to find Longson.

Clough shook his head. 'I must be mad. He won't agree.' He resumed his searchlight stare into Russell's eyes. 'Our chairman doesn't want to set any more world records. He told me to offer no more than twelve grand. If we can double that it'll be a miracle.'

Taylor returned, his hands raised. 'Twenty-four is absolute maximum.'

'Twenty-four?' Clough looked suitably astonished. 'Well, I'm blowed.'

Russell, thinking he had done well, eagerly shook hands with Clough. He would never know that Longson had agreed to £48,000.

Back in the Rolls-Royce, Longson was delighted with the raid. 'You've saved me twenty-four bloody grand, Brian! And you've bought the man I picked.'

Clough and Taylor exchanged grins. 'Now then, Sam,' said Clough. 'We've not done the deal yet. We've got an hour to kill.'

'Eh?' said a puzzled Longson.

'We've another job to do first. We've got to sign the player. But we mustn't get there before midnight.' He raised a finger. 'The witching hour, Sam.'

Clough and Taylor grinned even more at Longson's increasing mystification.

They arrived outside McFarland's house on the dot. There were no lights showing. Satisfied, Clough asked Longson to take himself back to the booked hotel. 'Thanks for everything. We'll see you in the morning. We'll get a taxi back to the hotel. Now don't fret. You've been fabulous.'

Longson, a shade disconcerted, stayed long enough to see McFarland's father answer the door.

'Sorry to come so late,' said Clough. 'Our car broke down coming from Derby. We've walked miles. We've seen Dave Russell and it's all agreed.'

'What's agreed?' Mr McFarland frowned at them both.

'They've not told you? Roy's signed for Derby? Dave Russell's done the deal.'

Roy was dragged out of bed by his father. 'You didn't tell us, Roy!'

'Tell you what, Dad?' A befuddled McFarland cleared his eyes, hitched up his pyjamas and tried to sort out what had happened. It was, indeed, the 'witching hour'.

Downstairs, Clough drove home the facts. 'You're going to be such a player you won't know what's hit you. You are going to captain Derby County.' Clough was unrelenting as he rolled out the rising nasal cadences, rhythmical and irresistible. 'Roy, you are going to take Derby County into the First Division. Dave Russell has agreed to it. His chairman's agreed to it. My chairman's agreed to it. Roy, you want what's best for you. I want what's best for you. You'll get more money. You'll play for England, but only with me. I'm going to turn you into a great footballer. Around you I'm creating the best team in Britain. You can't turn this down. Get off to bed if you want. But we're camping here all night till you sign. I suggest you decide now. What's it to be?'

'Dad?' Roy McFarland, shell shocked, appealed to his father.

His father shook his head. 'I dunno.' He looked at his watch. 'Eh! You know what time it is? I've got to get off to work in five hours!'

'We all have,' said Clough. 'So. Let's have your decision. See that cushion? My head's going down on that if we don't get one. It'll stay there all night. So? What's it to be young man? Will it be glory or bust?'

McFarland, confused, appealed once more to his father. 'Dad?'

Mr McFarland kept shaking his head. 'All I can think is, well, if they're prepared to camp here all night they must really want you. I reckon you should sign.' He broke into a weak laugh. 'If only to get rid of them.'

Clough and Taylor laughed in appreciation. The next morning 'Toad' Longson joyously drove the celebratory duo back to Derby, both men falling asleep within minutes of setting off. The Rolls was a particularly comfortable car to kip down in. For Ratty and Mole it had been an important part of the planning.

BANG, BANG, BANG. The drummer of Ilkeston Town brass band, at the head of a thousand people, set the tempo for Elgar's 'Imperial March', which reverberated within the narrow walled street. It was 1 p.m. Saturday, 20 October 1973. We had gathered in Tenant Street, off Derby Market Place, watched by police on horseback. Banners and placards filled the roadway, traffic diverted. The Movement, as a force, aimed to arrive at the ground prior to kick-off in the home game against Leicester City. Regardless of the game, win or lose, I was convinced that the real victory would be ours.

As soon as the emperor had walked around the stadium to the adulation of his people, Longson would have no choice but to resign and we would have won the day. Clough would be back.

Just as I was about to stride off a strange, cloth-covered brown creature came to walk alongside me. He said he was a Womble and, since his first television programme went out the following week and he needed some 'free publicity', would I mind? I didn't mind at all. It kept me amused.

Lining the streets were fans waiting to join in the march, expected to reach 3,000 in the last quarter mile. Police reserves were on standby along the designated route. Closer to the ground I could see that all the windows of the terraced housing along the streets had been boarded over as protection in case of rioting, creating an air of threat and insurrection.

As the marchers dissolved into the huge crowd at the ground I struggled towards the club entrance where the football reporters often gathered before a game. Phil Jenkins, a local freelance and someone with whom I'd had a free and easy telephone conversation less than twenty-four hours ago, stood outside.

'Hi, Phil.'

He heard me, but turned his head away and then moved off in the direction of the Osmaston end of the ground. It was a snub. I'd been given the cold shoulder.

'....Don Shaw's only doing this to write a film about me.' Clough's words came back. The 'rumour,' I thought, could only have been spread by the board, desperate as they were to weaken the Movement. I decided it was best to ignore it and show by example I was a genuine fan.

Unsettled, I spotted, pinned by the melee against the wall, David Lacey of the *Guardian* and another sports reporter I took to be Hugh McIlvanney. It would be unlikely that national journalists would have been fed lies by the board.

I introduced myself. Before they could answer a roar went up from a section of the crowd at the Osmaston end of the street. We stood on tiptoe to see what was happening.

Lacey smiled. 'Where's the guillotine?'

McIlvanney said laconically in dry Glaswegian tones. 'Lay you two to one God's arrived.' He smiled as the crowd in the distance indicated that 'He' was with us.

'Cloughie. Cloughie. Cloughie!'

Remembering, I took the tickets Clough donated from my inside pocket. Within seconds I was the target of a scrum of young men, crushing me against the wall, fighting desperately for each ticket. To each eager fan I gasped out the instruction. 'These are from Cloughie. Behind the directors' box. Shout up.' As the last ticket was snatched from my hand I breathed a sigh of relief, letting my head rest back against a window frame. I felt it vibrate. Windows, doors, anything constructed of wood or glass, from the directors' entrance down past the general office to the large wooden double gates that barred a mass exit point, were trembling. As the crowd's mantra changed to: 'CLOUGH BACK, CLOUGH BACK, CLOUGH BACK' there was a general closing of ranks by the police in nervous readiness.

Then came a rumbling noise, faint at first, then growing louder to become a drumming. It came from the adjacent stand inside the ground, from hundreds of feet stamping on its wooden flooring. With the speed of a bush fire, it spread to other stands, in waves of rolling thunder. Out in the street more protesting fists added to the din, banging on the wooden window surrounds, even on the windows themselves. It intensified. And all the way down the dingy street the chanting rammed home the demand: 'BOARD OUT! BOARD OUT! BOARD OUT!'

3
MUTINY

THE PRE-MATCH atmosphere inside the Baseball Ground, always warm and buzzing, was superheated that cold October afternoon by the twin emotions of frustration and resentment. Large red-and-white 'Clough' placards obscured much of the crowd, giving it the appearance of a medieval army hiding behind massed shields. It made one of the smallest grounds in the League feel even more claustrophobic. By seven minutes to kick-off none of the directors had dared make an entrance and only the Leicester players were on the pitch for the warm-up. I sat five rows behind the directors' box. The lads with the free tickets sitting around me were already shouting their pro-Clough slogans. Policemen walked around the ground with tense stewards in attendance.

The rumour that Clough would put in an appearance had men craning their necks, scanning the entrances to the stands. A handful of fans were on the pitch waving their arms, pursued by police. I caught a glimpse of a man being marched by stewards off the perimeter track just beneath me. For a brief moment I feared it was Clough himself. Suddenly a chorus of booing broke out, directed at three directors, the first to make their furtive entry into their wooden walled enclosure. Last came Sam Longson, creeping into his seat, head lowered.

It was six minutes to kick-off and still no Clough. The Leicester players were already on the pitch, but no players in black and white. I dared to hope McFarland and the lads were staying in the dressing room in protest.

Then, like a puppet on a string, Clough popped up in front of me, a few yards from the directors' box, holding his arms aloft in defiance. It was not a spot Nero would have chosen to greet the masses, standing underneath a low black roof, halfway up tiered seating and with a fading autumnal light further reduced by clouds of tobacco smoke. At least Clough had removed his disguise of flat cap and muffler, but only a small section of the crowd could identify, or even see him. There was some cheering, but the vast majority of the spectators were ignorant of his presence.

Bradley, the smallest director, realising the opportunity to convert protest into apparent support for the board, urged Longson to stand up in acknowledgment of the limited cheering meant for Clough. The directors' box being relatively well lit, Longson dutifully stood and was easily seen raising his arms, in contrast to his opponent's gestures. By now news of Clough's appearance had spread throughout the terracing and Longson caught the full blast of their acclaim. Suddenly, believing it was meant for him, he waved vigorously back. Clough, realising that his show had backfired, turned quickly away and headed for the staircase. Outside, Keeling had the engine running and whisked him away from the ground.

Longson sat down in great relief. 'There you are,' he said to his fellow directors. 'That proves who they really appreciate around here.' Then he glanced at his watch and was given a jolt. It was four minutes to kick-off and the Derby players had not yet appeared. Beads of sweat bloomed on his forehead as he exchanged anxious glances with his fellow directors.

Then they trotted out, McFarland, Todd, Gemmill and the rest of the players. Longson took out a handkerchief and mopped his brow. But would the team, having demonstrated their disaffection by being deliberately late on the pitch, now drive in the knife by throwing the match? There was a chance that their dilemmas of loyalty be transferred to their performance.

They had not long to wait for an answer. Gemmill, from the kick off, picked up the ball on the right wing, dribbled neatly past two defenders and crossed a low ball into the goalmouth, but just beyond the outstretched leg of O'Hare. Longson could relax.

McFarland, speaking to Gerald Mortimer of the *Derby Evening Telegraph* after the game, said that the team had put on a stylish performance of attacking football 'in tribute to our manager', inferring his appeal for Clough's return. But, if anything, it had achieved the opposite effect. It created a feeling of solidarity within the board, reinforcing the conviction that, though the reign of Brian Clough was over, Derby County could still thrive.

And although the crowd welcomed the victory 2–1 there were many, including myself, who would have preferred the players to have lost the match.

Clough's fear that an attempt to get on the perimeter track would have seen him ejected from the ground I could understand, but at the same time dismissed as unlikely. I'm certain that his show of brave defiance would have whipped the crowd into a frenzy of support.

Badly disappointed, I slipped away from the ground as quickly as I could. I had originally hoped to be interviewed by Lacey and McIlvanney, but now hadn't the heart.

Longson, still believing he had the support of the fans, was all smiles later in the boardroom. Holding his glass high he toasted the assembly of directors and their friends, 'To a new era.' He turned slowly around, his glass remaining steady. 'Gentlemen. I showed him. Thirty thousand fans showed who they really want. And the team was behind us.'

No one chose to disabuse him.

I SPENT THE rest of the afternoon imagining what should have been. Instead of seeing Clough popping up and down without effect in a badly lit stand, I saw him striding around the ground, the fans ecstatic. The fantasy reel ended with the pitch occupied by the crowd chanting their protest at the directors' box, the faceless men inside fleeing in fear. Pure self-torture.

Then, at 6.30 p.m. Clough rang me with a request that we meet that evening in Markeaton Park. His phone, he said, might be tapped. He didn't say who he thought the culprits might be. He added that there would be a major development in the next day or two. On the basis of what had happened at the ground maybe it did give credence to the theory that he 'winged' all that he did. Or was I doing him an injustice? I hoped, the fiasco of the afternoon would be wiped out by what he was now about to offer. Maybe, I tried to convince myself, his ineffectual appearance at the match would still keep the pot boiling. In cautiously revived optimism I set off for the meeting.

We met close to the Markeaton road island, one of the hubs on the A38 which made for busy traffic, linking up with the M1 to the north and the motorways in the south.

Clough had parked near the public toilet. I left my car for the short walk to Clough's Mercedes. A slim man with his back to me suddenly appeared at Clough's side window, tapping on it with his finger.

Clough slid down the window. 'Yes, young man.'

The man's pale, sensitive face dropped. 'Oh my God,' he stammered and turned quickly away.

Clough peered after him, watching him disappear. 'Well, he seemed to know me.'

I laughed and got into the passenger seat and closed the door.

'Now then,' he said. 'The players are going to sort it out. They've got their plan. Watch out for Monday. Today was only a token. I put down a marker, that's all.'

'What's the plan?' As soon as I spoke, I realised my mistake.

'Don't you worry. All will be revealed.' It was a rebuke, but put reassuringly. He might as well have told me to 'enjoy it, keep it up, but let me fix it'. Possibly he wanted to keep me reassured so I would keep the movement going as a front, representing public pressure, while he did the plotting for his return.

Clough glanced at me. 'Don't whittle. It's not me. It's the players. They'll do what's right.'

'Great.' I was content. He would only have to give the word and they would take action, whatever that might be. I could look forward to Monday, when the Protest Movement would be made redundant, its task fulfilled. I saw the events of that afternoon at the Baseball Ground in a new light. He hadn't failed in his demonstration at the ground, after all. He'd merely registered his protest, knowing that he had his return in the bag. I was surprised then, when he handed me an envelope and said, 'It's a list of all the directors and their phone numbers. If you think it right, ring them. Get your mates as well. They're a cowardly bunch, directors.'

I put the note in my pocket, wondering why he should give me a list of directors when it would all be settled, come Monday. 'You were right,' I said. 'Phil Jenkins gave me the cold shoulder. Must have been that rumour you heard about me.'

'What did I tell you?' Clough gave me a wry smile. 'Power crazy, Longson. He'll get up to other tricks. Keep a lookout.'

As I left his car I heard Sinatra's 'My Way' start up in mid-tape. 'Regrets, I've had a few…'

I wasn't worried any longer. I was the First World War soldier who sat back in his trench and said confidently, 'The war will be over by Christmas.'

THE RENAISSANCE OF Derby County in the late sixties gathered pace with the capture of three more players, again targeted due to the uncanny ability of Clough and Taylor to recognise their potential when their clubs had not.

Alan Hinton of Nottingham Forest was the first of the trio to be targeted. His manager, surprisingly, had declared him to be 'past it' at the age of twenty-five. Hinton did not enjoy the bodily contact side of the game, so much so that the cry would go up at the Forest ground, 'Where's your handbag, Gladys?' But Clough saw in him a rare talent. His ability to cross a ball could not be bettered by any other winger in the Football League and his follow-through made a strike so powerful that the ball would trace a low straight trajectory, as good as anything Peter Lorimer could produce at Leeds. His apparent laziness, and lack of 'physical' involvement in the game was put down by Clough to poor management.

This time, instead of approaching the manager first, as in the case of McFarland, Clough enticed the player over to the Baseball Ground, sat him down and gave him a cup of tea, so nervous did he appear. Clough began with a general chat, showing sympathy. 'Shame that Forest don't know how good you are and can be for years yet. Don't you think so, Alan?'

Hinton managed to crack a smile. 'Do you mean that?'

Clough nodded sternly. 'I mean every word of every thing I ever say, young man.'

Hinton had heard how Clough had dragooned McFarland into signing.

'I've got a chance to go to America and help start up football as a proper sport,' he said firmly. 'I've got contacts.'

He found himself held by Clough's stare.

'America? You want to go to America when you've got the best of your life to come as a player? America? They play rounders, not football.' Clough dismissed it. 'Now look. I'm creating a team of footballers. They'll play football on the ground, where it's meant. Ideal for you. I want skilled players, like you. And no thugs.' The latter remark appealed to Hinton. 'With you on song there's no winger to touch you in this country. I will make you play better than you have in your life. We're going for the top. And I need you.'

Hinton remained uncertain and hesitant. Came the witching hour, midnight. He was taken for a walk around the pitch and was mystified as the floodlights came on. Being alone with Clough in the dead of night on a football ground was a 'weird experience', he later said. It made no sense and he felt highly vulnerable. Clough had now switched from being a conversationalist to being a lecturer.

An increasingly tired Hinton, bathed in the glare of the harsh lighting, trudged around the perimeter, forced to listen as Clough outlined his creed. 'Football is half luck,' he said. 'But nobody seems to know it except me. If you have ten shots at goal, luck might see one go in. But if you only have two shots at goal, your luck's out. I want you to shoot when you can. And you'll get lucky. And you can cross the ball better than anybody. In my book that makes you one of the best players in England. If you believe it, you will be.'

Here ended the lesson. At one o'clock in the morning Hinton was taken back to Clough's office, handed a pen and told where to sign. Hinton, dazed and tired, capitulated.

The next morning Clough bypassed the Forest manager and went to buttonhole Tony Wood, the Forest chairman, a softer target. He learnt that Hinton's price was £40,000.

Clough looked suitably appalled. 'But Hinton's past it. He's tired. I just want him to help the younger lads along. I want his experience. He'll be a sub, mostly on the bench. I can't pay more than fifteen grand.'

Wood, forced to endure Clough's special treatment, like McFarland and Hinton before him, succumbed, but not enough. His final price was £30,000, he affirmed.

Clough said that the player wanted £1,000 for himself out of the deal. Would the chairman accept £29,000? Derby County would fund Hinton's side payment. The deal was done, though Hinton was never to receive his money since as he'd never asked for it, he therefore never missed it.

Clough was peeved when Longson, instead of praising him for reducing the price by over 25 per cent, actually complained. 'Twenty-nine grand for him? He's past it, isn't he?'

Clough let the season's matches get under way, allowing Hinton's display of skills to fashion a suitable riposte. Instead of admitting he was wrong, Longson happily told his cronies how he'd encouraged Clough to sign Hinton. Clough's respect for Longson dropped to a tad above zero.

Clough's next signing had to be someone who was fast in midfield to add urgency to a championship bid. Archie Gemmill was targeted for this job, a Scottish Under-23 international with Preston North End.

In another midnight raid Clough and Taylor turned up at Gemmill's house. Archie's shocked wife went upstairs to wake her husband.

'Archie!' she hissed. 'It's Brian Clough. Look at the time! I don't like him. You've seen him on television. You know what he's like. You don't want to play for him!'

Archie, never flappable, tottered downstairs to suffer the Clough treatment, at the end of which Clough pointed to the settee. 'Archie. I'm kipping down here until you sign.'

'I've asked you to leave.' Mrs Gemmill threatened to call the police

Clough poked his head inside the kitchen. 'You've not washed up yet.'

'We do it in the morning,' said the irate housewife.

'Pete, I'll wash, you dry.'

Mrs Gemmill watched open mouthed as the duo set about the washing up.

'You can do what you like,' she said. 'But you're not getting Archie.'

Clough's answer was to say nice things about the kitchen lay-out and how Barbara was campaigning for one similar. While doing so he noticed that an electrical wall switch was loose. Finding a screwdriver where he expected it, in one of the kitchen drawers, he put the matter right. He also told Mrs Gemmill that he'd weed the front garden in the morning and how lucky Archie was to have such a proud, lovely and loyal wife. 'You'll have a much nicer house than this, you know, at Derby,' he added. 'With Archie's wages going up.'

Five minutes later Archie Gemmill was on the books of Derby County.

THE GAME WHICH marked the start of the transformation of Derby County from a nonentity bogged down in the lower half of Division Two to a potential giant in the land took place on 2 October 1968, a Wednesday night. There was a buzz in the stadium before the game against Chelsea in the Football League Cup third round replay, Derby having forced them to a draw away at Stamford Bridge. Chelsea was a First Division club, the Rams a division below.

The Rams were expected to lose and when Chelsea opened the scoring, it diminished any expectation. But when Derby equalised with Mackay's low hard drive from the edge of the penalty area, it was as if the crowd had been gripped by static electricity. The pitch at the Baseball Ground was only a yard or two from the spectators, always giving the home side a great advantage in the crowd's ability to intimidate the opposition.

Derby put on a display of such fast, attacking football that it put them into a class of their own. The roaring of the crowd intensified as, in the brilliant glare of floodlights, Carlin, Hinton and Hector rode every tackle from the strong defence. Suddenly the ball was up field and the Chelsea goal besieged.

The static switched to a bolt of lightning, sparking even the oldest and the least extrovert of spectators to their feet. On the crest of delirium Derby delivered a second goal from Alan Durban of such quality that Chelsea heads went down in despair, beaten both by the crowd and their opponents.

The third goal, scored by Kevin Hector, created pandemonium as the stands banged and terraces roared in a cacophony likely to shatter eardrums.

I left, hooting my car horn with my fellow drivers. Bars and pubs were filled to overflowing. There was joy in the streets.

It wasn't that we had reached the fourth round of the Cup that caused the celebration. It was the realisation that the amazing forecast made by Clough – 'We'll be in the First Division next year' – highly improbable as it seemed at the time was now a racing certainty. Brian Clough went home that night to his small house in Ferrers Way, a mystic hero.

Monday dawned, foggy and moist, the day when things, according to Clough, would be 'sorted out'. I tried to do some work, but the excitement I felt made it impossible. I hung around until midday when frustration drove me to ring him. Barbara answered, telling me that he had gone to the Kedleston Hotel to see some of the players. I decided to go to the hotel too.

Clough spotted me as he came out of a private room. He sighed. 'Don. Don't get involved. We're all in there doing our best for you. Okay?' He went into the toilet, leaving me dumbfounded. They were doing their 'best' *for me*?

But, as unpredictable as ever, it was a conciliatory Clough who came out of the loo and bought me a drink. 'Okay, Don. All the players refused to train today. I can't tell you anything else yet as the meeting's still going on.' He would ring me later with the results. As he set off towards the private room he stopped and turned.

'You might as well say hello to the captain. Let him know what maniac's backing him.' He went into the room and, seconds later, came out with Roy McFarland, the Rams' captain. He was not as tall as he seemed from my view in the stand. Smiling, he shook my hand and wished me the best of luck. 'Keep up the campaign,' he said.

'Thanks, Roy. You too,' I said.

Clough promised to ring me after the meeting.

I returned home, confused. It was clear that he'd not told the players to go on strike else, surely, he would have told me.

On the other hand they may have decided to keep it secret before they took action, to ensure nothing went wrong. And a strike would not start for a couple of days, at least. The FA would come down like a ton of bricks were it to be discovered that the ex-manager had met them shortly beforehand.

As I sat in my study doodling, awaiting Clough's promised telephone call, I was bothered by another thought. Although apparently welcoming my campaigning, it was clear that Clough had disliked my intrusion. In fact his 'mother hen' display over the players left me thinking that, in some way, he'd actually *resented* it. In sitting in disguise at the back of the Grand Theatre he may have been doing something more than testing my integrity. He may have also been keeping an eye on me. If I stepped out of line he'd drill me back in.

As I waited for Clough to get back to me, events at the hotel had moved on. Roy McFarland had telephoned Cliff Lloyd, secretary of the PFA, the union of professional footballers, seeking his opinion about their right to strike and the likely consequences flowing from such action. Going on strike was unheard of in football. Footballers loved playing the game. It would take something very special to stop them doing that. But this situation *was* special. Each player, regardless of his feelings about Clough, recognised his genius. The tale had circulated around town that Archie Gemmill had been heard to say that he 'hated the bastard but I'd give him my last half crown'.

They were, they knew, the best team in England and possibly, soon, in Europe. All that could be lost with Clough's departure. It wasn't just a manager they supported but their own careers. They would be unlikely just to stand on the touchline when those careers were at grave risk. The thought gave me a rising hope.

Inside the hotel room the pensive team looked to McFarland to put the question. It was 2.30 p.m. and all their talk had boiled down to one question: 'Boss, do we, or don't we strike?'

Clough bit his lip and looked down in intense thought. He only had to reassure them that striking was their only real option and they would take that as an instruction. He could not give it. 'It's not that time yet. Let's try one more thing. A letter. To the board. You all sign it. Roy, take it to the club this afternoon. Make sure that Longson gets it. And demand an answer by half past four, no later. And all of you go down there, stay down there. Don't shift until you get an answer.'

'What if they say no, boss?' It was Gemmill who spoke.

Clough paused. 'Occupy the place. Insist the directors see you.'

The players nodded their agreement. Their blood was up for it.

'I've never asked you lot before. Any of you lot capable of writing a letter?' Clough grinned as they broke into laughter.

McFarland went out to reception and came back with a sheet of hotel headed paper.

For half an hour they worked on it, reading it back, adding a word, subtracting a sentence, until they were satisfied. It demanded that 'the undersigned, ask that Mr Clough and Mr Taylor be reinstated immediately'.

All the players signed the letter.

Five minutes later a convoy of cars left the Kedleston Hotel and headed for the Baseball Ground.

It was a misty, chilly afternoon, but the players were on fire.

The game was afoot.

4

ATTACK

CLACK, CLACK, CLACK. A hard metallic noise, as from the pendulum of a gigantic clock, penetrated the pall of smog that surrounded the Baseball Ground. Ley Malleable Castings Ltd was at work next door. The repetitive sound irritated Sam Longson as he came from an extended lunch break into his office. On his desk was an envelope with the words 'Hand Delivered', printed in block capitals, on its front. He sat down, stared at the envelope, was about to ask his secretary who had placed it there and then couldn't be bothered. He picked up his ivory-handled letter opener.

Mondays always found him in a bleak mood, a carry-over from his early life as a farm labourer. Mondays then were 'Wash Days', cold and miserable rituals when the house windows were opened wide, whatever the temperature, hard and laborious work. Longson knew that many of the fans who stood on the terraces had also lived that kind of life. He also knew that production in manufacturing industry in Derby – as in other industrial towns – always rose when the team was winning and fell when it was losing. As he slit open the envelope Longson was aware that morale was currently low in the Derby work force. Nevertheless, he sighed comfortably. He told himself that, before sunset the next day, his problems would be over. He was about to make a move that would shut up the infernal Movement, regain the confidence of the players and keep the fans happy. It did not involve Clough. He began to read the letter.

If Longson had the blues it was worse for the bereaved players of Derby County standing outside in the clammy cold air. Jimmy Gordon, the trainer, had taken the letter from McFarland but said they would not be allowed to wait inside the ground unless they reported for training. As they shivered through lack of exercise, the slow, ponderous metallic clack, clack, clack of the industrial machine racked up the tension. But the explosion, when it came, emanated from within the stadium.

'Bloody hell!' The muffled roar came from the Longson's office. He wrenched open the door to stand trembling in the corridor, clutching the players' letter, purple with rage.

'Who the hell do they think they are! We own this club! We pay their wages! They work for us!' In a trice Longson had encapsulated the problem that besets every football club. Does it exist for the fans or are the fans there to support the club? On this day, 22 October 1973, a week after Clough's resignation, the feeling among the players outside in the street was that they were more important than the board and Brian Clough was even more important than anybody or anything. The problem was that neither Longson, nor his pusillanimous board, saw it their way.

Clack, clack, clack.

Longson dragged his secretary into the boardroom to dictate his angry response. No employee of his had ever dared challenge his authority in this manner.

He began 'You, the players, will shut up and do the job you're paid...' Then he waved a hand and told her to strike it out. He made another one or two emotional starts and then cooled down. The result was a curt reply, reminding the players of their obligations under contract. He left his secretary with an order that she hand it personally to McFarland. He then slipped away by a side entrance, unbeknown to the players. After his departure the secretary took the letter to the main entrance and handed it to McFarland in the street.

'Hold on,' he said to the middle-aged woman. He scanned the letter, then read aloud its contents. It gave them an ultimatum to report back for training the following morning or 'face the consequences'.

'We stay here,' said John McGovern, stubbornly folding his arms.

'There's a light on in the boardroom,' said Colin Todd, pointing. 'It's a board meeting.'

McFarland nipped in front of the secretary to prevent her locking them out again. 'Come on, lads. We don't let them out until they bring him back. We stay here all night and all tomorrow. We're not shifting.'

The players flooded into the reception and started down the corridor. 'We don't work for you directors,' yelled Willie Carlin. We work for the fans!'

'Come out, come out, wherever you are!' they shouted, banging fists on walls and woodwork.

Stuart Webb, club secretary, poked his head out of his office, waited until he saw his opportunity and then made his way upstairs to the boardroom, a haven in a storm.

McGovern turned to the secretary. 'Are all the directors up there?'

'I don't know,' she said in a quick and scared voice and disappeared in haste.

'They're up there,' said McFarland, no longer captain of a football team but leader of a mutinous crew. 'Hiding.'

Wee Willie Carlin, banged a radiator with his hand. 'Like rats.'

'Okay, lads.' McFarland nodded his head. 'Yeah. Okay.' He took a deep breath. 'Calm down. This is what we do.'

IN 1968, less than a year since Clough had become manager of Derby County, his 'team to beat all teams' was being assembled carefully, piece by piece. Other managers would have rushed out and bought 'good' players based solely on their playing record, without giving any thought to their suitability in terms of temperament, sociability, vulnerability, immaturity and potential skills, all of which Clough considered before making his choice.

He needed a 'sweeper', a player who would stand steadfast behind McFarland and cut out anyone who passed him. That rock was to be Dave Mackay. Aged thirty-three, Mackay was already a legend in his lifetime. Everyone in the world of football knew what a giant he had been in the fabulous Tottenham Hotspur side of the sixties. To imagine them without the great Scot is to picture the Merry Men without Robin Hood or the cowboy movie without John Wayne. He exerted an awesome presence, his muscular thighs and a barn-door of a chest topped by features that were positively piratical.

He tackled like a granite rock, exuding a passionate will to win and consumed by a ruthless relish for his work. His player colleagues were stirred by his personal example, as were the Scots in battle led to the skirl of the bagpipes. Though lacking speed, he was a non-stop mover between attack and defence, winning the ball, sending a pass, then bursting forward to receive the return. On reaching shooting distance he could finish in deadly fashion. He had another weapon in his strong armoury – he had a prodigiously long throw.

But that was yesterday. The old warrior was now in the twilight of his career. He was, in the jargon of footballers, 'past it'. He had twice suffered a broken leg and was now, clearly for all to see, tubby out front. No one in their right mind would sign him on as a full-time player. Mackay wasn't Taylor's idea of a sweeper. It was Clough who saw, where no else could, the advantage of converting the slowing midfielder into a sweeper. Yes, he wanted Mackay for his physical strength and skill in ball distribution but, more importantly, he wanted him to inspire the young defenders around him, teaching them the art of calmness and technique under pressure.

The Scotsman, Clough discovered to his alarm, was about to sign for Hearts, the Scottish side, as player-manager. Clough struck with the speed of a cobra. At the crack of dawn he set off down the M1, bound for White Hart Lane. He reached the Spurs ground at 8.30 a.m., and marched into its offices demanding to see Bill Nicholson, the manager. He demanded a brandy but was given a coffee instead and told to wait.

Nicholson, on arrival at the ground, was confronted by an impatient Clough, not waiting to be introduced. 'Bill. I'm Brian Clough. I've come to buy Dave Mackay. He's over the hill but we could use him. How much?'

Nicholson was one of the few who didn't bristle at Clough's abrasive and abrupt manner. Beaming in delight he put out his hand. 'Brian Clough! Well, let me shake your hand. Always wanted to meet you!'

Clough grinned, delighted to have his hand pumped by 'Bill Nick'. It prompted an apology. 'Sorry Bill, hardly any sleep, just driven down from Derby.'

'Brian, you scored five goals for the Football League side against Ireland. I was there. I'll never forget it. Damned bad luck about your knee. Sit you down. What can I get you?'

'Brandy. Bit chilly today,' Clough said, rubbing his hands.

Nicholson went to the drinks cabinet. 'Yorkshire men. Nothing if not blunt.' He gave Clough a wry smile.

'So, what about Dave?' Clough looked at his watch. He was behind schedule.

Nicholson poured out a measure of brandy and handed it to Clough. 'Sorry, Brian. You're too late. He's going to Hearts. He's signing today. It's out of my hands.'

'No, he can't do that. He'd be stupid. Whatever they want to pay him, I'll pay more. And I don't want him as an assistant to me; I want him to play for me. I'd like to talk to him.'

'He's not here. He's at the training ground.'

'Where is it?'

An hour later Clough stood on the touchline at the side of the training pitch, watching Mackay, muddied and panting, coming towards him, his breath steaming in the cold air.

Clough was direct. 'Dave. Brian Clough. I want you to get showered. We need you more than Hearts. How much they paying you?'

Mackay stared. 'Er…'

'It doesn't matter. We'll double it. You're coming up to Derby with me. We'll pay for your train back.'

'Er…'

'I'm Derby's manager. I'll give you ten grand. Now. In cash. We'll get promoted this year and we'll win the First Division championship. I'll tell you about the team. Great lads. You'll love 'em. So get changed, have a shower and I'll see you in half an hour.'

'Er…'

'We're going to win the League. And we'll be in Europe in four years. Forget Spurs. Think Rams.'

'Er…so you want me to play for Derby County?' The slow Glaswegian voice at last managed to issue from his mouth, accompanied by a shake of the head and a disbelieving smile.

It was Clough's sheer confidence and no-nonsense attitude that finally swayed Mackay, though he didn't remember much of the journey north. He was fast asleep as soon as they hit the M1.

Arriving at the ground he was introduced to Taylor and escorted into Clough's office. 'Coffee or tea, Dave?'

'Tea. Brian, I canna sign for you. I canna call you boss. I'm older than you are.'

Clough nodded. 'Grant you. Don't call me anything – except bastard occasionally.'

Mackay laughed. 'Aw, come on. This is a joke.'

'Did I bring you all the way up here for a joke? Dave, I want you as sweeper. Behind Roy McFarland. He'll play for England soon.'

'Er…who's McFarland? Eh. Is this April Fool's?'

'No. Roy Mac's the next England centre half. He's a great bloke, on the field and off. Forget Jack Charlton. And Norman Hunter. We've got Kevin Hector, Alan Hinton and John O'Hare. I only have players who I like and who the players like.'

'You're joking. I'm fat and tired and I'm thirty-three going on thirty-four!'

Clough pursed his lips, made no response, got up and left the room. Mackay heard the key turn in the lock.

'Can you hear me, Dave?' Clough's voice came from the corridor.

'Er…you've locked the door!'

'That's right. You're staying there till you get to your senses.'

Mackay sat down heavily, eyebrows raised, shaking his head and bursting into laughter. He picked up a magazine. 'Fuckin' maniac,' he grunted, then came another outburst of laughter.

'Dave?' The voice came back. 'You won't have much running about to do. All we need you for is to stroll about, sweep up behind Roy Mac.'

'My legs have gone!'

'We don't want your legs. We want your brain, your mouth and your heart. They're all bigger than anybody's.'

There was a pause.

'How much did you say I'd get? For signing?'

The door was unlocked. Clough re-entered.

'Five grand.'

'Fifteen.'

Clough narrowed his eyes, peered at Mackay. 'Fifteen. But spread over three years.'

'Er…done.'

Mackay's signing posed a threat to Clough's standing in the eyes of the younger players. Mackay had been right. He could hardly call his new manager 'boss'. It was a mark of Clough's flexibility and instinctive understanding of the needs of every player that, following the fast-track signing, he never tried to browbeat or trick Mackay in any way. He even ignored the older man's habit of only turning up for training when he felt like it. Like Hinton, Mackay took on a new lease of life. He was born again, an inspiration to his teammates – as Clough had expected.

After Hector he became the crowd's favourite. Whenever I think of him I see a big chest clad in a white shirt that was turning crimson from a broken nose. Many a player would have left the pitch, but not Mackay. He was battle hardened, resolute and dynamic in every way. He repaid his wages and fee in his first season.

When Longson first heard about the signing he was astonished. 'Brian, do you know we've signed the most expensive and unfit player in the whole of the Football League?'

'And the best,' said Clough.

Ironically, Longson's elevation to football scout by Clough at the time of McFarland's signing had fed his ego too much. He could not believe that Mackay, 'overweight and slow', could possibly justify the money spent on him and said so forcibly. Clough ignored his grumblings, allowing each game in which Mackay played to speak for him. They did, loudly.

Mackay's arrival marked the beginning of the greatest years in the history of Derby County. The younger players looked up to the Scot as if he were Clough on the pitch alongside them. They took his directions and followed his example. Not since the days of Carter and Docherty would there be such talent working together in such harmony. It soon became, indeed, a 'beautiful' team.

Clough told me that he had been conscious of taking a risk with Mackay, but that to achieve anything in life worth achieving was to involve some form of gambling. All he did was try to reduce the odds against failure. This was the nearest he ever came to 'winging' his way to success.

Mackay's signing was to prove a turning point in the Longson-Clough relationship. Longson was forced to accept defeat. It left him with a sour taste. He began to see Clough more as a rival than as a putative son.

'SHOW YOURSELVES! Come on out!'

'You're not going till we get this sorted!'

Players drummed and rippled radiators with pens, coins, anything they could lay their hands on, the noise carried by the central heating pipes into the boardroom. David Nish and Colin Todd approached it. They banged on the door with their fists. 'Open up. We're serious. Open the door!'

Downstairs covering the exits were Colin Boulton and Ronnie Webster. Other players roamed the corridors, searching for any director who might be hiding. For the staff, women as well as men, it was a scary experience. They kept their office doors shut.

Clack, clack, clack went Ley Malleable Castings.

Rattle rattle went the radiators.

It was dark now and the siege of the Baseball Ground was in its third hour. All this time the players erroneously believed the board was meeting to appoint a new manager and thereby kill the Protest Movement. If they'd known there was only one director present, Jack Kirkland, brother of Bob, plus the club secretary, Stuart Webb, they would not have bothered.

McFarland stood looking up at the boardroom window and then at a drainpipe close by. He grasped it in both hands, pulling himself upwards. Halfway through shinning up the pipe his foothold slipped and the pipe felt loose. He descended quickly and jumped the last few feet to the ground, uninjured.

In the boardroom Webb poured out a third cup of coffee from

the machine and handed it to Kirkland. Webb had become Clough's bête noire within the club. Both men were slim, good-looking and smartly turned out. They were also equally ambitious. But in other terms they were chalk and cheese. Whereas Webb stood for rational organisation and efficiency in the workplace, Clough tended to create chaos, which had appalled Webb on their first encounter. Clough disliked Webb for his quiet, charming demeanour behind which, he thought, was a scheming mind. Webb declared that he had his job to do and not even Clough would be allowed to walk over him. In response Clough told his friends and allies that Webb was bent on building himself a 'little empire' within the club. Having successfully built up a local travel agency, Webb had grounds for thinking that Clough treated him badly because, in Clough's eyes, he was a typical businessman who exploited football for his own ends. The bottom line was that no club secretary in England would have found it easy to tolerate Clough's careless habits and dictatorial manner in dealing with office staff.

Webb and Kirkland, sitting at the boardroom table, hoped the players would give up and go home. Kirkland, the owner of a large plant hire and building company, found skulking from players demeaning. Suddenly he found it too much. 'What can they do to us?' he whispered. 'I'll ring the police.'

Webb, aware of the bad publicity that might arise from a police visit, was not keen on the idea. Kirkland, on reflection, had to agree with him. 'You're right. The police guarding directors? I can see the headlines. We'd be a laughing stock.'

Kirkland and Webb fell silent.

Gemmill left David Nish guarding an exit to walk into a neighbouring street where Clough's car stood. The window slid down and Clough looked out. 'How's it going, my wee laddy?'

'Okay, boss. They're still in there. Soon as anything happens I'll be back.'

Clough nodded and slipped in his second Sinatra tape of the afternoon.

Archie returned to the ground.

Clack, clack, clack.

'I need a piss.' Kirkland grimaced at Webb. 'I've wanted one for the last hour.'

There was no toilet off the boardroom. Webb got up and went to the bar, returning with the ice bucket. 'Remember not to drink out of it.'

Kirkland was much relieved. It was 5 p.m.

Whoooo! The Ley factory joined in the communal hooting as factories all over town disgorged their workers.

Inside the boardroom Kirkland and Webb kept their silent vigil. The rattling had ceased and the voices of the players were silenced.

'I think they've gone,' whispered Webb.

'They heard the bull,' Kirkland smiled. 'Home time.' He looked at his watch, then at Webb. 'Want to make a break for it?'

Webb nodded. 'Stick together.'

Kirkland opened the door quietly and stepped into the deserted corridor, Webb behind him. Cautiously they edged their way to the staircase – to meet McFarland and Todd ascending.

For a split second the defenders and attackers stared at each other. Kirkland made the first move, roughly barging his way between McFarland and Todd.

'Kirkland's got out!' yelled Todd looking down. 'Stop him!'

He turned to face Webb, who looked calmly back at him, straightening his tie with a faint smile, giving out a calm confidence that he didn't feel. 'I want to help,' he said. 'What can I do?'

McFarland and Todd exchanged hesitant glances. Finally, McFarland stood aside and allowed Webb, breathing a sigh of relief, to walk down the stairs.

On the ground floor, Kirkland faced David Nish and Ronnie Webster, both defenders, their job description making them appropriate to the task of barring his exit. 'You're not going till you get the boss back,' said Boulton.

Kirkland nodded. 'Look, lads, you don't know what you're doing. I'm going out of that door.' He turned to see Webb joining him, behind him McFarland and Todd.

'I've called the police,' said Kirkland sternly. 'You're committing a criminal offence of holding a man to ransom. I suggest you back off.'

'Mr Kirkland, all we want to do is talk to you,' McFarland said urgently. You've got to know how we feel!'

Kirkland ignored him and barged past, evading clutching hands to quickly exit.

'Sod it.' Nish and Webster chased after him. Kirkland reached his car, opened the driver's door and got inside.

Boulton and Webster tried to stop it closing.

Kirkland shouted as he fired the engine. 'You're going to get a surprise in the morning!'

He drove away, Webster still grasping the open door, Nish banging on the side of the car with his fist.

Kirkland entered the road and accelerated, Webster, forced to release the door, stumbled and fell to the ground. With a screech of tyres Kirkland swung his car into a turn, the lateral force banging the door shut.

Webster and Nish were joined by McFarland and Todd. The street was now deserted. They were left staring at each other in defeat, heads going down slowly.

'All that wasted time,' said Todd bitterly.

'What did he mean, we'll get a surprise tomorrow?' Webster posed the question.

McFarland sighed. 'Let's go and see the boss.'

Clough was nodding off when a tap came at his side window. He jerked to awareness, saw McFarland's face and pressed the button, the window lowering.

'There was only Kirkland there,' said McFarland. 'He said we'll get a surprise in the morning.'

Clough momentarily shut his eyes. He knew what it meant.

They all knew what it meant.

5

COUNTER ATTACK

THE CLOSE OF THE '68 season saw Derby County promoted to Division One, the Rams closing out with an eleven-match unbeaten run. The sense of euphoria in the town, which had started with the victory over Chelsea in the FA Cup, had continued throughout the season and brought new fans flocking to the Baseball Ground.

Longson's reservations about Clough were lost in all the excitement. He treated Clough in the manner of Caesar receiving home a victorious Roman general. There was champagne, celebrations, congratulations and presents for the manager and family. When one of the directors complained that the chairman had bought Clough a new Mercedes, Longson declared, 'He can have my Rolls if he wants. He's given us a bloody sight more than he's taken out.' In addition Longson had handed Clough a bunch of shares in Derby County FC* and a full-length suede coat. He bought a waste disposal unit for Barbara, and numerous toys for Nigel, Simon and Libby.

But something was missing. Not for the recipient of the bounty, but for the giver. It began with a television interview by Guy Thomas for *BBC Midlands Today*. Longson and Clough faced the camera in a two shot.

The chairman spoke first. 'This man,' said Longson, putting an affectionate hand on Clough's arm, 'he's not only a great manager, he's a prophet. Do you realise he forecast all this when he got here, when we were down in the dumps?'

He removed his hand expecting Clough to reciprocate. He had

---

* *Something he would regret at a later date.*

taken a big risk in appointing a manager from a lower division, hadn't he? Clough was bound to thank him for the trust that had been placed in 'the lad'.

'Yes,' said Clough. 'It's not been easy. I've a lot more work to do. We're not ready for the big top yet. We're still a bit stick in the mud, the way we do things. We need changes. But I'll make sure we get them.' He thanked no one.

Longson strode off in anger. Clough's lack of gratitude in private he had withstood, but on television, in front of millions?

For others on the board, Bob Kirkland, Bradley, Bob Innes and the rest, their suffering had gone on since Clough's arrival at the club. If he had not thanked Longson, he had not treated him badly. At least he recognised his position as chairman. For the ordinary directors, life at the Baseball Ground had been one humiliation heaped upon another. Clough loathed football directors, not just because they were businessmen, but because they paid to stand in his limelight. Their vicarious excitement at winning football matches, for Clough, was anathema. His rage knew no bounds when he was told by Keeling that one of the directors had been overheard saying that he'd rather be a director of a club in a lower division under a 'decent manager' than suffer under Clough in the First Division. Clough had to be restrained from bursting into the boardroom, on hearing *that* news.

The directors watched the *Midlands Today* interview, Kirkland muttering to Bradley, 'Bloody Napoleon, look at him.' It wasn't too silly a remark. Although Napoleon had been statesman, dictator and army commander, Clough, in a tiny microcosm of the world at large, had similar attributes as well as failings. Charm and popularity in abundance was theirs. They both had charisma. As Clough involved himself in the personal lives of his players, so Napoleon took an interest in every aspect of the lives of his countrymen. That dangerous inflator of ego, determined and single-minded ambition, had lured both men to the heights of success. Even after Napoleon's eventual defeat, his soldiers still considered him their true leader and had fought for him to regain control. It was the same with Clough, the players fighting for their fallen manager.

With the excitement over and the closed season upon him, Longson went on long holidays and in consequence saw less and less of Clough. Over weeks of having nothing to do but lie on sun decks he had time to reflect and feel again those sparks of resentment provoked by Clough's displayed lack of gratitude. It was only with an effort that he was able to damp down the anger.

As Longson lounged in warmer climes, Clough was constantly at work planning for his first season in the premier First Division.

ON A GLORIOUS spring morning, he went to visit his neighbour, the factory of Ley Malleable Castings. Ever since he had first sat down in the dug-out to stare at the Pop Side he had made up his mind to get rid of 'that bloody awful shed' and replace it with a modern stand as befitted a top club. Unknowingly, his move would annoy Longson and fan the flames of his resentment even more. He had been approached by Clough so frequently on the matter of the new stand that Longson had termed it an obsession. He wasn't averse to the idea, but he had strong reservations. 'Oh, we'll do it, eventually. Don't forget a stand there, Brian, would get rid of most of the Pop Siders' terracing. That's where they shout up for the team, where we get most of our support from. Fans in seats don't shout much, do they?'

And, of course it was all a matter of cost, including the purchase of land from the factory. Architects had to be consulted as well as the town planning authority. These were matters they could deal with, Longson argued, when the club made more money following a successful season or two in Division One.

But when Clough had an idea he felt strongly about, indeed it became an obsession. Consideration for Longson's feelings was the last thing on his mind when he walked into the works next door.

He was immediately recognised and surrounded by dozens of workers.

'Gentlemen,' said Clough. 'A pleasure to meet you all.' He handed out vouchers, which he'd had printed, into each grubby hand, guaranteeing the holder a free ticket on the Pop Side for a game in the new season in Division One. They were thrilled at the great Clough treating them in such a manner. It was witnessed by a frowning company chairman who was visiting the works that day, a fact that Clough had established the week before, through a spy in the factory.

The chairman scowled heavily and came down from his perch to find out what was going on. He met Clough, who gave him no chance to speak.

'Brian Clough.' Out went the hand. 'Mr Chairman, I presume? You got my letter?'

'Er…'

'You didn't. Never mind.' Clough, who had never sent any such letter, turned to address the crowd. 'The town, the club and all you great lads here.' He had their quiet attention for his address. 'Derby County Football Club has given you all more efficiency and productivity. Everybody knows how well you lads do when the club's winning. In return what have you done for us? You've been magnificent. You helped us to get promotion by belching out your black bloody smoke so Arsenal and Chelsea couldn't see our goal. Well done.'

Clough grinned as the workers broke out in laughter and delight. Clough handed the chairman a fistful of vouchers. 'For the wife, kids and anybody else.'

The bemused chairman then walked with Clough to the side of the works that ran parallel to the Pop Side. 'I estimate,' said Clough, addressing him, 'This is where we need your land. You don't use it. So whatever you get for it is a bonus. And what is that bonus? Millions of people watching you on television. Why? Because *Match of the Day* will be here more times than you can count! And what will the world be watching? Wait for it, they will be watching a great sign right across the stand. It will say the "Ley Stand"!'

Returning to the ground, Clough rang Longson in the Caribbean, telling him that he'd secured the land free of charge. Longson was unimpressed. 'That stand will cost us a quarter of a million, Brian, whether we get the land free or not.'

'Sam, it will raise the ground capacity to forty-one thousand. I've got loads of people already asking me for a season ticket in it. You'll get your money back in two seasons.'

Events would prove Clough correct. But Longson was left, once more after a dispute with Clough, grumbling to himself. It was another example of Clough getting too big for his boots he thought, as he lay back resignedly under the sun. He reminded himself that when he got home he'd sit Clough down and acquaint him with proper procedures. He would lay down the rules that had to be followed by company law as well as in the interests of efficient administration.

Clough left for home playing 'My Way' on his car radio. He was as pleased as Punch. He was due to take Barbara and the kids to Majorca that evening.

And so the land was acquired. The Ley chairman, however, would be greatly disappointed when he sat down to watch Derby County's first game on television with the new stand in place. The TV gantry was based inside the stands. The insignia, 'The Ley Stand', emblazoned across the top of the construction, faced outwards with the cameras. It would never be seen on television.

THE PLAYERS' SIEGE of the Baseball Ground, having failed due to a lack of people to be besieged, proved a turning point in the campaign. Hardly had they risen from their beds on the following morning when there came the worst news possible. Jack Kirkland's 'surprise', shouted out as he'd made his escape, was, as feared, an announcement of a new manager. And they had guessed, correctly, who that might be.

Roy McFarland was first to be told in a phone call from Longson himself. It quickly spread to the rest of the team. I was given the news by George Edwards. 'Have you heard? Dave Mackay's the new manager.' He was currently managing Nottingham Forest.

It was all over town. The newspaper seller at the corner of Victoria Street and St James Street sold out within the hour. The players' telephones buzzed angrily all morning. By lunchtime it was decided that the captain, McFarland, would ring Mackay and tell him he was not wanted. McFarland, a decent, likeable man, found it difficult. 'Dave. Look mate. Don't come to Derby. Please? We're all trying to get Cloughie back. You know, we're desperate.'

'Sorry, Roy. I'm not your mate now. I'm your boss.' Mackay had been over the moon to get the call from Longson. It was simply unbelievable. He had been given control of the best team in English football without even having to attend an interview. He could not possibly turn it down. As manager of nearby Nottingham Forest he didn't even have to move house.

'Roy,' he said ponderously in his slow Caledonian voice, 'what are you asking me to do?' He was in an obdurate mood. 'This is a job in a million. Come on.'

'Dave, managing Forest and coming here are two different things. You're in the Second Division and we're in the First. As a player you were terrific. But none of us want you as manager. Can't you see that?'

'Roy, I'm the only manager who can unite everybody, the fans, the players and the board behind the club. Can you not see that?'

'I know, but see it from our point of view. We don't think you'll be good for us. Simple as that. Don't you see? We want Cloughie back.'

Mackay refused to 'see' anything. He repeatedly told McFarland that every manager in the country would jump at the chance to manage Derby County.

McFarland gave it one last try. 'Dave, can't you see that Longson's picked you because he's frightened? He's done it to shut us up. You were handy, close by, an ex-player, you know, a great player. A popular bloke.'

'Aye. All the more reason I'm your manager! Roy, I've been offered the job and I've taken it. I've already signed. Now just bugger off and tell the players I want them in for training, tomorrow.'

McFarland was left holding a dead receiver. He put it down in dismay. Then he picked it up and dialled each player. The normally shy and retiring John McGovern gave vent to his feelings. 'That's a dirty rotten trick. Let's go on strike.'

Most of the players were for immediate action. However, Nish cautiously suggested that they held a proper meeting, ending with a vote for a strike. It was necessary, he said, to counter any claim by the club that it had not been a proper decision. It would also distance Clough from their cause, thereby sheltering him from any accusation that he was behind it. The sensible proposal was adopted.

It was a sunny and warm autumnal day and McFarland called the players and their families down to a hotel in Newton Solney, a pleasant village close to Repton. There, the men would pow-wow while the wives played with their under school-age children outside on the lawns. Clough would be there.

Meanwhile, I consulted McGuinness and Holmes. We decided to call another mass meeting for later in the week. It was a decision that didn't fill me with enthusiasm. I knew that Mackay's popularity in the town, on which Longson was counting, would go some way to mollifying the fans. But, by midday I was less worried, having fielded dozens of calls bringing assurances from the movers and the shakers that they would not be moved, nor shaken, by Mackay's appointment. I was considerably reassured when Roy McFarland phoned me to wish the Movement the best of luck and inform me about the players proposed meeting.

Clough, it transpired, had already lit the fuse by tackling Mackay with a phone call, reinforcing all of McFarland's objections. Didn't Mackay accept that a special relationship existed between himself and the players? What was the point of accepting the job as a stop-gap when the 'true boss' would be back soon? How could he get the players behind him when, clearly, they would not cooperate?

Clough summed it up. 'Dave, you might take over as manager in name, but never in spirit. You're stepping into a hornets' nest.'

'You sound as if you're threatening me, Brian,' said Mackay.

'Never. Not you Dave. Not with your big chest. You were a fantastic player but, I'm telling you, if you stay as manager Derby will go down the pan. It might not be next year or the year after, but they will drop.'

'Why did you resign then if you loved it so much?' Mackay knew he'd scored a bull's-eye by the hesitation in Clough's reply.

'You're right. I shouldn't have. But you do things in this life you regret. Joining Derby could be a big regret for you, Dave. Think about it.'

'I've thought about it, Brian. That's it. Bye.' He put the phone down.

When Clough told me what had happened I wasn't too disappointed, McFarland's briefing about the planned strike having given me cause for optimism. Clough's first meeting with the players may have ended with a miscalculation, the second a frustrating delay, but this – the third – meeting just had to lead to strike action. McFarland promised to ring me with the result.

The players, on arrival at Newton Solney, had still not heard from their union as to their rights in taking strike action. McFarland again rang Cliff Lloyd, its secretary.

'It's a new ball game,' he said solemnly, not recognising his innocent pun. 'We've never had talk of strike before. It's all to do with contract. Get legal advice on it. Make sure you're not endangering your careers.'

Some of the burning passion that had driven the players cooled somewhat at this response. But then, in strode an angry Clough, his three-quarter length raincoat flapping. He looked around at the trusting expressions. He only had to say the word.

'Gentlemen, this is not a defeat. This is a challenge.' Clough looked at the barman. 'Bubbly all round.' Champagne. To celebrate their journey together, their success and their bonding. As the drink flowed, they recalled great moments in Europe, laughing as all footballers do at minor disasters. Clough laughed as Taylor recounted the story of his arrest by an Italian policeman midway through the away game at Juventus. They even joked about Mackay's reaction when he scored a wonderful own goal in an FA cup tie against Queens Park Rangers. As they chatted, their feeling for Clough surprised even the dourest of players, Archie Gemmill. A united team, they forgot Clough's fines, his verbal beatings and saw him as the man who had turned their lives into a glorious adventure.

After the joking came nostalgic reminiscence. More than one player wiped an eye that Indian summer's day in the country. They felt like a band of brothers who had fought a war against all odds and who should have been celebrating victory, instead of mourning the loss of their leader.

Nostalgia spent, they mellowed into moments of silence in which bitterness began to show itself. McGovern was the first to denounce those 'morons' in the boardroom who only cared for their social lives in club hospitality. Clough now apologised to Henry Newton, a player he'd signed with the promise that he would never quit the club. Nish nodded. He was too full of emotion to say anything in return.

The players now witnessed a new Clough, one humbly confessing his guilt and acknowledging the pain he'd caused the players.

'I resigned because I was angry. Longson telling me I couldn't do this, I couldn't do that. What was I doing on the front page as well as the back page? My photo in the *Express* every day. So bloody jealous. I was publicising their club! And me so bloody stupid. I'm now apologising to all of you. I quit without a thought what it would do to you. I've let you down. I bloody well—' He couldn't continue.

It was stunning. Clough, close to tears in front of his team.

In the silence that followed the first words were spoken tersely by McFarland.

'We're not letting them get away with it.'

Other voices joined in agreement. Palms met palms, the smacking of hands ramming home their determination.

Clough snapped out of his weepiness. 'Come on. Outside,' he said roughly. 'Let's join the wives and bairns. It's a lovely day. Let's make the most of it.'

They followed him out on to the terrace to see the wives playing with their children in the still warm afternoon. Clough brought their attention.

'Wives and ladies.' There was laughter. 'I'm going to make a suggestion. These lads mean the world to me. I'm not dumping them. I'm going back to the Baseball Ground. I don't know how yet. But I will.'

Cheering. Excitement.

'Now why don't we all, all of us, kiddies, all the families. Why don't we pack our bags and get off to Majorca for a few days?'

'Yes!' was the communal shout. They talked rapidly over each other. East Midlands Airport was only half an hour's drive away, with regular flights of only a couple of hours. They would be round the swimming pool or on the beach tomorrow afternoon. They laughed, imagining the faces of the directors when they heard the news and the trouble it would cause Webb. Wives and players marvelled too, at their sudden strength in kinship. It was all so wonderful, so brave, so defiant.

'We'll come back together and stay together,' said McGovern. 'I'm not playing for them again. Why can't we strike like the miners? What's so different?'

David Nish shouted out. 'Read all about it! Rams herd flee with shepherd Clough!' It brought more laughter.

But also came a heeding voice. 'The boss isn't with us any more. He can't be seen travelling with us, can he?'

'Course he can,' said Nish. 'We bumped into him. He just happened to be on the same flight.'

'Yeah,' said Clough. 'And you lot just feel you need a break. It's not striking, is it?'

'Let's do what the boss says. Let's get off to Majorca,' said Ronnie Webster.

'Yeah, let's do it. Let's damned well do it,' was the consensus. 'We're Fire Proof United.'

'United we stand,' said Clough, remembering his working-class days in the industrial north-east.

And what a smack in the eye for Longson. The press would have a field day. What better demonstration of unity? This was the impetuous Clough, the one loved by the media. He ordered more champagne. They toasted their victories, then a succession of hopes for the future.

'To the best of the bosses.' McFarland raised his glass.

'To the best players in the land,' said Clough.

They toasted their wives, their children and their future. Webster started to sing the number one song on *Top of the Pops*. 'We're all off to sunny Spain, Viva Espana,' then faltered as he searched for a suitable lyric.

It was taken up by Willie Carlin. 'We're all off to sunny Spain, no more directors. We've had trouble from them all… kick them out the door.' Amidst more laughter, they all joined in the poorly scanned, but exciting verse. A few linked arms and began to jig around the lawn.

Someone inside the hotel struck a few piano chords and then accompanied them. Soon all the players joined in, including some of the wives. It could have been a large family group having a picnic in the golden days of Edwardian England. The singing flowed across the hotel garden and into the village where a genius of a talking African Grey parrot, sitting inside the open door of the Unicorn pub, entertained the customers with a proper rendering of the song: 'Y Viva España! España por Favor!'

It was getting late. The euphoric state, fuelled by champagne, had given way to a dull feeling. The larger party now broke up into small family groups. Wives talked with their husbands, low voiced because no one wanted to sound like a drag. Of course they all wanted to go. Of course they did. But of course they couldn't. They all knew it in their heart of hearts. The wives especially. How do you suddenly secure seats for tomorrow's flight to Palma – at least thirty people wanting to get on the same aircraft? And how do you book a hotel in time? And what about the cost? The players only earned £350 a week. And what about their children of school age? They could never bring themselves to take them out of school. They'd be shamed publicly.

The afternoon ended as the families departed in dribs and drabs. The sun was low in the sky when Clough collected Barbara, Simon, Nigel and Libby, handing over the car keys to his wife.

At 6 p.m. he rang me with the news that no decision about strike action had been taken. But 'the campaign went on'. He was 'thinking about what to do next'.

I was disbelieving, unable to understand the hiatus.

'Eh,' he said, sensing my mood, 'Nothing's over till it's over.'

Later, that evening, he rang me again. He'd just had news: he believed that the club trainer, Gordon, had turned against him by ordering the players back to work.

'I signed him on,' he said. 'But it was me who kept the players playing, not him. He's a good trainer but he hasn't a clue how I kept lads playing when he thought they were injured.' He spoke bitterly. He was not going to give up the fight.

It wasn't the first time he'd spoken about injuries. It was always a battle to keep the entire first team playing. I had been continually surprised, as had many Derby fans, that Clough had managed to lead a first team squad of only thirteen players to the League Championship. They were no more immune from injury than those of Arsenal or Manchester United with much bigger squads. Hector, for example, had sustained a back injury, but Clough had him playing in a match within twenty-four hours of undergoing spinal traction in hospital. Pat, Hector's wife, had gone to the Baseball Ground and given Clough a roasting for endangering her husband's career. Clough, always hating to upset the wives, apologised and sent her a bunch of flowers.

McFarland's ankle injury, however, sustained while on duty for England, transmuted into a groin injury due to an imbalance while playing. It was a mark of his courage and skill that few fans noticed any difference. From the tales I heard and from odd comments made by Clough, himself, I believe that he turned out injured players in defiance against the gods who had inflicted upon him a career-ending knee injury at the early age of twenty-seven. The team was a projection of himself. It didn't matter that he was their ex-manager.

He was part of them and they were part of him.

AFTER THE EUPHORIC day in Newton Solney, the players woke up to a dawn of cold reality. But still they refused to report for training, content with running around their local parks. Gordon, the trainer, Clough discovered, was now telephoning the younger players to warn them that, at the start of their careers, they could be suspended by the FA if they went on strike.

Clough rang me the same morning. 'I'm on *Nationwide* tonight. The BBC have asked if you'll go on with me.' I needed no bidding. It was a great opportunity to put his case. It would put enormous pressure on the Derby County board.

We took the 2 p.m. train from Derby, arriving in London by 4.30. A taxi was waiting. The driver was a Spurs fan, instantly recognising his fare.

We listened to his tale of how he saw his favourites go down heavily 5–0 at the Baseball Ground. For once, Clough said little, content to let the driver ramble on.

We sat down in the make-up room just before 6. Clough hated having his face powdered. 'Why can't I shine as I am?' he told the girl. 'I'm a star already.'

We watched the TV news before entering the studio. There was nothing about Clough. It was mainly concerned with the Yom Kippur war between Israel and Egypt.

Frank Bough greeted us in the studio, with a cheery grin. On air he went directly to me, asking why I was spending all my time working for Cloughie.

I took a deep breath and said that he was a great manager, the likes of which we would never see again at Derby County. I said he inspired his players as no other manager could, that he always got the player he wanted and that his charisma inspired everybody, fans as well as players. How could the directors simply throw away the greatest manager—

Clough interrupted me, with a deadpan expression, to say that I was on 10 per cent of his future salary. It produced laughter in the studio.

'So where do we go from here?' Bough genially asked Clough. 'What does the future hold for Brian Clough?'

'I go on. I've got what it takes. I can manage players. I can produce a winning team.'

'But Derby County have a new manager. Dave Mackay.' Bough raised his eyebrows at Clough, in query.

'Great player, Dave,' agreed Clough. 'Did everything I asked of him. Great player. Fantastic player.'

He stared challengingly at Bough, who skilfully but wisely, moved on to ask Clough if he had any ambition to take on the job as England manager.

As usual, Clough created no little surprise by his reply. 'Yes, but I want to stay as a club manager. I'd do both jobs. I wouldn't want to turn up at games just to watch players.'

We arrived back in Derby just after 10 p.m. Mike Keeling was at the station to pick us up.

He had bad news.

6

IN THE TRENCHES

MIKE KEELING SPOKE in a flat, resigned manner. 'Longson and the board – they've had their solicitor at the ground all afternoon. They say you've fiddled expenses.'

'Oh aye,' said Clough, sharply. 'What expenses?'

'They reckon you've done illegal transfer deals, given players unauthorised money and you've dipped into ticket sales and petty cash.'

'How do you know this?'

'Bradley told me.'

'Bradley. The rabbit.' Clough was contemptuous. 'He's the weakest link in the board, if it's of any help. Now that Mike has left the board,' he added, winking at me.

'I kept your flag flying, Brian,' said Keeling, turning the Mercedes into Slade Close.

'Not long enough. You shouldn't have resigned,' said Clough. 'Hang on a minute. I want a word with Don.'

We walked into my garden to look over the expanse of farmland towards Burnaston village. There, a pink-washed farmhouse glowed softly in the moonlight. 'You know what I like to do?' he murmured. 'Go home, lock the door. Take the phone off the hook and know the bastards can't get at me.' He paused and looked at me. 'You still need a haircut.'

I gave a short, polite laugh.

Clough tightened his mouth. 'I told you about that board. They've spread a rumour about you and now they're going for me.

Those expenses and transfer deals all happened before Webb arrived. They can accuse me because there was no proper club secretary. I had to carry the can.'

'Does it worry you?' I said.

He was grinning. I looked at him in surprise.

'Don, I'm not daft. I've kept records as well. They wouldn't dare. Eh.' He touched my elbow. 'You know what it proves? It proves you've got 'em worried. Even with Mackay there. They're getting dirtier. So what's their next trick going to be?'

When we got back to the car Clough sat inside, nodding at Keeling. 'If you can get proof of all this, Mike, I'm suing them.'

THE WAR BETWEEN Clough and the board intensified in 1969–70, as Derby's first season in Division One ended with them fourth in the table, a qualifying position for European football. It was an outstanding achievement in the short time since his take over of the club, which had then been languishing in the lower half of Division Two.

The new season was to see the introduction of a much needed club secretary. Longson, in his *Memoirs* wrote:

> We were all under Clough's spell. Unfortunately for the club, he took more and more control on and off the field. I told him time and time again that a football club is a limited company subject to company law and also subject to the rules and regulations of the Football Association as well as the Football League. He ignored me. But then came rescue in the form of a new secretary, Stuart Webb. Ironically, he wasn't my choice but Clough's.

The fans, in their ignorance of the readying for battle within, flooded into the Baseball Ground to see football the like of which had not been seen for decades. From my seat in the Ley Stand I witnessed clean and decisive play, delighting the crowd in the fast break out from defence into attack. In Kevin Hector, the 'King' of the Baseball Ground, the team had a player who could judge to a split second when a tackle was about to strike, at which he would skip over it, his balance and poise wonderful to behold. The majestic Mackay, shouting at his younger defenders, marshalling them under attack, urging them when to go forward, was always ready to trundle forward himself and shoot at goal or make prodigious throw-ins from either touchline.

McFarland, as Clough had forecast, was now the best centre half in England. Positioned in front of Mackay he was flanked by dependable defenders Ronnie Webster and John Robson, the pitch their chess board, always keen to foretell opposition moves. John McGovern, shy and self-effacing, never quite fluent in his staccato bursts – even ungainly looking – was always a highly effective link man. Colin Todd, with his fluid, clean and lightning tackles, nearly always came out with the ball and without hesitation would release it with a well-drilled pass. Gemmill, small and courageous, delighted the crowd with his mazy dribbling into the opposition's penalty area. Hinton's accuracy in crossing the ball was a constant threat to any defence. He was also the perfect striker, unleashing his shot with a waist-high follow-through that ensured accuracy as well as power. And O'Hare, with a chest almost as wide as Mackay's, was the ideal target man, strong on the ball and quick in the swivel or turn to make a vital pass to runners on either side.

Mackay's rock-like presence in defence and John O'Hare's strength up front, anchored the perfect football machine that was Derby County. Bubbling with confidence, the players could hardly wait for the next match. Once, having trounced Tottenham Hotspur, little John McGovern was ecstatic. 'Jimmy Greaves shook hands with me as we came off. I didn't wash them for the rest of the day!'

The most satisfying result for Clough, the players and the fans, would have been a win over Leeds United, the 'dirty mob' as Clough described them. He was deeply disappointed to lose to them in both the away and the home games, but swore he would get his revenge the following season.

ONE WEDNESDAY MORNING in May 1970, suddenly and unannounced, two accountants from the FA dropped in at the ground to carry out a spot check of the books. Clough, without a club secretary, had found it impossible to concentrate on football when the offices were in such a mess and in his frustration had contributed to the chaos. In this pre-Webb period what the accountants discovered was disturbing. Money was missing, players listed without being officially registered and money paid out without record. There was a haphazard recording of season ticket sales and petty cash had been paid out without chits. The result of this enquiry was that Derby County FC was fined £10,000 and banned from playing in Europe the following season.

Clough exploded, denied his entrance on to the European stage by a 'bunch of office wallahs. It's their job running the offices. I'm paid to win matches.'

Taylor kept quiet, but years later confessed, 'Perhaps Brian and me were a bit cavalier at times.'

Longson took the full force of the FA's criticism. In an emotional board meeting three directors, Bob Kirkland, Harry Paine and Ken Turner voted him out of office.

The shock was so great and his sense of loss so heart-breaking, that Longson, resenting that he had paid the price for rotten accountancy, decided he needed help in clawing his way back to the post of chairman. He hatched a plot, so desperate, so self-humiliating that, like Faustus, he was willing to sell his soul to the devil..

He sought the help of Clough. 'Brian, we've got to talk.' It was late one evening and only he and Clough were in the ground. 'Let's walk round the pitch.'

They set off walking towards the Osmaston end. For a time Longson found talking difficult, so self-humiliating was his proposal.

'Come on, Sam. Out with it.' Clough was tense, sensing Longson's dilemma.

'Right,' said a determined Longson. 'Okay. This is what you've been waiting for and you're going to get it.' He took a breath. 'I'm going to put you in complete control of Derby County.'

Clough looked at him with a dry expression. 'Oh yes. What have I done right?'

Longson ignored the jibe. 'To get it you take Kirkland, Paine and Turner. You take them one at a time. You make sure they resign from the board.'

'How do I do that?'

'You do what you're good at. You scare them,' Longson said roughly. 'You know what to bloody well do!' He was angry with himself. 'You get me back as chairman and you can do what you want. You tell me when you want to do anything and I okay it. I won't argue. So long as we can afford it.' He paused, his head lowering in guilt. 'But in return, any decision you make has to look as though it's come from the board, through me.'

Clough peered up into the Osmaston Stand. 'I get the glory. You get the praise.'

'No!' Longson clenched his fists. 'Respect! That's all I want! I can't work with you and I can't bloody well sack you, so this is how it has to be and I hate it!' He lowered his voice. 'I loathe it. But this club's my life. I'm not letting you take it away from me. It's the only way of working with you. There. You're the bloody boss. Everything you ever wanted.'

'Right. Okay.' Clough nodded. 'Fine. Okay. I'm now a hit man. What do you want me to use, gun or knife?'

Longson's response was to growl, wave a hand and walk away, back to his office.

IN THE KEDLESTON that night, Clough was elated. Taylor listened to his tale, eyes narrowed. At the conclusion Clough raised his glass. 'Pete. It means we're only a step away from taking over the club.'

'A tame board,' Taylor said. 'Could be good.'

'Could? It bloody well will be,' said Clough. 'Longson's deal, not mine. Pathetic old twit.'

'Could it rebound?' Taylor pursed his lips. 'We'll have to think about it. You sure you can get rid of Kirkland, Paine and Turner?'

'I've only got to look at them,' Clough said. 'Nobody will miss 'em. Least of all us.'

The three men had contributed nothing to the furtherance of Clough's ambitions. If anything they had tried to drag him down with their prevarication when it came to providing the money that he sorely needed. He didn't exactly threaten the three directors with being hanged on a lamp-post by the fans like Mussolini, but he left them in no doubt that he and Longson were joining forces and there would be no room for hangers on. The directors' hair didn't turn white, but they were quick to resign.

Longson became chairman once more, but to his horror found that Clough showed him no gratitude for his self-sacrifice, nor the respect he'd bought by his sacrifice of power. He failed to understand that Clough despised him utterly for what he'd done. In Clough's book respect could only be earned, not bought.

Clough took the players for a break in Majorca, during which time he contemplated his next move.

While sitting at his café table, regally waving to all who recognised him, he decided to appoint a club secretary who would keep a tidy office and ensure that the club wouldn't be denied playing in Europe a second time.

On his return Clough told Longson he was drawing up a list of candidates for the job. Longson agreed but – in accordance with their pact – reminded him that it had to look as though it had been done via a board selection, even though Clough might have picked the secretary himself.

On the day of interview Clough breezed into the boardroom to surprise the directors who were drinking coffee and chatting before the interviews began.

'Morning, gentlemen. May I introduce someone?' He went out and returned with a good-looking young man. 'This is your new club secretary, Stuart Webb.' He turned to him. 'Mr Webb, would you like to sit down and tell the board why I picked you?'

Webb's statement showed that he was the man for the job. But Longson, beside himself with rage, brought Clough back to his office. 'The deal was you made the decisions but you had to make it look as if I was in charge!' he shouted. 'You made me look a bloody idiot in front of the board!'

'Yes, well, I didn't want to waste anybody's time. Webb's ideal. Isn't he?'

Longson's bloodshot eyes narrowed in disbelief. He sat down suddenly, panting heavily, fearful for his heart. He spoke quietly. 'You're mad. You're insane. Get out.' After Clough had gone he opened a drawer and took out his hypertension tablets. Pain and misery, mixed with acute self-disgust, made him tremble. God, what had he done?

Clough added insult to injury by appointing a new trainer, Jimmy Gordon, again without informing Longson. On finding out he quit the stadium in a state of rage and bitterness, his Rolls-Royce clipping a stone wall, due to his emotional state.

Later, watching television, he was shattered to see his tormentor standing in an empty stand talking to a man wearing a suede coat and holding out a microphone. Fascinated in loathing, he watched his nemesis lecture the BBC's new football reporter. 'Young man,' Clough said to John Motson. 'When you've watched a few more football games you'll learn to ask the right question.'

Then, next morning at breakfast, there was Clough's cocky face staring out at him on the back page of the *Daily Mail*. Longson's self-disgust was even worse as he had once decided to bequeath part of his wealth to Clough, the son that he had felt him to be. He went out to tramp around his large garden, recalling what Peter Taylor had said to him. 'The side's so good, Mr Chairman, you could run it.' In his anger he forgot that Clough saw him as a mere rubber stamp in the club. His vanity was such that he told himself *he* would run the team, once he'd got rid of Clough.

He spent the whole weekend burdened by anger and frustration. How could he hold up his head in 'away' boardrooms if he achieved the near impossible by ridding himself of his now great manager? And how could he face the wrath of the fans? It would all be put down to petty jealousy, something he couldn't stomach. But of such notions seeds are sown. And turn into cankers which, one day, will poison any lingering sufferance.

Stuart Webb, in his first week at the job, was appalled at what he found in the office files and documents. It was impossible to sort out the chaos without information. Clough, who was leaving for the training ground one morning, suddenly found Webb confronting him. 'Mr Clough. Can we talk? The accounts and everything, they're in such a mess. I need to know—'

Clough shut him up. 'Young man, I recruited you to put it right. You don't ask me to put it right. Get on with it. I've got real work to do.'

Webb went back to work. He must have been seething. He could imagine what Clough thought of him, in military terms one of the 'men behind the front line'. He was to be tolerated, no more than that. He considered going to Longson to express his dismay at Clough's behaviour, but thought better of it. Best to wait until he had sussed out the lie of the land, wait until his feet were well and truly under his desk. Wait to find out who his allies might be. Best to simmer a while…

The following Monday morning Longson was sorting through his mail when Clough came to say that he'd awarded himself a pay rise. 'In accordance with our agreement. It'll be within budget. All you have to do is press the button.'

Incredulous, Longson paused before speaking. 'Brian.' He steadied his voice. 'You want more pay. At the same time you want a new stand. You've already broken our agreement twice. The deal's off. I'm back as the boss of this club. And money doesn't grow on trees.' Suddenly mad with rage, Longson shouted out, 'No! Now bugger off!'

Always a stickler for fair play, Clough, who had once stopped a bus because the conductor had left people standing on the pavement when there was space aboard, now applied the same rule to himself. He raised a warning finger. 'I deserve that rise. If I don't get what's mine I'm finished. Then see what they do to you when I'm gone.'

Clough marched out of the office, not bothering that his words had thrilled Longson to the core. Over the weekend he'd written down all of Clough's misdemeanours with dates and comments taken from his diary. If it came to Clough being put on trial he would have chapter and verse ready to offer in evidence. But a *resignation*! Oh how glorious that would be! Longson decided to call a board meeting to debate Clough's ultimatum, hoping to force him to quit.

Unfortunately, the new directors on the board – Mike Keeling, friend of Clough, and Jack Kirkland – who had taken over from Clough's victim, his brother Bob Kirkland – were not prepared to allow success to be thrown away so easily. Longson clutched his pain and misery as they awarded Clough his rise in salary. To increase his pain they approved the proposal to build Clough's ambitious Ley Stand, something that Longson had resisted. And the Osmaston Stand, built before the Second World War, and which had suffered from Hitler's Luftwaffe, still stood without repair. This was to be rectified.

Clough's proposals were put forward by Mike Keeling, who knew they would be passed, having consulted his fellow directors beforehand. Longson was further shamed when Clough's proposal that would-be season ticket holders in the Ley Stand be asked to pay two years in advance to help finance the stand was also adopted.

Longson, robbed of power as well as pride, wished he could turn back the clock in his agony. Why had he listened to Shackleton? There were no end of good managers who would have given their eye teeth for the job. He went home, committed to getting rid of Clough, but, short of murder, he knew not how.

He was bitterly licking his wounds when Stuart Webb came to see him. The young and efficient secretary had done his best, but felt it impossible to continue working any longer under Clough's jurisdiction. Something had to be done.

'Stuart, sit yourself down. Tell me all about it.' Webb's litany of problems was music to Longson's ears. Having heard the whole story, he sighed, saying, 'Now I know what Shack meant.'

'Shack?' said Webb. 'You mean Shackleton?'

'Aye. He told me to watch Clough, called him a right bugger.' He gave a dry laugh, unsure of what Webb's reaction might be.

Webb saw Longson's glass was empty. He got to his feet. 'Another whisky, Mr Chairman?'

'Sam. Call me Sam. Yes. Why not?' Longson, smiling, saw Webb as he had first seen Clough, a good-looking sort, possibly one he could call his own.

Webb, sipping water, said, 'Of course we have to have working systems in place else the FA will be down on us again like a ton of bricks. The manager has to conform. He's no option.'

'Damned right!' said Longson. 'Absolutely right.'

'I know he's done wonders here. But a manager can't dictate to a board of directors.'

'I've been saying that for years!' Longson banged his fist on the table. 'I'm going to have a word with him. Don't worry. I'm backing you. And you're backing me.'

'Mr Chairman, that's my job.'

They parted as comrades in arms. But Longson, after much thought, decided to do nothing. Instead, he would allow Webb, a nicely ticking time bomb, to suffer more from Clough's disruption of office management. At some point his position could become untenable, at which point one of the two men would have to go. It would not be Webb, Longson decided.

However, in the aftermath of a game against Arsenal, a crisis arose sooner than expected. Clough's loathing for directors was especially reserved for 'rich Londoners'. Overhearing one of them tell another that their team had been conned into giving away a penalty, Clough stepped in. 'Eh,' he said forcibly, 'my players con nobody. Now get back to your club lounge and your nightclubs and your cigars. Accept we're a superior side. Thank you.'

Longson, told of the incident, flew into a rage, but found that Clough had gone home. He offloaded his anger on to Webb, who was working late.

The secretary sympathised. 'I know, Sam. But perhaps better to ignore it, this time. I'm keeping a diary. If things go wrong, I want to be able to show evidence that I did the right thing.'

Longson paused, seeing a light at the end of his tunnel. 'That's good. That is really good. I keep a record of what goes on as well. If it comes to push we'll pool what we have.' Thrilled, he hesitated in the doorway. 'Stuart? Keep it safe. Don't let anybody see it. Except me.'

At this point in the war, a more cunning Clough might have considered making an approach to Webb in formulating a plan of defence against Longson. By promising Webb certain things he might have been able to create an alliance with him. But Webb was naturally gravitating towards Longson, given impetus by Clough's attitude towards him. He and his wife Josie, in creating a thriving travel agency in the town, were putting down strong roots in the community. Through his business contacts, Webb must have seen the possibility of elevating himself within the Derby County hierarchy. It was only natural that Webb sought backing from the chairman in whatever struggle lay ahead.

On the other side it was Taylor who warned Clough that Webb and Longson were becoming a force that might threaten their own ambitions. But, contemptuous as he may have been about Longson, Clough had grown to dislike Webb. There was never any chance he would seek Webb's confidence in any mutual plot against Longson.

Then something happened to bring forward the inevitable confrontation that could decide Clough's future and Webb's standing within the club. A row broke out over the payment of staff wages. Webb, not lacking courage, was angered by Clough's jibes about the mess things were in. The mess, Webb declared, was all due to Clough's behaviour, calling him 'a bull in a china shop'.

The next morning Clough arrived to find six wastepaper baskets stacked full of paper money in the general office, each dedicated to the wages of members of the staff: groundsman, office cleaners, etc. It annoyed him. Wasn't this type of thing why the Football Association had fined the club and why Webb had been appointed to deal with it? He ordered Michael Dunford, the seventeen-year-old assistant to Webb, to get rid of the baskets before 'somebody nicks something'.

When Clough returned to check ten minutes later, the baskets were still there. 'This is what's wrong with this club,' he said sharply. 'Where's Mr Webb?'

Webb could not be located, and so Clough seized a basket and took it to his own office to 'teach him a lesson' he told his secretary. He instructed her to count the money, make a note of it and lock it away in a cupboard. Shortly afterwards Webb appeared in the doorway. 'Money's missing,' he said. 'I've been told you've taken it.'

'Yes, I bloody well have,' said Clough. 'To show you what I said could happen.'

'You've also got the safe key,' said Webb. 'Under company law...'

'Eh,' Clough pointed a finger. 'I don't trust anybody. Not the way this place is run. Just find a way of not paying the staff in cash, all right?'

Webb stood his ground. 'I'm sorry, but if you don't give me the key and the money I shall have to call the police.'

'Call them,' challenged Clough. 'And I'll tell them this club's an open door for thieves.'

Having made his point, Clough returned the key and the money. Webb left, knowing he had won the skirmish but was smarting once more from Clough's rough riding.

Clough meditated for a moment. He had suffered a partial defeat and it was important that he restore himself. In his book someone had to pay and if it could not be Webb... he got up quickly and marched back to the general office where he sacked the likeable Dunford, Webb's assistant.

Webb, outraged, went to see Longson. 'Mr Clough is totally out of order. Dunford's done nothing wrong and I need him.'

'Give him his job back,' said Longson roughly, 'and leave Mr Clough to me.'

In reinstating Dunford, Longson had thrown down the gauntlet at Clough's feet. He had suffered enough. His pact with Clough had died before it even started and he'd been left in self-loathing ever since. He now decided to dedicate himself to getting rid of his 'bloody awful manager' and, in so doing, regain his pride.

But Clough's pride was the greater. And he had an agreement. He picked up the gauntlet and collared Longson. 'Dunford goes. I'm in charge, Sam, remember. Webb works for me.'

'No he bloody well doesn't. You had your chance. I've given

you too much rope. I'm back in charge. You keep out of it. Stick to the team. Let people who're trained do what they're trained for.'

'Sam, I am not keeping out of it.' Clough was on his way out, in a fighting mood. 'Because I *am* it,' he added in the corridor. 'I am all of it. Every bit of it. I'm the boss, remember. You appointed me.'

Longson was left panting in anger. He went to his desk to search out his blood pressure pills.

In this bitter triangular conflict it seemed to those listening to the row that it was only a matter of time before the club imploded.

THE PROTEST MOVEMENT, as autumn slowly faded in 1973, maintained its pressure. I gave daily interviews for Radio Derby which were transmitted down the line to BBC main channels. Nationwide, people sat at breakfast listening to what we were planning next with meetings, demonstrations, leaflet hand-outs at home games and press releases.

Clough asked me to meet him at the Midland Hotel. He was quieter than usual, a shade thoughtful and inclined to listen to my views on the progress – or lack of it – of the campaign. When I'd finished he looked about and lowered his voice. 'I'm telling you this because I don't think you need work any more. I'm suing the directors for libel and slander. I've got a case. Until it's done I don't think you need bother too much.'

I asked him how he saw it ending. It was simple, he told me.

'I'll win. The board will have to resign and I've got enough businessmen who'll bite my hand off to get on it. They'll be under me. I'll become dictator so I can watch the guzzling that goes on!' He chuckled at the idea.

A few days later, I heard from Keeling that Clough's solicitor had advised him to delay the case in order to gather more evidence. Counsel's opinion was that, on the basis of present information, the outcome would not be a guaranteed success. Clough was back to square one, with the Movement as his only hope. He rang me, requesting an urgent meeting at the health club, together with Keeling and McGuinness.

It was raining heavily as I arrived. Clough's car was parked outside the health club. He sat in the passenger seat, Keeling beside him. I got into the back seat, scuffing water from my face. Clough half-leaned backwards to speak to me. 'We've been firing off odd shots. We've got nowhere. From now on our best plan is to work together.'

At last. I was delighted at the news.

John McGuinness arrived and opened the door to the health club. Once inside he produced one of his best wines. We picked at a bowl of nuts as Clough outlined his plan. 'If we can drive a wedge between the directors, isolate one lot from the other, we might get somewhere. If we can get Bradley to pal up with Jack Kirkland they could turn that board against Longson. Bradley's a rabbit. Whatever you do, don't scare him off. Don't you approach him, Don. John? Somehow get Bradley trapped so he has to listen to both of you. But remember: don't scare him. He'll run a mile.'

McGuinness nodded. 'We'll do it.'

In the soft glow of a table lamp Clough's eyes were bright and shiny. 'Get him on your side, flatter him. Tell him how much I'll reward him if he can get Kirkland to join him and get rid of Longson.'

Clough turned to McGuinness. 'You know Bradley. His shop's near you.'

McGuinness nodded. 'We're in the Chamber of Commerce together.' Bradley was a respectable menswear retailer in the town.

'Okay. You lure Bradley into here. Don, you be here, waiting. Tell him I'll be grateful for any help. He likes to be liked, does Sydney.' Clough leaned forward in emphasis. 'But you can put a little knife in. Tell him I'm watching his every move.'

Mike Keeling was given the job of sounding out Jack Kirkland. As the brother of Bob Kirkland, who was scared off the board at Longson's instigation, he would jump at the chance of getting revenge, said Clough.

I was puzzled. Wouldn't Jack Kirkland also want to get his revenge on Clough as Bob's frightener? I put it to him.

Clough merely grinned. 'No. Because Jack Kirkland is still looking to build a new Baseball Ground. He still needs me to help him.' If Bradley teamed up with Kirkland against Longson, Clough reasoned, the chairman would have no choice but to allow himself to be bought out of the club.

Clough's trump card was that Longson had boasted for years that he only had twenty-five pounds' worth of shares in the club. 'I reckon a few grand would buy him out, the old twit,' Clough said, grinning mischievously.

'What about Webb?' I asked.

'Easy. As soon as the new board's in place he gets his marching orders.'

It all seemed so simple.

'Will Bradley listen to me?' I put the question in some trepidation.

Clough spoke firmly. 'He will listen. You make him believe. If you do your job properly, he will.'

It wasn't the first time in my encounters with Clough that I knew how the players would have felt in the dressing room, after he'd given them his pre-match talk: convinced.

'Just do your jobs properly and it will happen.' Clough nodded in emphasis.

I promised. Keeling, I noticed, said nothing.

I stepped out into the rain-swept shopping centre without fear or doubt. We few in the leadership of the Movement, committed as we were to him, never questioned Clough's ideas or motives.

I went home with his instructions my only thoughts, my head stuffed with an unthinking compliance. He had looked into my eyes and I had obeyed.

The next morning I set out on my mission.

7

OVER THE TOP

THE WAR AT Derby County rumbled on. Occasionally a skirmish involving Clough and Webb would flare up, followed by a tactical withdrawal by one side or the other. The rest of the staff was caught up in the conflicts, some taking sides according to their status. Sniping, with barbed comments, was a frequent occurrence. By 1971 both combatants seemed dug in for the duration.

Longson, having tried to accommodate Clough but failed, now looked upon him as his natural enemy, which bothered the victorious general not a jot. Clough was far too busy fulfilling his dream of fashioning the perfect football team to bother unduly about internal affairs. Such was his success that he felt he was beyond any direct threat. But in the intimate hot house of a football club, in which paranoia can breed and minds are poisoned, why couldn't Clough have seen where the situation was heading and patted Longson on the shoulder with a few kind words of appreciation? He knew that Longson was hurt. And, ultimately, Longson, backed by the board, had the power to dismiss him. Why build a stairway to the stars and then pull away its supports?

If Clough, especially, had been a little less brusque with Webb, events might have taken a different course. The same might have applied if Longson had stood outside and looked in on himself to realise that he was putting his pride above that of responsibility to the football team.

Longson was blind in a different way, less keen to possess what would have become Europe's best team than to get rid of its manager. The grumblings and the mutterings of them both had already turned into whispered conversations. Clough had created a formidable opponent in Webb but refused to worry about him. Such, at the basic level of all human endeavour, is vanity.

THROUGHOUT 1971 Clough continued in his search for new talent. He wanted an ace defender, a fast moving and strong tackler. Taylor had selected a Sunderland player. While briefing Clough on his intended target, he slipped in a tactful note. 'Best we tell the old twit this time, eh? This lad's too important to lose. I know how you feel, but why not butter Sam up a bit? We need that lad.'

Clough's respect for Taylor overcame his prejudice.

Longson was tidying up his desk, prior to going on holiday, when Clough knocked at his door to tell him that Colin Todd had become available at Sunderland, a player who would add strength to the defence, a lightning tackler who could snatch a ball from an opposition player like no other, clean as a whistle. Clough put the matter for Longson's approval.

Longson, satisfied that he'd been consulted, cautiously nodded. 'What's his price?'

'A hundred grand?'

'Hell's bloody bells. A hundred?'

'Well, ninety. We won't get him for less than ninety, I can tell you that.'

Longson grunted. He was off on holiday and he wanted to depart without any acrimony or worry about finance. 'Ninety's tops then.' He added, 'Good luck.'

As Clough left, Longson felt a stab of optimism, a rare occurrence in his relationship with Clough. For once the manager had shown respect for his office as chairman. If he could continue in that manner…? More than that, and which softened Longson even more, was that Clough had wished him a happy holiday.

'Why can't he behave like that all the time?' Longson, with a shake of the head, left his office, dreaming of a warm blue sea.

As he flew out of Heathrow he felt he could relax. Maybe he had misjudged his lost wunderkind. Maybe the prodigal son would turn into a normal, decent bloke, after all.

THE MOVE TO secure Todd had been planned with Clough's usual care and attention to detail, though any player worth his salt will want to go to a successful team. And so Clough only had to spend a few minutes eyeballing Todd and drilling words into his brain: 'You will never, ever win a Cup Final or championship medal with Sunderland or any other team. But you'll do it with me. And that is a guarantee. Do you understand?'

Todd, the most pacific and calmest of men, had nodded in acquiescence.

THE CARIBBEAN 'doctor's wind' clattered softly in the tops of the palm trees as the chairman of Derby County sat down for dinner by the hotel pool. It was 6.30 p.m.

At that precise moment the breeze dropped along the beach and finally died, the only sound being the croaking of frogs among the shrubs and the filter splashing in the deserted pool. Longson watched the white-jacketed waiter light his candle, its flame tall and strong. He gave a comfortable sigh and picked up the half pint of beer he drank before every meal.

'By the centre, Derrick. Look who's here!'

Longson looked up to see Arthur Wait, chairman of Crystal Palace and Derrick Robins, chairman of Coventry, grinning down at him.

After the expressions of surprise and a few words of banter, Wait slipped in a sly comment. 'You've been at it again, I see, Sam.'

'What?'

'Spending. That's all your Cloughie seems to do. You've got Colin Todd.'

'Good. I told him to go after him.'

'Did you give him a limit?'

'Yes. Why?'

Robins and Wait exchanged grins.

Longson winced. 'Don't tell me. A hundred grand?'

'And the rest.' Wait puffed his cigar to enjoy teasing Longson. He blew out a cloud of smoke and then spoke slowly and with relish.

'One hundred and seventy-five thousand pounds. It's in all the papers. It's a British transfer record.'

Longson choked in his beer. After he'd recovered he sent off a telegram to Clough, telling him he'd bankrupted the club. It had also ruined his holiday. On his return, Longson collared Clough. 'You did it with Webb, Jimmy Gordon, now this! I keep telling you, money doesn't bloody well grow on trees! It's not in the bank! I've got to go cap in hand now! You think all directors are loaded. Well, we're not!'

Clough smiled. 'I know, Sam. It shows by how much of your own money you've put into the club.' Leaving Longson fuming, Clough walked away.

FROM MY PERCH in the Ley Stand the new signing seemed to complete Clough's vision of the perfect team. Todd gave a dynamism that – I only then realised – had been a touch lacking. From his first appearance his speed of tackling and ability to emerge with the ball was unparalleled within the game. Todd frequently threw opposition defenders into confusion as they raced back to defend their penalty area. There was no other player in England who was faster in switching defence into attack.

The team now ran like the pride of Derby, a Rolls-Royce aero-engine, sweet and powerful. Clough's thirteen players hardly faltered in their race for the League championship. It was won within the year – as Clough had forecast.

I LEFT HOME on my mission to entice Bradley in Clough's plot and entered McGuinness's restaurant at the designated time: 12 noon. McGuinness saw me from the kitchen doorway and, smiling, limped across the room. He kept his head back as if ready to 'nut' me, a habit that reminded me of his willingness to 'sort out' the man in the back row of the Grand Theatre.

He checked his watch. 'Bang on time,' he said. 'Stay there, Don. I'll be back. Five minutes.'

He went outside into the shopping precinct. Through the

restaurant window I watched him make his lopsided way towards the fogbound London Road. A hundred yards along, opposite The Spot, a central point in town where two main roads joined, was Bradley's menswear shop. He was always present at noon on a Friday: 'wages time'.

Minutes later I saw Bradley, a small man tailing a fast limping McGuinness, pass the window. He had the look of someone who had been promised that there would be something to his advantage in the forthcoming meeting. He had no idea that he would be introduced to me.

They entered the restaurant. McGuinness ushered Bradley towards a seat opposite mine. 'Sydney, this is Don,' he said, giving me a sly grin.

'Hello,' said Bradley, as he shook hands, a little out of breath. It was obvious that, despite my photograph having appeared many times in the local press as a writer, and recently during the dispute, he didn't recognise me. He reminded me, in his stature and demeanour, of the type of timid shopkeeper so often seen in films of the Wild West.

McGuinness sat next to Bradley. 'We're trying to work out a way to keep Cloughie. We think, Don thinks, we can do it together. The three of us. There is a way, Sydney, if you help.' He broke off as a waitress placed a tray of filter coffee in front of us.

'Don.' I found Bradley staring at me. 'You're Don…?'

'Shaw. Sydney, don't—' McGuinness put out a hand.

But Bradley was on his feet, scraping back his chair, fearful and panicky. 'Sorry, I've just remembered…wages…'

'No. Sydney. Come on.' McGuinness, shuffling his chair backwards, had him trapped against the wall. 'Come on, Sydney. We're not going to bite. Sit down. Come on. Sit down. It's for your benefit. Cloughie's going to reward you. Sit down. Go on. Just listen. Nothing to worry about.'

Bradley hesitated and then sat down in defeat. 'Go on, then. Tell me. I've got to be off. Wages.' He kept his head down in a deep frown.

'Right,' said McGuinness. 'Now all we want, as you know, is to get Clough back. He's told us you'll get rewarded if we can get rid of Longson.'

'Rewarded?' Bradley looked up suspiciously. 'How?'

'Let Cloughie tell you. We'll arrange a meeting with him. It will be secret. No one will know.'

Bradley grimaced. He put a hand to his chest. 'I've got reflux. Acidity. It's when I get stressed. I've got to go and get my tablets. Please.'

McGuinness twisted his mouth in contempt. Finally he scraped his chair forward, allowing the little man to escape. I watched Bradley hold up his collar against the cold and scuttle past the restaurant window and out of sight.

'Cloughie gets it wrong,' I said glumly and then sighed. 'It's amazing.'

Mike Keeling's meeting with Jack Kirkland also ended, like mine with Bradley, as a wash out. There had never been any chance that Bradley, irrespective of Kirkland's cooperation, would have engaged in such a nefarious plan. He was too scared of Longson and had no appetite for boardroom battles. In any case, Kirkland would have been unlikely to join Bradley against Longson. He believed it would not be long before Longson quit owing to general ill health. His time would come.

I wondered if Clough's lack of concern at the failure of his plot meant that he had other schemes in the pipeline. He could have been handing out tasks to keep me busy and onside while he bent himself to some secretive master plan of his own.

At least I hoped so.

Now as I was young and easy under the apple boughs,
About the lilting house and happy as the grass was green,
The night above the dingle starry,
Time let me hail and climb
Golden in the heyday of his eyes.

The season of '71 to '72 became the salad days, when the young handsome prince of football, Brian Clough, was lord of all he surveyed. But, for Longson, it was a time of pain overcoming joy. The club had won the League championship, but the result had made it impossible for him to escape Clough's constant image in the press and on television. It seemed that every chat show wanted him and no football programme was ever complete without Clough living up to his reputation for outspoken and, sometimes, knock-about comedy. He amused, stimulated and shocked the nation.

Longson had *his* biggest shock of all when he saw a photograph of Clough with Muhammad Ali on the front page of the *Sun*. In March 1971, Clough had gone to America to see Ali fight Joe Frazier for the World Heavyweight Boxing Championship. After-wards, Clough was introduced to his hero, and they competed with each other to be the world's best in the art of boasting and talking your rival to death.

Ali won easily on points. 'I hear you've been impersonating me! You are not to do that. I am the greatest,' he ranted, wagging his finger at Clough with a big grin on his face. 'You are not the man. I am the man. You are an also-ran. All you are ever meant to be is my fan!' Ali broke into laughter and Clough joined him. It was the only time that Clough's gift of the gab had fallen before a greater talent.

It was not all painful for Longson. Now that Derby were League champions, the jokes in boardrooms about Clough's behaviour had been replaced by congratulations.

But the stress of dealing with Clough had begun to show itself in Longson's behaviour. Occasionally he would pick up the tele-phone and talk into the earpiece. The publishing of his *Memoirs* was a pathetic attempt to gain sympathy. Turned down by every publisher, he resorted to vanity publishing, handing copies to those he wished to impress. No Rams fan, as far as I know, ever read them. He wrote: 'I had a special relationship with my supporters. Most of them knew me as Sam.'

But, if Longson was at his lowest point, it was worse for Webb. He caught the full force of Clough's obsession with winning the

European Cup. Completely disregarding office protocol, Clough frustrated Webb at work so many times that, finally, the club secretary was forced to confront Longson, 'I can't go on like this. He's interfering with everything.'

'Are you saying either the manager goes or you? Go on. Out with it.'

Longson eagerly awaited what he was sure would be Webb's ultimatum. It was the moment he had long been anticipating.

THE DAY AFTER Keeling and I had failed to bring Clough success with his 'Bradley and Kirkland' plot, the protagonists in the Movement met to orchestrate mounting pressure on the directors. Armed with Clough's list of the home telephone numbers of board members, approximately a hundred protesters volunteered to make their own, individual phone calls to each director, a first wave followed by a second and then a third covering four weeks in total. At the same time we would send them numerous letters and petitions, the desired effect being to irritate and annoy them into rebelling against Longson.

It had the opposite effect. Longson called a meeting of one or two selected directors, a meeting in which no minutes would be kept, but much vitriol expended. Webb was excluded. It would have been far too dangerous to allow a salaried employee to listen to what Longson had to propose. The result of the meeting was a vicious counter attack upon the Movement, entailing briefings of misinformation to influential people in the media, together with open letters to the press and interviews on both radio and television. The simple message was that the Movement was deliberately sabotaging the team's efforts, not for the re-instatement of Clough, but out of revenge.

The effect of this insidious campaign was shown in me receiving two phone calls, one from a freelance journalist and the other from a sports reporter in local radio. Both sympathised with our aim but maybe it was time to draw a line, in case our continued campaign damaged Derby County? Within days other voices spoke up, one or two even from our own ranks. Now doubting the return of our hero they, too, spoke of the need for unity.

Clough took it all in his stride. 'Don, when you're fighting for what's right and good, what do you expect? You get casualties and you get turncoats. This is a power struggle. Longson lives for Derby County. He'd die if he lost. But that's his problem, not yours. Keep up the fight.'

Then something happened which gave the conflict sinister over-tones. Clough rang, asking me to meet him in Allestree Park. 'Don't want any nosey parkers on this one,' he said briefly. It sounded ominous.

There was a scattering of snow on the ground and a freezing north-easterly as I entered the park, clad in sheepskin jacket, scarf, hat and wearing gloves. I saw Clough marching towards me from the northerly entrance. He still wore his customary thin raincoat, inap-propriately open at the top. He didn't stop as we met, but kept walk-ing at the same speed forcing me to turn quickly to keep up with him.

'Hope you're keeping a diary, because this is real drama, not your *Z-Cars* stuff,' he said grittily in staccato bursts into the bitter wind. 'Longson's been at it again. Anonymous letters written to Chief Constable, the press, Radio Derby, Mayor, and Alderman Jack Bussell. Letters claim you and your mates phoned each director. You said you'd evidence they stole petty cash and transfer deal money. If they took me back evidence would be destroyed.'

'Bloody hell,' was the first thing I said. Then added, 'Straight from the Longson Ministry of Propaganda, I bet.'

'Not a bad gamble.' Clough suddenly stopped walking, bring-ing me to a halt. He looked around, saw a woman walking towards us, towed by a large French poodle. He buttoned up the top of his raincoat. 'It shows how scared they are. You're winning.'

'We did phone the directors. We did send letters. But nothing like that. It's ludicrous.'

Clough nodded. 'Yeah, but they know who gave you the list of director's phone numbers. I'm the only one who's got it apart from Longson and Webb. Got to give the old twit credit. Neat, eh?'

'Machiavellian,' I said with a smile.

'Him as well.' Clough started walking again and kicked a tennis ball lying in his path. He suddenly grimaced, flexing his knee.

'Have you seen any of the letters?' I asked.

'No. Stansfield – Chief Constable – says they're all the same. He gave his to Detective Superintendent Burgess. He just asked if I wanted it investigated or press charges against anybody. I said no. So they dropped it.'

He waited while the woman passed by tailing the poodle. 'Reason I don't want any fuss is because it shows they're panicking. That's a risky thing Longson did. When they realise it's had no effect on the Movement he'll up the ante. Stand by for fireworks. And let's hope the board blows itself up. I reckon one more push and they'll fold. That's what we want: some action. Been too much pillow fighting anyway.'

As he said goodbye, urging me to keep up the campaign, he had a gleam in his eye. This, together with the way he'd marched and talked like a battlefield commander, indicated he was enjoying himself for once. Maybe his frustration had been uncorked by the war taking a new turn. Perhaps his 'pillow fighting' remark meant that, for him, the warfare hadn't been bloody enough.

8

OPEN WARFARE

LONGSON DREADED the celebration dinner to mark Derby County winning the 1972 League championship. Finally, he cried off, saying he was suffering from toothache. But he forced himself to attend the shorter boardroom presentation a day later, a task that pained him as much as it bored the recipient, Brian Clough. How Longson hoped that the manager would mention his name, just offer a few words of thanks in his acceptance speech.

In the event Clough thanked the club, but no specific person. Longson's heart shrivelled into a husk. Beta blockers slowed down his emotions, but not enough to drive out his need to unburden himself of his misery.

By chance, it seemed, Derrick Robins, chairman of Coventry City and the bearer of bad news in the Caribbean, invited the board of Derby County FC to lunch at their ground. It was normal for club directors to engage in this kind of hospitality, thus Longson had no idea that Robins had an ulterior motive, which was to sound him out as to where he stood with his errant manager, hoping to poach him if possible. The wolf in sheep's clothing posed the question over the prawn cocktails.

'Why so gloomy, Sam? Cloughie getting you down again?'

Longson seized his opportunity. Here was a ready-made counsellor, an outsider who knew what it was like to be faced with failing or difficult managers. He launched into his grisly tale of betrayal.

'Beyond redemption, Derrick,' he moaned. 'Cloughie drives me nuts. He's pure murder. Heard his latest shocker? About Storey-Moore?'

Of course Robins had heard of it. The whole football world was agog with it, but he shook his head, wanting to gauge the depth of Longson's despair and desperation. 'No, I haven't, Sam. Why? What happened?' he said in a show of concern.

Longson, with a martyred expression, took a breath and launched into the diabolical story of Ian Storey-Moore, the Nottingham Forest winger. Wanted by Clough, he'd been snapped up by O'Farrell, manager of Manchester United, with a bid of £210,000. O'Farrell and the Nottingham Forest secretary had met to finalise the agreement. Clough, resigning himself to losing Moore, heard over the grapevine that the deal had been held up by the player failing to agree terms. At this news Clough rang Moore, speaking rapidly in his compelling monotone.

'You will not sign for United because you're coming to Derby. You don't even have to move house. You say nothing, do nothing and sit tight. I'm coming over. This is the biggest moment in your short life as a player. Do not let yourself down.'

Clough's voice drove into Moore's head like a jackhammer. He then phoned Moore's agent, one of the first of a species that would forever change football from being a game played by working men and watched by working men.

'Eh, you. Listen,' ordered Clough. 'Your job is to do the best for your player. You cannot do better than bring him to Derby County. You don't deserve a penny if you don't do that. Got it?'

Clough got into his car and sped off towards Bingham, a village near Nottingham. Moore's wife answered the door and stepped back in amazement at the sight of Clough. 'I've come to sign your husband,' he said, stepping inside. 'No time to waste.'

Again, a player was confronted in his own home by a finger-pointing Clough in full lecture mode. 'You do not want to go to Manchester United. (Clough would never say 'Man U'. He hated abbreviating titles. He wanted the chance to emphasise each syllable.) They are going nowhere. We are. Come on, pack your bag, you're coming with me.'

Moore, dazed as Clough had intended him to be, tried to buy time, to make sense of it. 'But – I'm being signed by Matt Busby. He's—'

'Don't mess about,' cut in Clough. 'This is the chance of a lifetime. I'm not leaving this house. I'll sleep down here until you agree to get into my car.'

Moore swallowed nervously. 'I should speak to my agent, shouldn't I?'

'Eh.' Clough put his face into Moore's. 'The only agent you want is me. Got it?'

Clough drove the bemused player to the Midland Hotel in Derby, where the Rams players were spending the night before their home game with Wolves. Clough now set about phase two of the operation. Each player was introduced to Moore individually and left alone for a chat. The aim was to ensure that all the players would get the feel of him. Afterwards they would each be quizzed as to their opinions, standard Clough practice, based on the methods of SAS recruitment. 'If the guy isn't liked by the squad then he's out.'

Meanwhile Clough instructed the hotel receptionist that if a 'Mr Gillies' called – Moore's agent – on no account was she to allow him anywhere near the club's special guest. The receptionist, a twenty-five-year-old with a crush on Clough, assured him, earnestly and breathily, that Mr Moore would be safe from all marauders.

At 10.30 p.m. the team members were dismissed to their bedrooms, having assured Clough that they were unanimous in agreeing that Moore was a suitable bloke for passing a ball to, someone who would share a laugh and play a good game of pontoon. On this positive news Clough marched into his bedroom to place the regulation forms in front of Moore for signature. He duly signed. Clough had gambled and won. 'We're down in the lounge. Come down and have a cocoa with your wonderful mates.'

Moore was thrilled. He was now a Derby County player. The world, literally, was at his feet. Later, with all the players tucked up in bed, Derby's assistant coach was instructed to stand guard in the corridor outside Moore's unlocked door. If he heard the phone ring inside the bedroom his order was to leap inside and prevent him from answering.

The night passed peacefully.

Phase three of the Moore operation began at 2.55 p.m. the next day, Saturday. The pre-match music stopped over the PA system at the Baseball Ground and Clough's words were heard by the huge congregation of the faithful, including myself. 'Ladies, gentlemen, boys and girls, this is your manager, Brian Clough, speaking to you!' He waited for the burst of cheering to subside. 'I have a special announcement. Yesterday, I signed a new player. He is someone who will take us onwards and upwards! I want you all to stand up and applaud your new player, Ian Storey-Moore!'

Clough timed his announcement so that the outburst of cheering and applause would unsettle the Wolves team, then standing in the tunnel. In the event, Derby won 2–1.

Afterwards Clough took Moore back to the Midland Hotel and locked him inside his bedroom. 'My apologies, young man, but there are conmen about. This is for your own safety.' Clough then searched the hotel to ensure that Gillies, or anyone from United, was not in the building. Again instructions were left at reception. 'On no account must Mr Moore be seen or talked to by anyone without my permission, other than his wife.'

At this point in telling the story Longson's face resembled that of a contender in the annual 'Gurning' competition to find the best puller of the ugliest face. 'Oh, Derrick, I can't tell you. It was bloody awful. Clough's insane, did you know that?'

Robins, who was getting increasingly excited, shook his head in the deepest of sympathy. 'Go on, Sam,' he said tenderly. 'Carry on.'

Longson continued with his dreadful tale of piracy and betrayal. Clough's kidnap could not have remained a secret, he said. Someone in the hotel had sold the story to Raymonds News Agency, which had then contacted Manchester United's manager, Matt Busby. On hearing the news he had immediately ordered his driver to take him to Bingham.

Two hours later he arrived at Moore's home with flowers, telling his wife that her beloved Ian had been kidnapped by a piratical Clough. He gave her the hotel phone number.

The Midland receptionist had to hold the receiver away from her ear as the loud shrill voice demanded to speak to her husband.

The upshot was that Moore was released from Clough's 'prison' and whipped away to Manchester.

On hearing the news Clough bellowed 'What!' and rang Old Trafford. He was put through to the club secretary. 'You've stolen my player,' he intoned. 'I want him back here by four o'clock. If he's not back I'm reporting you to Hardacre at the FA for kidnapping.'

The secretary spoke calmly. 'I understand you kidnapped *our* player.'

'Right! You're in for it.' With no sign of Moore being returned, Clough waited till 4.15 p.m. and then rang Hardacre to make his report. 'And do something that's not just sweet FA,' he said.

Meanwhile Busby advised Mrs Moore to ring the police regarding the illegal abduction of her husband and also to contact her solicitor with a view to taking action against Derby County FC.

Longson paused in his story, to shake his head wearily. 'Guess what Clough did then? He sent a telegram to Alan Hardacre asking the FA to investigate Manchester United and Forest for an illegal signing. Can you imagine?'

'I can imagine,' said Robins vacantly, already working out what he could afford to pay Clough. He smiled sadly at Longson. 'What next, Sam?'

'Alan Hardacre said they wouldn't investigate, because they bloody well knew, like any right thinking man, that Clough had kidnapped Moore! I told you he was insane! He then...' Longson broke off, gulping, in distress.

Robins thoughtfully replenished Longson's whisky tumbler. 'What a bad business,' he sighed.

'Oh, Derrick. Can you imagine?' Longson looked pitiful in his deep shame. 'Can you imagine how I feel? Christ Almighty, he is mad. Absolutely crackers. I know he gets results but...Jesus Christ!'

It took Robins a further minute before he could elicit the rest of the black and evil saga. Clough, outraged, his pride severely wounded, had fired off a long and virulent telegram of complaint to Alan Hardacre, which left no room for doubt what Clough thought about the spineless FA.

As a friend of Hardacre, Longson was outraged. He broke off telling his story, emotionally lanced. He resumed in a flat voice. 'I was flattened, Derrick. I hated myself. But I had to defend the club. So I sent off a telegram to Alan Hardacre to say Clough's telegram had nothing to do with Derby County. Nothing at all. And I apologised for Clough. I apologised again for my own manager. I'm always doing it and I'm pig sick. Dear God.'

Longson could say no more.

Robins didn't need to hear another thing. He went home, doing his arithmetic.

Here, once again, was exposed the sharp difference between Clough's perception of what was right and proper and the rules and regulations that so bugged him on his pathway to glory. There was no doubt in his mind that Moore was a Derby County player. The lad had signed, had he not? All that was needed was the Forest secretary's signature. And, given that the player *wanted to play* for Derby, it should have been a formality.

His sense of unfairness drove Clough to sit in his office, drinking brandy, fuming with the alcohol. He had been made to look a complete idiot in front of the fans. It never occurred to him to realise it had been all *his* doing. Common sense should have told him to wait until the Forest secretary had completed the formalities.

The day after Moore's snatch back, a morose and intense Clough paced the corridor inside the ground considering his failure, a rare occurrence in his professional life. Catching sight of Longson's cheerful, almost cocky grin – though fleeting – made him deeply suspicious. He was about to charge after him, but was intercepted by Keeling who insisted they went into Clough's office.

'Sam's sent a telegram to Harding at the FA. He says he disassociates himself from your telegram.'

'That's why the old twit was grinning!' Clough, realising that the smirk he'd seen on Longson's face had been a smile of revenge, burst back into the corridor intent on seeking him out. At this point Webb had just walked out of his office and unfortunately caught the rage of a rampaging Clough. Arm pointing, Clough bore down upon him like a knight on a charger. 'You did that. You sent that telegram!' Webb instinctively flinched and took a step backwards, flattening himself against the wall.

'That player was ours,' raged Clough. 'Until Busby butted in. Moore agreed to come here. Now I'm made to look a bloody laughing stock!'

Webb bravely denied the accusation, advising Clough to check his facts. He then quickly went back to his office.

Clough, burning, strode into Longson's office, banging the door open. 'Mr Chairman. I sign players. That was the deal. Busby stole Moore from me. I complained to the FA. You stood with Busby. You're telling the FA that I'm in the wrong when it's you. You're a traitor to Derby County!'

Longson stood, quivering with rage. 'No, I'm not the traitor. You are! You let us all down with your bloody kidnaps. You're as mad as a hatter. You can't keep players prisoner! You forced his signature like a Gestapo man getting a confession from a bloody spy! You're insane!'

Clough focused his anger into a penetrative stare at Longson. Speaking slowly, he began quietly. 'I was doing that not for me but for the club. Moore didn't complain. If he does I'll apologise. He signed the forms to come here. He *signed* the forms. He told me we were a better bet for him than Manchester. He *is* a Derby player.'

'No, he's not. And you listen to me. You can't send telegrams to Alan Hardacre criticising him. This time you've gone too far. You're a bloody disgrace!'

'Okay, sack me!' The snap challenge echoed around the building.

The staff, eagerly listening behind their half-opened doors, waited for the explosion.

It never came. Clough stared long enough to register his disgust and then turned to go back to his office. Longson remained staring after him. Whoever heard of a manger being sacked in his League championship year?

Mired in depression, the chairman went to sit alone, brooding in the semi-darkness of the boardroom. He knew that the story of his spat with Clough and the FA would get out. Clough stories went round dining tables like the port and brandy, everyone always eager to sup while chuckling at 'Sam's latest'. He wished now he hadn't been so forthcoming with Robins at Coventry. It had helped get it off his chest, but the Moore tale would now certainly do the rounds, if it hadn't already. Once again, there would be those directors waiting for the visit of Derby County, ready to poke fun at him. He hung his head in misery.

Then, letting out a huge sigh, he looked up at the photograph of the Derby County side that had won the FA Cup in 1946. They were all honest, decent men. The manager had been a decent man. At that moment, cast down, Longson would willingly have exchanged the club's position at the top of the football world for a lowly position in Third Division North.

Then he remembered the exciting journey back from Scotch Corner and the wonderful two years that had followed. Images of glory came and went – the FA Cup tie with Chelsea, winning the Second Division championship, the magic of the European Cup, his affection for a manager he once regarded as his son…

Longson grimaced. The ungrateful bastard wouldn't get a penny. Not a penny. He tossed back a shot of whisky. In the darkest and deepest part of his heart he loathed Clough and all he stood for. He'd tried, oh, how he'd tried – and what had he got in return? No honest man should have to withstand the arrogant, strutting egotist that was Clough.

In his intense bitterness Longson gave no thought to the club's status as champions of England, nor to the glory that lay ahead. Winning the European Cup was no carrot to a despised donkey. Suicide would be better than suffer the plaudits that would be aimed at a European Cup-winning Clough. And how dare Clough accuse him of being a traitor? *He*, Sam, was Derby County. Clough was a tenant for only as long as his contract lasted.

Longson's fist tightened on his glass. He would prevail. When the time came, which he knew it would, he would be sitting at the head of the boardroom table supervising Clough's departure. He would die achieving that, rather than fail. 'And leave your car keys on the table!' he would declare, his voice ringing in triumph. It was a comforting dream. With this palliative thought he went home, ruing the day he had followed Shackleton's advice.

Clough spent the next hour closeted in his office with Taylor, who was trying to get him to see the future, not get bogged down in the present.

'Brian,' urged Taylor. 'Think about it. Longson's only an elected chairman but we've got the real power. That comes from achievement. If he makes a move against us the fans will gut him for breakfast.'

Clough remained embittered. 'The old twit was more bothered about how Hardacre felt than about us losing the player. He's obsessed with his own bloody ego.'

Taylor resisted an ironic smile at the comment. 'Brian, Sam's not going to last long. He's tired. He's knackered. We've got years of doing great things here. He's yesterday's man. We'll take over this club one day. We've been almost there. It will come again. But only if we play our cards right.'

Clough nodded, not really listening, preoccupied as he was with his fierce instinct for fairness and loyalty, both thrown in his face by a vainglorious old fool.

Taylor sighed. 'Now look. I'm off to the training ground. You do what you've got to do here.' He looked at his watch. 'At four o'clock let's bugger off and go down to the Kedleston. Let's really think this out, once and for all.'

'Think what out?' said Clough.

'Let's work out how we're going to take over Derby County.'

'Tell me now.'

'Simple. We win the European Cup. That's all we have to do. On the back of that we raise our battle standard. We force Longson out. We put in our own men. We set Mike Keeling up for it. We'll make him chairman.'

'Pete.' Clough smiled faintly. 'You're always the voice of bloody logic and reason.'

'Well, some bugger's got to be. That okay? We win the European Cup first?'

Clough shrugged. 'Yeah. Dead easy.'

'Yeah. So let's ignore Sam. Eh?' He knew that Clough's strength was also his weakness. As with Longson, it was pride. If he were manager, Taylor told himself, he'd have slapped Longson on the back long ago and thanked him. He longed to tell his partner that there were two Derby County clubs, Longson's and Clough's, neither of them realising that their parallel universes managed to jog alongside each other at the moment, but were always in danger of a severe collision, wherein lay disaster.

He picked up his coat, ready to go out.

'That's why we work so well,' said Clough.

Taylor hesitated in the doorway. 'How do you mean?'

'I'm action man and you're a bloody philosopher.'

WITH TAYLOR AT the training ground Clough looked about for the brandy bottle, found it and wondered why it had contents of less than a finger. Forgetting that he'd drunk from it earlier in the day he searched for another bottle, to no avail.

'Bastards!' Believing it was Webb who had robbed him, he had half a mind to go down to his office and bring back whatever he fancied. But then, accepting that emotions had been stirred enough for one day, he made one of his more rational decisions which was to sit back, clear his mind and, like Patton, remain toughly resolved and gung-ho for the future. He toasted himself with another wee dram.

When Taylor came back from training he was taken aside by Keeling. 'Just heard. Longson's told Kirkland he's going to get rid of Brian, even if it kills him.'

Taylor went to tell Clough. They looked grimly at each other before setting off for the Kedleston.

The war was now total.

9

ENTRAPPED

I sat in my car outside the entrance to the Derby Rugby Club ground. Two boys passed by, each holding a candle-lit, hollowed turnip with holes cut out to produce grinning masks. The strong musty odour of oily fat and burnt turnip still hung in the air as Clough pulled up alongside. I locked my car and nipped into the Mercedes.

'What's happened?' said Clough, giving me a penetrating glance. The meeting had been at my request.

'Mike Keeling rang me.' I hesitated. 'He told me that the board might sue me for damages.'

'Why?' Clough switched off the engine.

'We lost to Sunderland three none. They reckon I tapped up Roy Mac. I talked to him when he got home from that day at Newton Solney, but we never talked about throwing matches. There's all sorts of rumours, though.'

'That's all it is. Rumours.' Clough scoffed at my dubious expression. 'Who told you this daft thing?'

'George Edwards rang me. He told me the board were after me.'

It silenced Clough a moment. 'Well, yeah,' he said. 'Could be. I warned you about their tricks. It's great news.'

'What?' I stared at Clough.

'Yeah! They're clutching at straws. You've got them on the run. The players aren't chucking matches. It's because they're pissed off with Mackay and Longson. If they're playing rubbish it's because I'm not there. That's my team. Not theirs. I know how to turn it on. They don't.' He gave a contemptuous sniff. 'I was a good player and now I'm a good manager,' Clough stressed. 'Dave Mackay was a good player, that's all he was and ever will be. 'They played for me, those lads. They won't play for Mackay. End of story.'

He was right, of course. The tough and dour Dave Mackay had been a rock on the pitch but could never replace Clough. No manager could emulate his achievements. Mackay might find success at some point with the present squad, but it would be with what was essentially Clough's team.*

I still remained worried. I told Clough that I'd spoken to my solicitor, who had told me that the club could initiate proceedings and that alone would cost me a small fortune.

Clough would not be moved. 'Okay. They're trying to scare you off. They want to take your eye off the ball. You won't get sued. Now look. You tell George Edwards to get out a story that the Protest Movement's not stopping until the players ask you to stop. That'll sort the old twit out.'

From bitter experience I'd taught myself – or so I thought – to pause whenever Clough gave me an idea. So I thought about it. Yes, it was a neat notion. It meant that if the players didn't ask me to stop they were still backing me. I was impressed. 'Are you coming to our meeting tomorrow night?' I referred to the publicised mass meeting. We would be packed to the rafters. But it needed Clough's presence. It would give notice to Derby County that we remained united and strong.

Clough pursed his lips. 'Dunno. Got something on. Things happening.'

'More important?'

'I've got to go down south.' He wouldn't elaborate.

I drove home frustrated. Clough reminded me of 'Deep Throat' from the recent film about the Watergate conspiracy, hinting and suggesting, either leaving me puzzled, or on tenterhooks.

* *Mackay's Derby County, featuring mostly Clough's players, won the First Division championship in 1975 but then went into a steady decline.*

IT WAS 10 P.M. when John McGuinness let me into the side entrance of the health club. It was quiet and deserted. He took me to the restaurant where the coffee machine bubbled steadily.

'Well, Don. This is it. Tomorrow night.' He raised a hand as if toasting the success of the forthcoming mass meeting.

I told him about my latest dialogue with Clough and the issues arising from it. McGuinness thought that Clough might be busy working on Bradley and Keeling. I doubted it, said I thought it was a dead duck.

We sat down with filtered coffee. 'Don,' McGuinness's voice was soft. 'Don't forget the players are coming to our meeting tomorrow night. The press will be there. Can you imagine how Webb and Longson will react to that?' His grin widened as I thought about it. 'Think.'

I thought. And nodded. 'They'd have to surrender.'

McGuinness kept grinning. 'All we need is Cloughie to turn up with them. And bingo.'

I was worried. 'Yeah, but he told me he was going down south tomorrow.'

'What for?'

'He didn't tell me. I think it's something big.'

'He'll miss the meeting?'

'He said he might.'

The telephone rang, forcing McGuinness to answer it. A police siren wailed in the street outside, drowning his voice.

He came back angrily. 'Roy Mac rang the player's union. They said a strike was all down to contract. Gave them no encouragement. Mackay's picked up on it. He says if the players turn up at our meeting they'll go in front of a firing squad.'

NOVEMBER 1 1973 was to go down as the most momentous day in the campaign. It began with me taking a phone call at midday.

'Don. It's Brian.'

'Brian! Where are you?'

'I'm at Brighton. I've got half the nation's press outside.'

'Sorry, Brian. What?'

'I'm at Brighton and Hove Albion. They want me to sign on as manager. I said I had to talk to you, first. Do I sign or don't I? If you don't want me to sign, say so.'

Brighton? My mind raced. Brighton were in the Third Division! Hold on, hold on. This can't be Clough. It's a trick. It's an impersonator, Mike Yarwood even, for a TV programme. He did a wonderful Clough.

'Brian. This sounds weird. How do I know it's you, it's not Mike Yarwood?'

'Eh. Here's Pete.' His voice went faint as he passed the phone. 'Don thinks I'm Mike Yarwood.'

I heard Taylor's dry laugh. There was no mistaking his gruff tone. 'Hiya, Don. Yeah, it's Mickey Mouse and Donald Duck. Here's Brian back.'

A rustling sound, then Clough spoke again. 'I told them I needed to talk to you first. If you say no, then I won't sign. It's up to you.'

I froze. This was unbelievable. Was he hoping I'd say no, so that the publicity would shake Longson and Webb?

'You'll have to hurry up, Don. What do you want me to do?'

Thoughts rushed through my head. What game was he playing this time? Had he deliberately chosen lowly Brighton because he could easily quit as soon as the door opened back at Derby? No one would blame or criticise him for it, or was he merely marking time, keeping in practice as a manager? Or, did he feel he had to work and had chosen an easy option? I needed advice. And I couldn't get any. I had no time. No time. No time at all.

'Don, hurry up. I've got to go. They're popping cameras at me through the window.'

He had intentionally given me no warning. Half an hour would have been sufficient. I could have sounded out opinions. I felt a prickly rush of heat to my hands and cheeks. 'Brian,' I stammered. 'I've got to talk to the Movement. I've got to talk to them. I just can't—'

Clough cut in. 'Don, listen. It's simple. If you don't want me to sign I won't. Whatever happens I'll be at your meeting tonight, whatever happens here. Do you get that?'

'Yes, I just don't know. Obviously we don't want you to join another club.'

'You don't want me to, but you're not stopping me?'

'Brian, I can't tell you what to do. It's your career. You have to do what you think right.' Christ, what had I just said?

'Okay, Don. See you tonight.' The phone went dead.

There are innumerable novels and films in which bad news leaves the guy continuing to hold the phone to mark the impact the call has made on him. I held it as long as in any drama. In which time I decided to ring George Edwards.

He responded to the news. 'Blimey. Let me check, I'll be back.'

Within five minutes he rang me back to say that the newsroom had just picked up the story. The *Derby Evening Telegraph* would splash it on its front page. Edwards, a mild-mannered man, sighed. 'I didn't think he'd go to Brighton. I thought it would be a London club.'

'But why Brighton, George?' I sounded pained. 'He could have signed for any local club. He's not going to stay at Brighton, is he? It could have been Mansfield or Chesterfield. On his own doorstep!'

'He ticks differently to us, Don. Who knows what he's up to?'

I went into the kitchen for a spot of lunch, then the phone rang once more. I raced to it, but took a breath before picking it up, desperately hoping against hope that it would be Clough again, his mind changed. But it wasn't.

'Don? It's Roy McFarland.'

'Hi Roy. How's it going?'

'Not good. Don? It's in the papers you said you'll stop the protest if the players ask you to. Is that right?' His voice sounded strained.

Oh God. 'Yes,' I answered, in dread.

There was a pause. 'Well, we're asking you to stop.'

His taut tone and formality meant that he had people standing over him with some kind of threat.

'Don? You there?'

'Yes. Yes, I am, Roy.' I tried to think. It was almost laughable. For the second time in five minutes I'd been thrown into a new dilemma at the hands of Clough. There was not one decision that he'd made, since the campaign began, which had moved us forward an inch. If anything we were going backwards.

'Just a minute, Roy,' I said. 'I've got the kettle boiling.' I thought desperately for some words that would amount to an ambiguous statement, satisfying McFarland's tormentors, yet not surrendering to them.

I spoke with deliberate slowness. 'Roy. Is it that you *genuinely* want us to stop. Do you?' Stressing 'genuinely' was the nearest I could get to spelling it out in code.

There was a silence. 'No. We just ask you to stop. You said you would if we asked you to.'

I could prevaricate no longer. 'Okay. But we're still having the meeting tonight. I was told you and the rest of the team were coming.'

There was a pause. 'Can I have a moment?' His voice was faint as I heard him speak to someone. I thought I heard Mackay's voice.

After a pause McFarland was back. 'Don. We were coming: you know, all the players. All of us. We'd have been there. We can't now, now that he's signed for Brighton. You do understand that?' There had been a catch in his voice.

'Yes. I understand, Roy. Thanks.' I heard the phone go dead.

NEWS TRAVELS FAST when it's hot. George Edwards was back within ten minutes of McFarland's call. 'I've just talked to Dave Mackay. He says Roy Mac's asked you to give up the Movement. Have you?'

I took a deep breath and tried to explain what had happened, that I hadn't admitted defeat and that the meeting was going ahead.

Edwards interrupted. 'But the club have put out the statement that you have. We're running with the story that you said you'd stop the protest if the players told you to.'

'Yes', I said, explaining as carefully as I could the subtext of my phone call with McFarland.

'I get that. But the news doesn't go out in subtext, does it?'

The only good news was that Clough was coming to the meeting and Edwards said the *Telegraph* would be there with cameras and notebooks ready.

I next rang McGuinness and said I felt as though I was trapped in a spider's web.

'Webb tied you up, did he?'

His pun didn't amuse me. 'No. It's Cloughie again. Another idea bites the dust.'

McGuinness said he would talk to all the leading members of the Movement, leaving me free to deal with calls from the media. The Clough–Brighton story would capture all the leading sports pages as well as some of the front pages of the tabloids and draw ironic commentaries from the likes of Hugh McIlvanney and Brian Glanville in the broadsheets.

McGuinness became sympathetic. 'Look, Don. We've got the meeting tonight. We'll make it big. With Cloughie there who knows what might happen?'

Yes. Indeed, I thought with heavy irony. With Cloughie, who knew anything?

I ended the call and switched on the radio to hear Radio Derby lead with the story that 'Don Shaw, at the request of the players, has agreed to suspend the Protest Movement but tonight's meeting at the Kings Hall will go ahead as planned.'

I looked at my watch. Two hours to go before I had to face the public.

McGuinness rang back. 'Don't worry, Don. I've been talking to people. You can't stand us down. The Movement isn't a registered company. The protests will go on as long as he's available to return to Derby. The rest of us can do what we want. Tonight I suggest you make a personal statement and then I'll back you, okay?'

I sat down to watch the BBC TV news. Kenneth Kendall began with the latest on the Israeli–Egypt conflict. Three-quarters of the way through the newscast the familiar, sprightly and smiling Clough appeared, standing next to the flamboyant Mike Bamber, the Brighton chairman, jubilant in his catch. It was bizarre. Brian Clough was now the manager of Brighton and Hove Albion Football Club.

The news reporter asked Clough a question. 'What brought you to Brighton?'

Clough replied. 'I like the sea air. But I'm here to do a job of work. I'm a football manager. And listen. I don't want any Regency dandies messing with my players. And this club's Brighton *and Hove Albion*, not Brighton, understand?'

Just as I was leaving for the meeting at the Kings Hall, the phone rang. I nearly left it to Liz to answer, but picked it up.

It was Clough. 'We reckon we'll be with you about eight. Eh, don't worry. Listen. The players are going to the meeting. They told me last night.'

'They won't, Brian. Haven't you heard? Roy Mac rang me this morning. They forced him to ask me to abandon the protest. I had to agree.' I bit my tongue. I nearly said 'It was your idea.'

There was a pause. 'I didn't know that. Got to go. See you later.'

The phone went dead. I replaced the receiver only for it to ring within seconds.

It was Bill Holmes. He told me that Longson had issued a press release which said that Don Shaw had ended the Protest Movement because he 'was fed up with Clough's behaviour, as they all were, and wasn't it time they were all united, protesters and club officials in the interests of Derby County?'

'Oh…' I despaired. But actually, it was nearly true.

10

RAIDING PARTY

In a state of apprehension, I arrived early at the Kings Hall, keen not to be recognised, well, not immediately. I wanted space and time in which to think what I would say in my 'personal statement'.

I hung about in the foyer of the grand building, constructed between the World Wars as the town's main swimming baths. Inside, a number of supporters were arranging chairs over the wooden covered pool. The hall was decorated with the – by now familiar – large placards featuring Clough's face in red and white, reminiscent of a Soviet rally. McGuinness appeared, gave me a pat on the arm as he guided me to the platform. 'Don't worry, Don. You'll be okay. You make your statement and everything's fine.'

By 7.30 p.m. the hall was packed, with hundreds outside, waiting for Clough to arrive. I'd feared that my surrender to McFarland's request, plus the little matter of Clough signing for Brighton, would have resulted in the meeting being an abject failure. But the first setback had been discounted. It was generally accepted that McFarland had a pistol held against his head when he called me. And the Brighton story, it appeared, had been dismissed for the obvious reason that there was no fan base in that south coast resort the like of which Derby enjoyed, and so little chance of them ever breaking into big-time football, even with Clough at the helm. He'd chosen Brighton, it was commonly held, as a stop gap. If he'd signed for Arsenal or Manchester United, on the other hand, it would have been a smack in the face, with little chance of seeing him back at Derby.

I was struck by a sudden irony. Here we were, fighting for Clough's return to Derby County, ranging ourselves against the bastions of power at the Baseball Ground, when two of the individuals I could point to as having damaged our prospects were Clough himself, and me, Don Shaw. It was almost funny.

The hall was packed ten minutes before the start, people jammed in the double doorway and in the foyer leading out into the street. As the clock touched the half hour McGuinness stood up, welcomed everybody and announced that Don Shaw had a personal statement to make. I took the microphone and apologised for my gaffe in giving Longson and Mackay the means of shutting us down. I made no mention, of course, that it had been Clough's idea. I picked up confidence as I drew some initial, if scattered, applause.

'I don't speak for the Movement. You decide what the policy is. You've decided you want Cloughie back. That's why you're here.' That brought some cheering. Encouraged and relieved, I adopted Clough's voice and manner. 'Now look here, young men and young ladies. I was wrong. You were right. Eh.' I wagged my finger. 'We're in this to win. I've only signed for Brighton because it's got a railway line back to Derbee!'

No sooner had I sat down to general laughter, than a burst of cheering from outside the building caught our attention. 'It's Cloughie! It's Cloughie!' was the cry taken up inside as fans stood to peer towards the entrance.

It wasn't Clough who appeared, but eleven attractive women who passed through the crowded doorway, then marched down the aisle with determined strides. 'It's the wives.' In the echo chamber of the swimming baths the shouts and the applause reverberated as Barbara Clough led the women to sit in the reserved front row of seats where photographers eagerly awaited them, flashes going off.

What next? I exchanged glances with McGuinness and Holmes. Ten seconds later I got my answer as Barbara stood up and led the wives out again, to even louder applause.

They had made their statement of support. They had told the world that, although the players were not there in person, they were present in spirit.

The atmosphere built to a keen expectation. What would

Clough say, what would he do, when he arrived? I glanced at my watch. Ten minutes to go, according to his forecast.

A sudden loud cheering from the foyer could only mean one thing. Amidst a joyous uproar I left the platform to meet Clough halfway down the aisle. He strode towards me with a fixed smile on his face. As we shook hands to the flash of cameras his eyes had a far away look.

IT WAS OCTOBER 1972. The Baseball Ground at midnight was a dark and silent place as Clough let himself in, careful not to make a noise. He went straight to the work shed and brought out two large-diameter hosepipes to set about the job of connecting them to the mains. He then hauled them out to stretch them over the pitch, one lying in each half, then went back to open the cocks. Listening to the water gushing forth, he jumped down on to the concrete terracing and sat down. He looked at his watch. He would give it fifteen minutes. As he listened to the rhythm and flow of water his head gradually lowered to his chest.

He awoke with a start, the splashes around him confusing. Then realisation hit him like a brick. He rushed to the stop cocks, feverishly turning them off. As fast as he could he retrieved the hoses whilst up to his ankles in water, the deluge dripping on to the low-lying terraces. He glanced at his watch. It was 1.15 a.m.

Sixteen hours later on the same day Longson stood in the board-room, introducing Sir Stanley Rous, President of FIFA, to Brian Clough, his manager. The international soccer chief was to be a spectator at the European Cup game that night.

'Brian?' he said frowning. 'I can't understand why the pitch is so muddy. We haven't had rain for days.'

'Hah.' Clough smiled back at him. 'You've not heard of the Trent valley peculiarity, known by the Met Office as Trent pressure?'

Sir Stanley confessed his ignorance.

'Well, it's well known by the farmers. We get sudden downpours, you see. It's to do with the low pressure and humidity from the river Trent – and the Derwent, come to that. The water table under the pitch is lower than that in the street, so we can't drain off, you see. In fact we're famous for being in the mire!' Clough laughed, encouraging Sir Stanley to smile back, albeit hesitantly.

Longson didn't know where to put himself, such was his embarrassment. It was true that the Baseball Ground pitch had a reputation for getting waterlogged. Putting in layers of cinders had proved of little value. 'Wait till we get you down to the Baseball Ground,' was the cry at Arsenal or Tottenham fans following a rare away defeat in September. The players knew that, come January, they knew how to cope on a sticky pitch. Tommy Powell in the fifties, had been one of the best wingers in the country, a craftsman in the business of controlling a muddy ball.

Derby County easily beat Benfica 3–0. Sir Stanley clapped both sets of players off the pitch, difficult to tell which team they belonged to, in their mud-plastered kit. Clough smiled benignly at Longson, who didn't know how to react.

Clough once told me that he'd intended merely to 'soften' the pitch in the manner of a cricket groundsman preparing the wicket. At the end of the day both teams had to play on the same pitch, didn't they? He clearly didn't think of it as cheating, but his cheeky smile was vastly amusing.

The bizarre incident illustrates Clough's global attention to detail as a manager, a job at which he was unique in almost every aspect of the job.

One lunchtime at the Midland Hotel, I prompted him to explain his actions – or lack of them – during a match. Why, for example, was it that he rarely demonstrated his pleasure at scoring a goal?

He told me that it was a player's job to score goals, the end result of a pattern of play for which he himself, as manager, was responsible. He disliked the idea of congratulating himself. 'And jumping up and down for joy would wreck what's inside here.' He tapped the side of his head. 'In there I've got a camera and notebook.'

Unlike managers we see, eyes down, busily note-taking during a match, Clough missed nothing. He could remember whole sequences of play and rewind them through memory. He took in every move and every quirk in a player's repertoire and could reel them off analytically at half-time, followed by terse orders as would befit an infantry officer in battle. Unlike 'ball watching' spectators, he would disregard the immediate action to focus his attention on the alertness and movement of players 'off the ball'. Were they reading the game and anticipating the next pass, or the next pass but one? It required a fast-moving eye and brain to decide if players were in the wrong place, or running a fraction slower than demanded. Clough had the ability to make fractional computations in that regard. If a player was judged to have fallen short of this responsibility, he would be acquainted with his misdemeanour forcibly, either at the interval or after the match. At Hartlepool he'd observed a winger glancing more than once at a spectator close to the pitch. Clough recognised the man as an undertaker who had arranged the recent funeral of the player's father.

He quickly substituted the player who, significantly, was not disciplined for his lack of attention. Like the occasional player who was allowed a cigarette to calm his nerves before a big game, he had felt oddly grateful to 'the boss'.

Clough's motivational powers employed all manner of stimuli. The days before a game which are normally devoted to training, were interspersed with what he termed 'group therapy' sessions. These could take place on the training ground, in a tearoom, dressing room, on a public park or on a beach. During his morale boosting talk Clough kept a keen eye on the players' reactions and body language.

It was as much about bonding as anything else. The sessions had been his idea initiated at Hartlepool, after visiting the fish and chip shop on returning from an away game. He and Peter Taylor became experts in the art of relaxing the players in the dressing room.

Roy McFarland told me that 'Cloughie was a brilliant psychologist. What I remember most are the laughs we had before a game.' He said, 'We turned up two hours early at Benfica. Cloughie realised the long wait would increase stress – lactic acid builds up in the leg muscles – so he and Pete Taylor told us jokes and had us playing card games with laughs thrown in. The time went quickly. I was still laughing as we walked down the tunnel on to the pitch.'

Clough disregarded 'tactics' which, he said, were 'the best thing to talk about if you want to ruin a team's rhythm'. Blackboard analysts were condemned as counter productive. 'Tactics aren't for me,' he declared. 'They're things teams dream up because they're scared they might lose.'

He admired George Best who had openly admitted that talk of tactics went in one ear and out the other. 'You don't teach genius,' Clough said approvingly. 'You watch it.'

To send out a team cautious about the opposing force, he maintained, was to create tension and nervousness. In the minutes before they entered the tunnel, Clough put the final touches to his week-long programme. His players were ready for battle, believing they were superior to the other side. In the minutes before a game Clough would give his team instructions, but they were simple, so as to keep their focus. And they were brief, as to O'Hare: 'Hold the ball as long as it takes Kevin or Alan to get level with you and push it ahead.' And to Hector: 'Watch John all the time. Be just ahead of him ready to pick up his pass.' Alan Hinton was invariably told to 'stay wide' and 'Don't be scared of shooting when you feel like it.' Clough's instructions were not much different to those given at schoolboy level. 'You pass the ball and you keep passing the ball, and when you see the goal, if there's nobody better placed, have a go.'

'Try to keep your shape,' said most managers. But not Clough. He maintained that shape would be kept if the rhythm and accuracy of passing out of defence was set in motion from the starting whistle. It didn't matter how good the other side's reputation was – if you played to your potential in the simple belief that the other side would find it hard to match you in the basic skills, then you would win.

Liz and I went to Birmingham to see City take on Derby in that glorious season of '71–'72. I remember overhearing a Blues supporter saying to his mates around him, 'Look at Derby. The passing. It's like the tick of a clock. A metronome.'

It was no coincidence that clean play was demanded from every player. Clough was always aware that 'dirty' play and disruptive behaviour only served to slow down a side's momentum. It was also bad sportsmanship. Clough would fine a player if he committed such a crime. There were very few of these to deal with at Derby County, which, consequently, had the reputation of being the cleanest side in the division.

He hated Leeds United for their deliberate fouling and underhand methods, laying the blame squarely at the door of their manager, Don Revie.

Scouting and choosing a player was an art form in itself. It did not stop at midnight raids and press-gang signings. That was merely the target end of the operation. Beforehand, Clough carried out checks as a credit company might evaluate the worth of a debtor before lending him money. Once the player was signed he would commence an intimate search into the player, at the end of which process Clough felt he knew him. It was vital, he said, that he understood how a man ticked. He had to be open for examination, not by physical pressure as in the case of the army, but psychologically. Clough searched for character traits and patterns of behaviour, which, once grasped, gave him a power over the player intended to induce fear initially, out of which would come obedience and respect. He gave me the analogy of SAS selection because his method of training players was based on military-style indoctrination. Although a Labour voter in a time when left-wingers dominated the party conference, Clough believed in a code of disciplined behaviour and obedience to authority in the community at large.

He told me a tale so breathtaking in its psycho-dynamism it would have been unbelievable had he not told me himself.

Colin Todd was the perfect defender, fast and accurate in the tackle and a wonderful distributor of the ball. He was also the first to arrive for a training session. He was never heard to grumble or cause dissent in the dressing room. He lived quietly with his wife and baby Ian in Dean Close, Littleover, a pleasant residential suburb of Derby. He never swore, nor did he 'rubbish' other players or even joke about them.

In the whole of the Football League, there could have been no player more virtuous and dedicated to his game than Toddy. Even when Billy Bremner of Leeds United caught him with a vicious tackle, which could well have resulted in serious injury, Todd merely hobbled around a bit, made no protest to the referee and got on with the game.

Clough found it annoying. He did not believe in the 'perfect player'. There had to be a flaw somewhere. Taylor found Clough's insistence on penetrating Todd's shield of virtue amusing. 'Toddy's a good lad. He's dead straight. Why worry about him?'

Clough would have none of it. He couldn't understand Todd's lack of emotion. Even when the final whistle blew on a victorious European match, he had remained cool, calm and collected. Clough decided to test that degree of serenity. He fined Todd ten pounds for allegedly turning up late for a training session. Todd had not been late. In fact he'd arrived early. With the players goading him to protest at the injustice, Todd did nothing. He merely paid his fine.

Clough was furious. 'He's a bloody inhuman robot!' he shouted at Taylor. Todd, it seemed, had defeated him. Clough, never the loser, was more determined than ever to 'get into Toddy'.

Following the game against Benfica in Portugal, Clough chose his moment. That night, at the celebratory dinner with the players and their wives, Clough stood up, wagging his finger and said forcibly, 'Toddy. I do not like you, nor do I like your missus. There's something about you!'

Todd, shocked to the core, could not finish his meal. He nodded for his wife to leave with him.

'Good riddance,' shouted Clough, as the couple left the dining room. Taylor sat open mouthed. In all the years of their relationship Clough had never behaved like this. The rest of the team continued the meal in silence.

The following day Todd demanded to speak to the boss. Without showing emotion he stood in front of Clough. 'I don't mind what you say about me, but leave my wife out of it. I want an apology.'

Clough, grinning, got up from his desk and shook a startled Todd by the hand. 'Toddy, you're human after all! And you're a great player. But I needed to know you. I tried every way and last night I had to do something radical. Now I've sent flowers to your missus, with a note. I've explained. And you're getting a pay rise. That's the end of it. Well done, young man.'

Todd, bemused, smiling a little and shaking his head was leaving the office when Clough stopped him. 'Eh.' He narrowed his eyes. 'There's still something I don't know about you. Some little secret. What is it?'

Todd thought desperately. 'I don't know, boss.'

'Think about it. I'm on to it. Off you go.'

Clough's unerring instinct – by antenna, telepathy or whatever – was vindicated. He was driving through Littleover village when he saw Todd enter a public telephone box. Since he had a phone at home, a quarter of a mile away, why should he choose to do that? Clough decided it had to be one of two reasons. It was either to make a call to the 'other' woman or it betrayed a vice that afflicted many footballers, owing to the time they had on their hands.

Clough quickly established that Todd was not playing away and concentrated on the other, more likely reason. Albert Whittaker, a local bookmaker, found Clough visiting him for a chat. It transpired that Todd owed £700 to the bookie.

Another manager would have torn a strip off the player, telling him to pull himself together and start paying off the debt. Clough was more subtle. He paid the debt himself, telling the bookmaker to ring Todd and say it had been paid by a benefactor who wished to remain anonymous.

Todd was immediately scared at the news. It had to be Clough, he reasoned, who had wiped out his debt. But he daren't approach him. What if, by an amazing long shot, Clough wasn't the benefactor? In which case Todd would have revealed, unnecessarily, that he was a gambler.

Clough enjoyed Todd's nervousness and awaited the next game with interest. He was highly satisfied to see him play 'out of his skin'.

Clough's bizarre brand of 'man management', as he liked to call it, had cost him £700, but had been worth it.

I put it to Clough, with grovelling tact, that it wasn't absolutely necessary to know *everything* about a player, was it? His reply left me in no doubt that he was a latter-day Svengali. 'That's my team,' he said abruptly. 'They're mine. You've got a house you run. You know everything in it, else how can you manage? I've got a team. Ditto. Next question?'

John McGovern was the longest serving of Clough's army, having played at Hartlepool. He was small and a bit awkward on the pitch. Many Rams fans thought him not the best of players. Clough knew differently. McGovern's father had been killed in a road accident and so he lived with his grandmother. She adored Clough, regarding him as a 'charming young man'. Clough had no problem in signing him and she invited Clough for tea as a way of giving thanks. As they sat in the parlour Clough was struck by the polite and calm behaviour of young John, never speaking out of turn and observing both his grandmother's and Clough's needs before and during the meal. Clough went home, telling Barbara that he wanted his two sons, Nigel and Simon, to grow up in the same way, well mannered, polite and kind.

Nevertheless, McGovern did not escape close scrutiny. Clough took to dropping by at late hours, or telephoning, to check if Johnny was tucked up safely in bed and not out drinking and womanising.

While McGovern was at Derby he would warn each new recruit, 'He'll shout at you if you win and he'll do nothing if you lose. You might play a blinder and he'll give you a cuff round the back of your head. You know why?'

The new player would shake his head, puzzled. 'No. Why?'

'He doesn't want you thinking it's easy. He can't stand players coming off satisfied. You've always got to keep getting better.'

Throughout McGovern's career under Clough, although knowing that the boss thought highly of him, he never knew that Clough also loved him like a father.

Clough's treatment of his players varied according to the individual.

Alan Hinton, one of the best wingers in the club's history and whose lack of appetite for the contact side of the game was known to be at variance to that of the rest of the team, came in for special treatment from Clough. He lived in constant fear of being sent for. Whenever the message was delivered that the boss wanted to see him, he would hyperventilate and start to sweat. He knew what to expect. Clough would bark at him, lecture and browbeat him to such an extent that he would return white-faced to training. Even so, his name rarely was missing from the team sheet each week. As a result Hinton never failed to get stuck in as best he could. His crossing of the ball was as impeccable as ever. Occasionally he would unleash a shot at goal to rival that of any from hotshot Peter Lorimer of Leeds. Clough told me that Hinton, neglected by Nottingham Forest, was his best buy in terms of cost effectiveness. Hinton not only helped Derby win the Second Division championship but also the First, as well as helping Derby get into Europe.

Roger Davies, a tall centre forward, was another player to be given the treatment. Bawled at one day, the next day given a pat on the back, he would then be allowed a cigarette to calm his nerves just prior to leaving the dressing room for a big game.

Clough's measures were devoted to one result: winning matches. If the player knew that Clough was paying such close personal interest in him the result was, as intended, unsettling. He would ask himself: 'If he wants to know all this about me I must be important. I've got to show him my good side.' It meant using every fibre of his body in striving to win a game.

I LED CLOUGH on to the platform at the Kings Hall, with Peter Taylor following up behind. McGuinness handed me the microphone. All eyes were on Clough, who sat elbows on knees, his head lowered as in deep thought.

'We all know what happened today.' My voice vaulted to the high roof of the swimming pool, echoing down over the packed ranks of seats. 'Roy Mac asked me to halt the protest. We've decided to carry on. Brian has signed for Brighton. We've decided to ignore it.'

Laughter broke the tension. I put out a hand towards Clough. 'Our manager, Brian.' I sat down.

The tumult that greeted Clough had him standing and shaking his head. He stared down at his tightly coiled right hand as if, therein, lay the words. When they came he spoke in a regretful tone. 'Ladies and gentlemen, boys and girls, fans and friends.' He paused. It was now silent in the hall. 'I've made mistakes. We all make mistakes.'

A wag called out, 'That bring heartbreaks all over nothing at all.'

Laughter brought a smile to Clough's face. 'Yeah. A great song that. I wish I...' He hesitated.

'Could turn the clock back.' The wag again.

'And that. I want to tell you lot something.' The laughter died in anticipation. 'I want you to know we'd have won every prize there is in football.'

'Well, stay and get 'em them!' The man was small, with a wispy beard.

'The best prize is getting rid of Longson!' someone else shouted.

'Yeah. Give him a wave. So long, son!' came another voice.

More laughter.

Clough smiled and nodded. 'You know why we would have won everything going? You lot. You don't know how much you mean to...' He broke off. His smile had vanished, his lower lip was trembling. He took a deep breath, regaining his voice control. 'That's why I've enjoyed every moment at Derby.' He gave a twisted smile. 'On the pitch.'

Laughter.

'Not so much off it. As you all know. You lot and the players. I don't know what will happen. But I'm not moving from Derby. I'm staying here. This is where we live. I'm not being kicked out of my...' His final words were drowned by the noise of people on their feet clapping, shouting and whistling.

A female voice shouted 'We love you, Brian.' The hall rapturously endorsed the sentiment. The wave of emotion swept on to the stage and embraced him.

I noticed Taylor, who was sitting beside me, watch with concern

Above: Clough, aged 23, snapped before Middlesbrough took on Fulham at Craven Cottage. The enigmatic smile and self-assurance already in place.

Right: A reflective and solitary Clough in the Roker Park dressing room in 1963. The knee injury which cut his playing days short was perhaps the very thing that later made him such a driven manager.

Above: Young and hungry. Playing colleagues since 1956 and now the country's only management team, Clough and Taylor watch Hartlepool in 1965.

Below: Cat that got the cream – Derby chairman Sam Longson unveils the duo as the new management team at the Baseball Ground in 1967. To the far right is Len Shackleton who had recommended Clough – 'He's a young bugger, Sam, but by God he gets things done.'

Above: Clough poses with the team in the
background at the start of the 1969/70 season,
excited by the prospect of First Division football.

Above: Clough shakes hands with his captain Dave Mackay – the rock on which he had planned to build Derby – after they had beat Bristol City to win the Second Division championship in 1969.

Below: More silverware – Sir Stanley Rouse hands Mackay the Watney Cup in August 1970, after a 4-1 defeat of Manchester United.

Right and below: Building Derby in his own image – key signings for Clough included Roy McFarland (below) and three years later, Archie Gemmill. Clough secured both players by going to their houses unannounced and refusing to leave until they agreed to sign for him.

Above: Colin Todd is unveiled by Clough in February 1971. The fee of £170,000 made the deal a British transfer record. Longson, the chairman, had agreed to a maximum offer of £90,000. He claimed that Clough had bankrupted the club.

Below: Clough with 'kidnapped' Ian Storey-Moore in 1972, shortly before he paraded him on the pitch proclaiming him a new Derby player. This was one of the few times his mesmeric tactics failed and Moore eventually signed a few days later for Manchester United.

Above: Clough oversees yet another record
transfer – that of David Nish in August 1972.

Above: The Holy Grail – Clough and Taylor hold the
First Division championship trophy aloft in May 1972.

Below: Trainer Jimmy Gordon takes his turn, while the
players show off their medals.

Above: The players had been on holiday in Majorca with Peter Taylor when they heard that results elsewhere had made them champions. Here they celebrate with an impromptu jam: Jim Walker on guitar, Colin Boulton on drums, Ron Webster on tambourine, Alan Hinton on saxophone and John Robson on vocals.

Below: Clough and Taylor sign an improved deal in 1972 with the board looking on.

Opposite: The reigning champions line up for a new season with Clough far left in tracksuit. (Back row, left to right) Hennessey, Webster, Boulton, Todd, Robson, Peter Taylor and Jimmy Gordon. (Front, left to right) McGovern, Gemmill, O'Hare, McFarland, Hector, Hinton, Durban.

Above: Now in full celebrity mode, the ego landed in New York in 1974, but soon finds his match in Muhammad Ali.

Below: Old Big 'Ead gets some last minute make-up for his debut as a pundit on ITV's On The Ball, August 1973. His media commitments and 'bigger than the club' persona would become an increasing bone of contention with the Derby board.

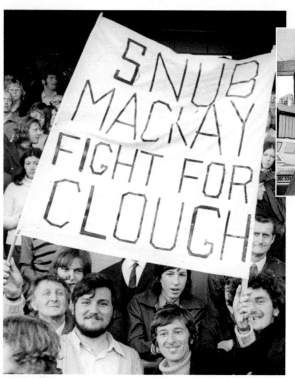

Above: Rams winger Alan Hinton holds up the letter signed by the players demanding the reinstatement of Brian Clough and Peter Taylor.

Left: The fans make their position clear at the Baseball Ground during the weeks of October.

Above: Surrounded by the rest of the team, Kevin Hector studies their letter to Sam Longson and the board.

Above: I may be smiling as I guide Clough to the Kings Hall platform, but I'm worried about what had happened earlier in the day when Clough had signed for Brighton.

Above: I listen to Clough's speech at the King's Hall, Derby, during the defining meeting of the Protest Movement, 1 November, 1973.

Above: Brian Clough, at his most content, away from it all on a walk in the Derbyshire countryside in 1982.

Right: Clough in happier days at Derby with his two sons in early 1973, Simon and future Rams manager Nigel (right).

Left: Now manager of Brighton, Clough arrives at Heathrow, breaking his holiday in Majorca to discuss the possibility of becoming Leeds United manager with chairman Manny Cussins.

Below: A man apart – Clough leads out Leeds United at Wembley for the Charity Shield. Clough's disastrous flirtation with Leeds United lasted just 44 days.

as Clough brought his tightening right fist to the side of his face and quickly brushed tears away with the back of his hand. He then lowered the fist and stared at it, the knuckles shining in the spotlights. 'I don't know what's going to happen—' He broke off, his voice choking.

Taylor stood up, looking alarmed.

Clough swallowed hard. 'But one thing's certain—'

Taylor had a hand raised. 'Brian,' he said sharply.

Clough turned to see Taylor grimace, as if urging him to measure his words.

Clough turned back to the audience. 'Look. What Peter and me want you lot to do is support Roy Mac and the lads.' His voice began to waver again.

A voice shouted. 'Board out! Clough back.'

It was taken up by the thousand inside and then by the throng outside the hall. 'BOARD OUT CLOUGH BACK BOARD OUT...'

The chanting was repeated and repeated and not denied by Clough's raised hand, palm outwards. He shook his head. 'Okay. A contract's a contract. It doesn't rule my life. I am not giving up and neither should you.'

'Brian. May I have a word?' Taylor got up and beckoned for the microphone, showing quiet determination.

Clough, surprised a little, stood to one side. Taylor moved in and bent his head to the microphone. He looked serious. 'We've got to cool it. Okay?' He waited for the chanting to die down. 'We've got to just calm down a bit. Let's just calm down and look at the situation. Then we'll decide what to do. We've been up since six this morning and I'm knackered. I know Brian's knackered, so we're going now. We thank you. You're the best fans in the land. Love you.' He looked at Clough with a hard searching look.

Clough nodded back at him.

Taylor shook my hand and put his mouth to my ear. 'Sorry, but you know.' He turned to raise his hand at the fans, addressing them. 'Keep the faith. We're not deserting you. But we have to step back a bit and do a bit of thinking. Okay?'

He turned to escort Clough from the platform. As he did so the packed hall stood in applause.

Clough stopped for a quick word with me. 'I'll ring you.'

He followed Taylor off the platform and down the aisle. The applause was sustained. We could have been at the end of an orchestral concert. No shouting, no whistling. Just massive applause.

Then the singing broke out spontaneously. 'Brian Clough, Brian Clough, we'll support you ever more.' It rose to a crescendo. It could have been the Kop at Liverpool. The song vibrated around the metal arches of the roof. It was taken up outside as Clough and Taylor were enveloped by the crowd.

I was grabbed for interview by John Hall of Radio Derby. As we made our way through the throng my shoulders began to ache from back-slapping fans calling out words of encouragement.

They thought Clough was as good as back. But I couldn't shake the look on Taylor's face from my mind.

11

ESPIONAGE

JOHN HALL ENTHUSED as we broke through the crowd outside the Kings Hall and began the short walk through the murky night to Radio Derby: 'He's definitely coming back, Don. If he'd stayed longer I reckon he'd be back tonight. You'd have had the crowd carry him down to the Baseball Ground.'

Across the road a beery crowd stood outside the Olde Dolphin pub belting out 'You'll Never Walk Alone' in celebration of Clough's return. Competition came from the adjacent Cathedral with the Choral Union's joyful rendering of Verdi's 'Sanctus'.

'They'll be ringing the bells next,' said Hall. 'I think you've done the trick, Don.'

I was less than ecstatic. It was only nine hours since the Brighton phone call and I felt nothing but a growing resentment at being a pawn in a game I barely understood where the rules changed from day to day.

As we entered Radio Derby's reception I came back, yet again, to the paradox that was Clough and the popular view that he winged everything he did. My frustration increased the more I dwelt on it. Feeling as I did at that moment I would have happily dismissed all the stuff about his mystical brand of 'man management'.

I was so preoccupied with cosseting my annoyance that in the dim light I hadn't noticed a man crouched over a desk at the far end of the otherwise empty newsroom.

'Hi, Don,' he said, lacking in enthusiasm. I peered in his direction and recognised the bulky figure of Graham Clarke huddled at a typewriter. We'd known each other since childhood.

He played cricket for my village team, had worked in the National Westminster bank in Irongate and did some local sports reporting as a hobby.

Hall punched the air at Clarke. 'I think we've got Cloughie back. You missed something. Christ, it was like a revivalist meeting. Martin Luther King, Billy Graham, take your pick.'

Clarke merely grunted. 'You don't know what's going on, Don.' He looked down at his copy. 'You don't know the half of it.'

'Half of what?'

'What went on at the Baseball Ground. With Cloughie. Nobody could work with him. He was out of hand. He had to go.'

'I don't care,' I said. 'When you've got the best manager—'

'He's not the best manager.' Clarke had a friend who worked at the ground and who fed him with the gospel according to Longson.

'Of course he bloody well is.' The anger I felt over Clough I thrust at Clarke and then shook my head. Good grief. Despite my irritation with Clough I was now defending him.

I went through a door into the studio, the red light on. The interview would go out on the local news that night. At the same time it would be sent down the line to Broadcasting House for the national network. The gist of what I said was that nothing had changed. The Protest Movement would continue.

I got home at 9 p.m. Liz said, 'Cloughie rang.'

I rang him back.

'Don. Just to say don't worry about today.'

'How do you mean, Brian?'

'I can quit Brighton any time. I told Bamber that.' He referred to the Brighton chairman. 'Me signing there's got nothing to do with me wanting to get back to Derby.'

'That's great news, Brian.'

'I'm still backing you. Just keep the Protest Movement going. I've got an idea. Let's meet.'

Ten minutes later I drove through the rain along the ring road to the Kedleston Hotel set in countryside near Quarndon village. I found the lounge bar empty. Shortly afterwards Clough walked in. I had his drink ready, a brandy. He sat down and looked at me seriously.

'I took that job because I didn't want any other First Division club trying to poach me. They might have succeeded. I'm only human. Big money might have grabbed me. Then how would I have got back here?'

I told him that the Movement at large had already assumed that had been the case. 'Glad it wasn't Arsenal,' I said dryly.

'Me at Arsenal? With those plutocratic directors?' He gave me a derisory grin, took a sip of brandy and sat back. 'Nothing I did today changes anything. I can leave Brighton at the drop of a hat. Bamber agreed on that. They'd be happy for me to manage Derby and be a consultant there for a hundred quid a week.'

More drinks came. He raised his glass. 'To Derby County.'

I reciprocated. 'Derby County.'

'I respect Bamber,' he said warningly, in case I harboured scepticism. 'I'll stay at Brighton until I get the chance to get back here. But that means Longson and Webb will have to go. I picked too smart a bloke in Webb. I don't like him and I can't deal with him.'

Clough, as a pendulum swinging along my resentment scale, was moving back from red towards zero. He'd planned his move with care. You'd think you had him sussed and bang, like the English weather, he'd changed yet again.

'That was a great do tonight. Fantastic.' He broke off, twisting his mouth to keep control. 'Bloody marvellous.' He paused. 'Can you set up a meeting with me and McGuinness?'

'Yes, what for?'

'Got an idea. You'll find out. You can be there.' Clough added casually, 'Do you know him well?'

'Not really,' I said. 'All we do is talk about you.'

'What it's like to be loved, eh?'

I joined him in laughter. Clough sat back, relaxed. 'You're a writer. Do you listen to stories as well as write them?'

'Go on.'

'You'll like this. It's the tale of two cities, Coventry and Derby.'

He told me his story.

IN 1972 THE keenest observer of the conflict at Derby County had been Derrick Robins, Chairman of Coventry City. Following his accidental meeting with Longson in the Caribbean he'd kept himself informed of the state of relations between Clough and Longson. By mid-'72 he decided it was time to act. He told his doubting board that Clough was a marvellous manager who had to be allowed total control, whatever the club.

The Coventry motto would be: 'Let the beast have his day.' Clough would be invited to all board meetings and have the casting vote on any split decision. In that way the pressure cooker would stay with its lid kept on. The role of the directors, simply, would be to sit back and enjoy the fruits of Clough's success.

Robins had met Clough at a service station on the A38. On his return to Coventry he'd smugly told his board, 'I just listened. That's all you have to do. Listen and do what he says. Longson's too proud. He presses all the wrong buttons. You've got to give Cloughie a free rein. Then, enjoy the ride.'

I stopped Clough in the middle of his story. 'How do you know about what went on at Coventry?'

Clough smiled wryly. 'I've got a spy there. I told Robins how pissed off I was at Derby. I told him I wanted a board that would let me do what I was there for. To manage. I wanted a big salary, a house, and a car. Robins said I could have anything I wanted. He thought he'd got me.' Clough's grin was mischievous.

'But you didn't take the job.' I shook my head in bewilderment.

'I didn't want it. I wanted my rights at Derby.' He raised his eyebrows, teasing me.

I tumbled. 'You were using Robins to get a bigger pay rise at Derby, playing one club off against the other.'

'And why not? I deserved it. I told the old twit if he didn't pay what was my right I'd be off to Coventry. I said Robins had tapped me up. I said if he didn't match Coventry's offer I'd resign.'

'Longson paid you what you wanted.'

'No. He didn't. So I resigned.'

'You resigned? You've done it before?' I was astonished. 'But, why didn't Longson accept it then? Why wait for a second resignation?'

'Because we were heading for the League championship then. No chairman will sack a manager in that run up. It was different this time. We were already champions and in Europe.'

Still enjoying my bewilderment, he carried on with his story. 'Longson decided to accept my resignation to test if I was serious. That's what I believed. And I gambled on it. And I was proved right.'

I was open mouthed. 'Good God.'

'I let him stew a bit then I went up to his house to ask for my job back. I told him he'd have to pay me what Coventry had offered. That way I'd withdraw my resignation.'

I shook my head at the revelation.

Clough grinned. 'You saw *Sleuth*, that film last year with Laurence Olivier and Michael Caine? It was just like that. I'm in Longson's big house, a young whippersnapper against the big man with the big money. He goes on about how he's proved himself in business, how he'd handled a big work force and what had I done? Got a few lads to kick a ball about. Can you believe? I took him right to the very edge, him knifing me, and me with my little needle. It was a game I knew I'd win. He gave way and paid up. Except...' He paused, the pain of disappointment on his face, his voice dropping. 'This time I resigned once too often. He pushed me into it. He knew I couldn't stomach having to crawl to get his permission every time I went on TV.' He gave a wry smile. 'And all it needed from me was to clap the old twit on the shoulder and say "Thanks, Sam, for bringing me to Derby." Why didn't I? Go on. Ask me. You've been bursting haven't you? So. What am I, stupid or mad?'

'Neither. You just couldn't do that.'

'Why not? Only a stupid idiot or a lunatic would get himself kicked out just because he couldn't say thank you. So, what am I, stupid or mad?'

Seeing my confusion he relented. 'You're right. I couldn't do it, no. He didn't bring me to Derby. It was Shack who did that.'

He stared bitterly at the rain pouring down the window. His expression hardened. 'Shack got nothing from Longson for getting me here. Well, a box of bloody biscuits. Miserable old sod.'

'So what happened next?' I was enthralled.

'Longson found out that Robins had told me the deal was off before I went to see him. He shouted at me. How I'd lied, conned him, used him – as I had. He was entitled.'

I chuckled. 'All these directors falling over to get you.'

'Oh yeah. I had Barcelona, Sunderland and Everton after me, all at the same time. I played one off against the other, seeing how much I could get. Great fun, better than playing Monopoly. The money I was offered, you've no idea. I had a letter from the Greek government boss of sport. He said the Greek national side needed me, pride was at stake, that type of thing. Offered me a bloody great house overlooking the sea at Glyfada. I'd been there. Not a patch on Scarborough. I led him on. In the end I took pity, said I can't understand what you say. It's all Greek to me.' His grin widened. 'The Barcelona guy, he flew over to meet me. Met at the Hilton hotel in London. Had a great meal. I said I'd join. Next day I rang him back, changed my mind, told him I didn't know Spanish and I couldn't learn it because I couldn't even speak the Queen's English properly.'

I laughed along with him. His 'director, chase me' game was his way of exacting revenge, born as he was into a working-class community still suffering from the aftermath of the Great Depression. Michael Parkinson had brought it out in his TV show when Clough had said he had more affinity with the Derby fans 'than a million directors'. He'd worked as an apprentice fitter at ICI. He knew what football meant to the working man.

The sharp eye had mellowed and the familiar raised pitch of voice was absent as he wound up his director baiting tales with a wry smile.

'What they don't know is my family comes first. I'm not dragging them over to Greece or Spain when they're happy here.'

In that respect he hadn't changed. Ever since his first encounter with Sam Longson, who was eager to sign up with the young tyro from Hartlepool, Clough had remained a stick-in-the-mud. He hadn't wanted to move from Hartlepool. And he hadn't wanted to move from Derby. His children were happy at school and Barbara was highly content with their new house in Ferrers Way. It was true what Shack had said about him. The amazing and mercurial Clough was only comfortable in a steady domestic situation surrounded by familiar faces.

He suddenly noted a mark on his glass and summoned the barman to change it. It occurred to me that the tale of his dealings with Robins pointed to another paradox. He was thought to be honest to the point of hurting people with his blunt and uncompromising plain-speaking. He was never considered devious. But his manipulation of Longson and directors from other clubs and countries presented another picture.

Suddenly he looked tired. I wasn't surprised. In the space of one day he'd gone down to Brighton and back, 330 miles in total, after which he'd gone through the emotional wringer at the Kings Hall.

Mike Keeling entered. He'd given Clough a lift and had now returned to pick him up. 'Hello, Don.' He looked his usual self-effacing self. 'Sorry I couldn't come to the meeting.'

'That's okay. Brian did,' I said.

'And the fans. That's what mattered.' Clough led us out to the car park.

As he got into Keeling's car, he turned to me.

'Don't forget. McGuinness.'

'I'll do it.'

THE NEXT MORNING I left home, bound for the health club, without any misgivings. I didn't think twice. That was how it was. He gave an order and the result was pre-ordained.

Twenty minutes later I walked off London Road into the paved square and then pushed open the door to the restaurant and stepped inside.

McGuinness, at the cash till, saw me approach and beamed his big smile. 'Don. Sit down, I'll get you a coffee.'

'Thanks. Cloughie wants to meet you. Asked me to fix it up.'

'What about?'

'Wouldn't tell me. He says I can join you. We'll find out together.'

'Hah.' McGuinness nodded. 'A secret, eh? I wonder what that's about?' He shook his head. 'He's a strange man. Everybody thinks they know him. Well, they don't.'

Having reached the same conclusion myself only the previous night, I asked him why he thought that.

McGuinness summed it up neatly. 'Everybody thinks with him, that what you see is what you get. Blunt and honest. Everybody thinks he's an open book. He gives it you straight in the gut. Says exactly what he thinks.' He paused. 'Do you think that still, Don? I don't.' He tapped his head with a finger. 'Cloughie's thinking. His mind's always ticking. Ticking away. Yeah, he's a strange guy, all right.'

12

STRIKE

'YEAH, HE'S A STRANGE GUY, all right.' McGuinness rubbed his hands together, shifting his weight from his longer leg to the shorter one. 'How is he so successful when the things he does with us go off at half cock?' He suddenly beamed at me. 'How about at my place Barrow upon Trent? I'm home tonight. I'll ring Cloughie. You come as well if you want. Both come for a meal. Should be interesting.'

That evening Keeling picked up Clough and then me, driving us to a timbered eighteenth-century riverside house in Twyford village. McGuinness and his bubbly Irish wife greeted us. A savoury hot pot was our treat and McGuinness was a solicitous host, endeavouring to impress with the fine wines that he brought up from the cellar. During the meal Clough was quietly polite and considerate of Mrs McGuinness, who had prepared the meal.

Later, we went upstairs, into a large beamed roof space converted into a gymnasium. McGuinness pressed a switch somewhere and the pure piano notes of Bach's 'Goldberg Variations' filled the air. He made a proprietary gesture at the room in general. 'Did it all myself.'

Clough looked up at the ancient oak roof trusses arching over-head. 'Marvellous.' He gave the gym equipment only a cursory glance. 'I don't get it, John. You've got a gym in Derby and one here. Why?'

McGuinness enjoyed the moment. 'At sixteen I weighed eight and a half stone. I was picked on by lads at school. I made a vow I'd beat them all up one day. Want to try me at this?' He sat down astride a low exercise bench, ready to perform some exercise. 'My polio leg against your good one?'

'No. I've just eaten. John, I want to ask you something.'

McGuinness swivelled his withered leg back. 'What's the problem?'

'I've been told you're going into business with Webb.'

McGuinness narrowed his eyes, crossed his arms and stared at Clough.

'Well, you are or you aren't.' Clough extended the palm of his right hand and appeared to study it. 'I've also been told you're not a Derby supporter. You're a Glentoran fan.'

'Yes.' McGuinness spoke slowly. 'In Belfast. Here, I'm a Derby fan'. He stood up. 'Why do you think I've been chasing around, having meetings and all that stuff if I didn't want you back at Derby?' He began to breathe rapidly. A blue vein on the side of his head began to palpitate. 'Ask Don, the time we've spent trying to get you back.' He stomped towards a dormer window. 'Fuck's sake!' Swivelling round, he confronted Clough. 'I invite you for a meal and I'm accused of working for Webb!'

'I didn't say that, John.'

'You bloody well meant it! What else did you mean?'

Clough raised the palm of his hand. 'I'm talking about business. Nothing to do with Derby County.'

McGuinness stared back, his eyes wide, his chest heaving.

'John. Just listen. No, listen.' Clough spoke calmly. 'I said that to see how you'd react. There's been rumours. But I believe you, so I can now make the proposition.'

'What proposition?' McGuinness was still angry.

'If Webb wants you in business with him could you get a quid pro quo?'

'How do you mean?'

'The power at Derby isn't Longson. It's Webb.' Clough paused to give emphasis. 'They can vote out a chairman but Webb's made himself indispensable. Good at his job. Now your business is nowt to do with me. But if you're thinking of going into business with him – I'm not asking you to do yourself down – why not tell him you'll cooperate if he uses his influence to get me back at the Baseball Ground?'

McGuinness stood up and limped around the gym, still burning with resentment.

'I don't like that. Telling me I'm not a Derby fan. So why have I got a season ticket in Ley Stand?' He stopped to deliver a broadside at Clough. 'And I don't like somebody telling you about my bloody business if you want to know!'

This was a rare moment. I'd not seen anyone stand up to Clough in an argument, let alone a row.

Clough was unperturbed. He raised his finger a notch higher. 'It wasn't me. It was a rumour. You know how rumours spread.'

'Well, it's bollocks. Don't you realise that businessmen have different agendas to…to football managers! Webb's got his own business as well as working at the club. He's not bothered with me!' He thumped the wall with a fist. 'You tell me I'm not a Derby fan! Jesus. I've been spending days and weeks with Don trying to get you back!' A white dab of spittle flecked on the edge of his lower lip.

'John.' Clough bowed slightly. 'They're just rumours. I don't want to know your private affairs. I don't want to know if you're doing business with Webb. All I'm saying—'

'I know, Brian. But let's be fair. That's all. You know?' He stomped about a few paces, sighing and breathing heavily. 'Okay.' He made an awkward gesture, trying to cool down. 'Okay. I'm sorry I got upset. But, you know…'

Clough looked at his watch. 'Now I'm going to thank your lovely wife for a lovely meal.' He turned to go. 'Nice gym. Doesn't smell of sweaty socks. That's a first.'

'Brian.' McGuinness picked up a black exercise weight, sat astride the bench and placed it on his withered leg. 'They say you make players believe they can do anything you want. Bring them here. Let them try this.' He raised his outstretched and weighted thin leg slowly over the bench and back again.

Clough nodded, impressed. 'Great. Not even Mackay could do that.'

McGuinness stood up proudly. 'My dad worked at Harland and Wolff. He did jobs on the *Titanic*. He was only thirteen. Life was tough.' He indicated the bench. 'Go on, Brian. Have a go. You've never turned down a challenge in your life, have you?'

'Oh yes I have. I hate losing. And you've been practising. I haven't.'

'KEEP IT ON the grass, Martin! Not in the air!' It was the following afternoon and Clough and I were watching Simon, Nigel and Martin practise a quick passing game on Allestree Park.

'Do you think McGuinness will tap up Webb, go into business with him and get me back?' He turned to look at me.

'No. He was really upset. I don't think he's in any deal with Webb.'

I did a double take. Clough was grinning at me. 'What?' I said dumbly.

'I know that. Because I made it up.'

I stared at him.

'I didn't tell you, but I've been suspicious of him from the start. Just a feeling he might be in league with Webb, doing his best to sabotage you. So I set a trap. If he was spying for Longson he'd have lied. He'd have said "Yes, I am doing a business deal with Webb." And he'd leave it a day or two, pretending to think about my suggestion. Then he'd have rung me and said "Yeah, Webb's agreed. He'll try and get you back." Do you know why he'd say that?'

I thought hard. 'No. I don't. Why?'

'Well, what would your Movement do while we waited for Webb to work his magic?'

It dawned. 'It would have shut us up. We'd just wait.'

Clough nodded. 'And wait. You'd wait a long time. And Dave Mackay's legs would get stuck under my desk even more and Longson and his mates would be rubbing their hands and the Movement would be dead from boredom by New Year.'

I nodded. 'So if McGuinness contacts you about Webb it means he's working for the board.' I was impressed by Clough's cunning.

'He won't. You're right. He's not working for the board.' Clough folded his arms. 'He's okay.'

I smiled. 'Clever.'

'Spoilt it, has it? The pigeon hole you've put me in?'

'Sorry?' I didn't follow.

He kept grinning. 'Everybody does. Everybody wants to know what makes me tick.'

'Oh.' I gave an embarrassed chuckle.

He lowered his voice. 'I've got another secret. This is just for you, nobody else, okay?' He touched the edge of my jacket.

'Promise.'

'I lied. I didn't sign for Brighton to stop bigger clubs getting me.' He shouted at Nigel. 'Running off the ball! In front!'

He turned back to me. 'Think. What's Cloughie doing commuting nearly two hundred miles to a Third Division Club on the south coast?' He still enjoyed my confusion – I was still grappling with his former revelation. 'When I rang you from Brighton what did you think?'

'I was surprised. Arsenal, yes. But why Brighton?'

'Right. Why Brighton?'

'You didn't want to go?' I said, fearing the answer.

'I bloody well didn't. It was Pete Taylor. He wanted to retire at the seaside. He saw it as a job for life. He begged me to help set the club up. Negotiate a good pay deal for him. He's a mate. So I had to say yes. The deal was whenever I got the chance to come back here I'd leave him in charge.'

'So when you rang me… if I'd said no, don't go to Brighton?'

'Bloody hell, Don. I was dying for you to say no. The Movement was the perfect excuse. You let me down.'

My stomach fell.

'Now sort that out.' Clough grinned mischievously. 'Eh. How's that book coming on about me?'

'I'm not writing any book about you.'

His grin disappeared as he saw Nigel juggling with the ball between Simon and Martin, both of whom were trying to get it from him.

'Eh,' shouted Clough. 'Nigel! No showboating!'

Nigel caught the ball on the back of his neck, let it roll around his shoulder, then let it drop, catching it on his instep. Yanking it upwards, he caught the ball in his hands and smiled at his father, who gave him a dry 'thumbs up'.

I went back with Clough and the boys for tea, sick in the knowledge of what I'd done. It was now obvious why Taylor had shown alarm at Clough's emotional breakdown at the Kings Hall. He'd killed the emotion because it had threatened his dream. And Clough had not taken the Brighton job out of any fear or insecurity. He'd acted out of loyalty to Taylor, his partner, that was all.

Clough's unpredictability meant that assumptions you'd make about 'normal' people were with him impossible. A day or two ago, in a fit of pique, I'd written him down as lucky. Now, on my way home, I had no doubts. He was impetuous, but he was also a planner and a plotter, manipulative as well as scheming.

I came to the conclusion that it was time to stop messing about. There was only one way by which we could succeed and that was through the players themselves. I still couldn't understand why he hadn't told them to strike already. The players, surely, would never betray him.

As soon as I reached home I picked up the phone, intending to call McGuinness, but was caught momentarily by a photograph I'd cut out from a newspaper and stuck on the wall in my study. It showed Muhammad Ali shaking hands with Clough. Ali's eyes are hooded, almost unseen, Clough's bright and shiny. I had to be as assured. I had let down our army of fans. The only way to put it right would be to get the players out on strike. And if it cut across any of Clough's plans, so be it. The ludicrous, stupid thing was that I couldn't – I daren't – tell Clough what I intended to do. Given the variable winds orbiting around his mercurial nature, any response of his might well destroy the attempt.

I was to be proved right not to keep him informed.

'MEN IN A HURRY' shouted the *Sun* newspaper, its front page bearing a huge picture of Clough and Taylor running down the concourse at St Pancras station en route to their Brighton connection. The few words of copy at the bottom of the page were notable for the adjectives. 'Dashing and debonair', 'The golden boys of football', were some of the epithets used.

On the inside page there were more pics of Clough and Taylor strap hanging on the tube, then running out of the station at Brighton for the taxi to take them to the ground. 'Clough and Taylor, flying troubleshooters' read the inside caption.

At the Baseball Ground someone showed a copy of the newspaper to Sam Longson. He grunted in contempt. 'Men in a hurry? They were always in a bloody hurry. Hurrying to the top. Bugger everybody else.'

MCGUINNESS PROVED he was innocent, as Clough had expected. It was a few days later and he'd not made contact in connection with Clough's suggestion that he offered a deal to Webb. Instead he had telephoned me twice to see if I knew what the 'secret' reason for Clough's visit had been all about. He was still hurting from the way Clough had treated him. 'I invite him for a meal and he behaves like that. I now know what the players must have felt like coming off the pitch, having played a blinder, to be cuffed round the head.'

I confessed to being no wiser and he dropped the subject. We agreed that our next meeting of the Movement, due to take place at the Pennine Hotel, would be delayed in order to give time for the players to go out on strike.

'John.' I was anxious to get off the phone. 'The meeting with the players. Where do you want to have it?'

'Here. At the health club. They can come and park at the side. Round here's deserted after dark. We'll do it through Roy Mac, eh?'

'Okay. But if we're going to do it, best it's done quickly.' It was unintentional but, as I spoke, it reminded me of *Macbeth*.

And look at how that turned out.

I FELT SORRY for the players. For the most part they burnt with a desire to get Clough back. Their desperation had already been shown by the siege at the Baseball Ground. That alone should have moved the board to re-open the door. As far as I was concerned, they had treated the players with contempt. And how mean, miserly and curmudgeonly they seemed, those who had little financial interest in the club, yet appeared to rule it as their fiefdom. Their first duty was to the fans, who loved the club and kept it solvent. Their second duty was to the players, whose physical and mental state had to be maintained. Overall, they had a duty to their manager who had brought them fame and glory. They failed in all respects.

Clough's great achievement had been to give his players infinite self-belief.

This had made them champions of England. One had only to look at the match results since Clough's departure to see that self-belief and team spirit had plummeted.

Even if they were not bent on 'throwing' matches, they were affected psychologically and physically by Clough's sudden removal. At a time when they should have been enjoying the fruits of their labours they had been plunged into a long period of uncertainty.

I wangled an evening with Todd, on the pretext of talking football but intending to raise the subject of a strike. We watched Liverpool play in a European game. Throughout he kept yawning and looked dispirited. Mackay was not to blame. It's doubtful if any manager in Britain could have kept the well-oiled machine that was Clough's team still humming.

After the match, I put it as casually as I could. 'Are you and the rest of the lads going to strike, do you think?'

Todd shrugged. 'We're talking about it.'

The phone rang. He went into the hallway to answer it. On hearing who it was he shut the door to the living room so I wouldn't hear the conversation. He returned half a minute later. 'Cloughie. Did you tell him you were coming here?'

I shook my head. 'No.'

Todd nodded. 'I didn't tell you, but he doesn't like us talking to you on our own. He's coming over.'

I took the hint. 'I'd better go.'

A day later McGuinness told me that he'd persuaded the players to agree to a meeting. The agenda had only one item: Strike. We conspirators and players were to get together on Sunday night, 4 November, the eve of 'gunpowder, treason and plot'.

I emphasised the importance of keeping it secret from Clough.

NOTHING ANGERED Clough more than cheating, whether in the workplace or when playing football. In 1965 three players, Tony Kay, Peter Swan and David 'Bronco' Layne, were convicted of conspiracy to fix matches after betting against their own team, Sheffield Wednesday, in 1962. Seven other players and former players were also convicted of fixing lower-division matches as part of the same betting ring. They were all banned from playing football for life and sentenced to four months in prison. Kay had been Britain's most expensive footballer at the time he left Wednesday for Everton later in 1962, and both he and Swan were England internationals.

Clough's playing career had ended by this time, ruined by injury. Characteristically he bounced back from depression and was a part-time coach at Sunderland when the case came to court. The criminal actions of able-bodied players, while he languished as a 'has been' tormented him. When he became a manager – 'when', not 'if' – he vowed to root out any kind of cheating in *his* football club.

It needn't be cheating for money. He would apply zero tolerance, so that any kind of deviousness would be stamped out. It included reprimanding a player who had pretended to be involved in the game, when he was actually 'hiding'. 'Diving' in the penalty area and other black arts, even shirt tugging on the blind side of the referee, Clough would punish by a fine and a blistering lecture.

Clough's determination to get into a player's mind, to ferret out if he had any vices, had been part driven by the villains in the Sheffield Wednesday case. Nobody was going to accuse him of winning by such methods.

Ironically, the worst example of cheating he came across not only impacted upon his dreams and aspirations, but was perpetrated by an entire team and, to make it worse, made more unpalatable by the perceived favouritism of the referee. It was Clough's bad luck that he had to face Juventus of Italy in the European Cup competition.

By 1973 Clough had a Rams team that was world class in performance. On 8 April they had flown to Turin, highly confident they would win, or at least draw, the first leg. It wasn't sheer bravado that they exuded. Each player knew they were capable of defeating the Italians. They had left Derby in great spirits. They had no idea of what awaited them.

They lost 3–1, a 'diabolical' result in the truest sense of the word. Afterwards, the match became the subject of an in-depth investigation by the *Observer* newspaper. Its report to the European governing body, UEFA, resulted in an investigation which cleared Juventus and nothing was done to explain, in Clough's written words, 'a rotten night, stinking with corruption.'

'I don't mind being beaten fair and square, but not by Italian cheats,' he stormed.

Many managers rail against referees, often accusing them of myopia, particularly when they make decisions that result in their player sent off or penalised. And, of course, managers complain all the louder should they lose the match. Thus, to anyone not attending the game, Clough's protestations were not to be viewed as anything out of the ordinary. Except that, even in the context of Italian football which has always been notable for its scandals, the game was outstanding for the behaviour of the Juventus players.

Within minutes from the start Clough's blood pressure was driven sky high as he watched Juventus players diving and throwing themselves to the ground in apparent agony, to be rewarded by the whistle blowing in their favour. What made it more shocking was the continuing and arrogant disregard for fair play in the shirt tugs, trips and even dangerous tackles by the Italians, without any of them being cautioned.

Instead, McFarland and Gemmill had their names taken. These two honest, decent players, neither of whom had any reputation for dirty play, were thus banned from the return game with Juventus at the Baseball Ground. It got even worse. At half-time, Peter Taylor became suspicious when he noticed the referee being escorted to his dressing room in friendly fashion by Haller, a fellow countryman and Juventus player, his arm draped over the referee's shoulder. Incensed, Taylor followed them and asked if he might listen in to their conversation.

A row broke out and a policeman was summoned. He promptly detained Taylor. Clough, who knew nothing of this, came out to a second half minus his assistant manager. Finding that Taylor was under arrest, he blew up.

Shouting and raging at the Juventus bench and any Italian official who happened to be within range, Clough, also, was threatened with arrest by the police. Taylor was eventually allowed to rejoin Clough but not before having had his 'collar fingered'.

Clough later wrote: 'I close my eyes and think of that bloody awful night in Turin and what I see is the majority of the opposition flinging themselves all over the place and apparently conning the referee, their twelfth man.'

Clough looked forward to the return match, intent on revenge. He prepared his players as always, with psychological precision. Tactics, of course, never even got a mention. Much of his focus was upon the methods by which Juventus had won the first leg. He called the players to a 'group therapy' session at Newton Solney where they were allowed their single pint of beer or glass of wine. Relaxing, Clough did not sound bitter, but addressed them with a smiling, dismissive contempt for the enemy. 'They're a bunch of cheating bastards. The whole bloody team hasn't got the talent, you, Kevin, or you, John, have got in your big toes.' He paused for laughter. 'That's why they had to cheat. When you go out next Wednesday night you'll slaughter them. You'll be so good out there they won't know who to kick or when to fall down! The Baseball Ground will swallow them whole. They'll be so deaf from the crowd by half-time they'll want to go home to their bloody godfathers! You lot are fantastic. Even you, Alan! And even you, John!'

Hinton and O'Hare grinned as the players kept laughing, feeling good. It could have been King Henry inspiring his army before

Agincourt. They were ready for battle. They would show those Italians how to play football. They'd dazzle them so much they'd go into a tizzy and disappear up their own backsides.

The Derby fans, including myself, were aware that Clough had been angered by what had taken place in Turin. But the details, as released to the press, were sketchy. Clough, on his return to Derby, was instructed by Longson – who had been briefed by the club solicitor – not to make any rash statements in any media interview. On this occasion Clough was happy to obey. His feelings would be more than adequately expressed where it mattered, on the pitch during the game. Victory, no less, was demanded of the second leg due to take place on 25 April at the Baseball Ground.

The game was looked forward to with an anticipation and growing excitement, the like of which I could not recall. Not even when Derby won the FA Cup in 1946, nor the League championship twenty-six years later, had the town buzzed so much.

Men, and some women, walked about the streets with a spring in their step. The talk, apart from the weather, was all about the Rams. Production soared in the factories, hotels took unprecedented bookings and children in the playground kicked the tennis ball at the 'Juventus' goal, drawn by chalk on the brick wall.

Clough later wrote: 'The heartbreak was to become even more intense, unbearable, by the time the second leg came around. It just happened to be my birthday. My present was that the bastards were at it again. We had Roger Davies sent off for nothing. As a result the game was drawn without score. It gave Juventus victory over the two legs.'

His misery was fully compounded when, later that night, he was given the news that his mother had died. In his tribute to 'Our Mam' he said that she was responsible for his success. She had given him the drive and desire. More than that, she had given him the belief that only decent people deserved to win at anything in life. She had drilled a need for honesty and fairness into the young Clough, qualities which made his loathing for Italian 'football' the greater.

In the ensuing years since the travesty of Turin, most of the top clubs in the 'Serie A' League of Italy, have been fined and had points deducted for bribery and corruption. Including Juventus. When Clough heard that news he kept a straight face – as he always did when Derby scored a winning goal – and stuck a finger in the air.

ON SATURDAY 3 November, I met McGuinness to be told that two players – McFarland hadn't named them – were unhappy about going on strike and the meeting the following night might have to be cancelled. The team, he said, would only consider strike action should they be certain it would have the required effect. Of this they were not satisfied, given they were not unified. McGuinness said, however, that he was still 'working on it'. I told him I wasn't happy with the delay.

'John,' I said. 'I'll ring Roy Mac. I'll tell him to be ready for a strike any time. We've got to arrange it with only a few hours' notice, else somebody will tip off Cloughie. We've got to move fast. Every day that goes by Mackay's digging in, as well as the board.'

After meeting McGuinness, I rang McFarland. He accepted the need for urgency, but confirmed that there were one or two players not keen on striking. 'If Cloughie hadn't signed for Brighton we'd have been all out,' he added.

It was depressing news. 'Roy, do you think one of the players keeps Cloughie informed about what we're up to?'

He was silent for a moment. 'I don't know. Honestly, I don't know. But to tell you the truth, we're all a bit fed up.' He sounded rather dispirited.

I pressed him as to what he meant, but he failed to elucidate further. I rang McGuinness, stressing the need for even greater urgency to mount a quick strike. Then I spoke to Bill Holmes on the general matter of how he thought a strike might affect the players in terms of their welfare.

So far Holmes had not played any direct part in dealing with Clough, nor the players, but had put in a great amount of work in terms of publicity. Later that day he joined me at the Derby Crest

Hotel. The silver-haired brewery executive was more like a bank manager in the measured and earnest way in which he conducted his briefing. With his urbane manner he could have been discussing a public relations strategy.

'I think the best way is not to call the players to a meeting about striking. We won't use that word. Why not make it more general, say calling it "Ways of getting Clough Back"? Words are emotive. The players are very sensitive. They're young, and vulnerable. We've got to approach it carefully.' Holmes placed his glass of wine carefully on the glass topped table and paused before carrying on. 'Don, I'm on TV tomorrow. They want me to talk about the Movement.'

'Why you?' As the leader of the Movement I was always the one to be interviewed. It wasn't my ego that raised the query, just surprise. Maybe the media had got fed up with my constant appearances and wanted a fresh face.

He shrugged. 'No idea. Do you watch the programme? It's *Star Soccer*.'

I nodded. 'Yes. I watch it every week. It's on a Sunday. Two o'clock. What are you going to talk about?' I said.

'The Movement, I suppose.' He shrugged.

I rang Clough when I got home. He listened to the news about Holmes going on TV and, uncharacteristically, said little. 'Don, I want to make a couple of phone calls. I'll ring you back.'

Half an hour later he rang me again to suggest we met. 'I'm not telling you over the phone. Get ready for a surprise.'

Half an hour later, Keeling pulled up the Mercedes outside my house.

Then we drove out of the village into the dark countryside, wending our way to the hotel in Newton Solney. It had started to rain, some sleet mixed in with it. The windscreen wipers thumped. I noticed Clough nodding off in front of me.

When we reached the hotel it was in amazement that I saw Clough step out from the car wearing socks but no shoes. The manager of Brighton and Hove Albion FC led me towards the hotel entrance, totally unaware of my embarrassment.

'Brian.' I had to say something.

'What?' Clough had a hand on the door.

'Your feet.'

Clough looked down at his sodden, sock-covered feet. 'I'm trying something out. Experiment.' With no further explanation he opened the door.

The hotel manager took the three of us into a private room with a red-leather button-backed settee and two winged chairs. It was lit by weak wall lights and a fire burning in the grate, its light flickering on our faces as we clustered round it. Clough removed his socks and stretched out his feet to dry.

Keeling drew nearer to the fire, luxuriating in its warmth.

Clough stared hard into the flames. His brandy and my pint of bitter arrived. He waited until the barman had left.

'Bill Holmes isn't a Derby supporter. He supports Nottingham Forest.' The quick and flat statement shook me.

I stared at him. 'What?'

'Holmes is a Forest fan. But he's not working for the board. Now why do I know that?'

I shook my head, dumbfounded.

'Because Longson has set him up for tomorrow's interview. If Holmes gets shot down on TV you're down as well. They discredit him, they discredit you. That's what Longson wants.'

I was disbelieving. 'Are you saying that ATV is conspiring with the board against the Movement?'

'No. Course not. It's just a good story to them. It's Longson. He's given them a damned good story. Why not? Can you imagine a Spurs fan leading an Arsenal revolt? No, Gary Newbon will have Holmes on, ask him how you're doing and then they'll spring the question. Good bit of TV. Egg on Holmes's face and on yours for being so daft as not knowing about it. So what are you going to do? Stop him going on?'

'Yes. I'll warn him.' I was incredulous. 'A Nottingham Forest supporter? What's all that about. What's he up to?'

Clough looked into the flames. 'No idea. There's some odd

things going on,' he said. By his lazy speech I guessed he'd been drinking beforehand.

I shook my head in bewilderment.

Clough rubbed his hands together, then held them out facing the fire. 'Mind, you could take a risk and let Holmes go on. See what happens. You never know, it might be good for us. You might find out things from it. Thought of that?'

I confessed I hadn't. I was trying to untangle my thoughts to arrive at some proper perspective.

Clough raised his hand. 'Mind. No names. No pack drill.'

'Brian. Are you sure there aren't people at ATV who're on the side of the board?'

'Absolutely. Mike, tell Don.'

Mike Keeling nodded. 'I get all the news from the ground. It was Longson. Somebody tipped him off about Holmes. So he gave *Star Soccer* a damned good story.'

'But why should Holmes…?' I broke off, a more pressing question surfacing, one I had been dying to ask him for a whole week. 'Are you planning to get the players out on strike?' I spoke abruptly, almost impatiently.

Clough turned his head towards me, put a closed hand up to his face, brushed the side of his nose with the back of his hand and lifted a crooked finger. 'What I want you to do is keep the Movement going. Let me worry about the players.' He broke off to drag back a sock on which a spark from the fire had fallen. 'You've done as much as anybody could. If I get back I'll give you a free season ticket for life.'

'You're joking.'

13

BLOODY SUNDAY

'I'M SORRY, DON. Bill left for Birmingham half an hour ago.'

I sighed inwardly, thanked Mrs Holmes and put down the phone. That was that. There would be no hope of getting a call through to him at the TV studios. A message could be passed to him. But what would it say – *Don't go on the programme?* I doubted that anyone at the studios would pass on such a message.

It was 10 a.m. Sunday morning. I sat in the kitchen on my second mug of coffee. The previous night I'd tried Holmes's telephone number every half hour until 10 p.m. without result. And now, it being a Sunday morning, I'd delayed making my call to allow him time to surface and then paid for my consideration by missing him.

I glanced up at the kitchen clock, time running out. I looked at the raindrops rolling listlessly down the windowpane. I felt as if I were in a slow-motion film, disaster imminent.

At 1.30 p.m. I dragged out my huge and heavy U-Matic video recorder from a downstairs cupboard, stabilised it upon its trolley and then wheeled it into the living room, as a hospital orderly might trundle around an early dialysis machine. It would be years before the advent of the cheap VHS video recorder. I had bought the U-Matic from a university simply to tape my TV dramas. I recorded a couple of minutes of ATV's midday programme as a dummy run. It worked.

At 2 p.m. the wide band tape started to turn inside the machine.

After the jingle that accompanied the opening titles of *Star Soccer* Gary Newbon, the young and dynamic presenter, appeared on screen. 'Today we're going to look at how Wolves, lying tenth in the First Division took on Arsenal yesterday…'

The programme ran on for half an hour until, suddenly, there was Holmes, sitting left of screen, smiling as he was introduced, wearing a dark suit, blue shirt and silken yellow tie.

Newbon began in a measured tone. 'Mr Holmes, you're one of the leaders in the Movement trying to bring Brian Clough back to the Baseball Ground.'

'That's right.'

'How are you getting on? Have you made any progress?'

'Things are happening. I can't say quite what. But we're very hopeful.'

'I'm sorry,' said Newbon. 'Why can't you say what you're doing? Isn't yours a public movement?'

'No. We don't want to reveal our hand. People in business don't tell their competitors of their plans, do they?'

'Mr Holmes. You're trying to restore a manager who resigned. Why is that?'

'Because he was forced to resign. It was made impossible for him.'

'How was that? In what way?'

'Well, it's common knowledge that the board kept putting obstacles in his way. He couldn't manage properly.'

'Really?' Newbon looked surprised. 'The information that I get is that there was a problem in working relationships, not that obstacles were put in his way, but that he became frustrated, lost his temper and resigned. The board felt it was in the interests of the club to accept his resignation, brilliant manager though he is. Wasn't that what happened?'

Holmes hesitated. 'You've just made the point. He is a brilliant manager and we don't want to lose him.'

'"We?" Who are we?'

'The fans, obviously.'

'Are you a fan of Derby County?' Newbon put the question mildly.

'Of course I am.'

'Really? Well I'm reliably informed that you're a supporter of Nottingham Forest.'

Holmes's mouth opened slightly, words failing to come.

Newbon waited. 'Are you or aren't you?'

'Yes. I support Forest as well as Derby.'

'That's unusual, isn't it? What do you do when they play each other? Stop at home?'

'No, but—'

'Were you aware that Clough had resigned once before?'

Holmes looked shaken. 'No. I wasn't, but—'

'And the board had allowed him to withdraw it when he asked? Did you know that?'

'No, but what's that got to do with—'

Newbon cut in. 'Is that really a board acting unfairly, the board you're trying to bring down? They let him back once. It doesn't sound like a board anxious to get rid of him. Why did you join the campaign, Mr Holmes?'

Holmes hesitated. 'The reason I joined the campaign was because I don't like the way that British companies treat their top managers, whether it's football or manufacturing.'

'Oh. So you're somebody who just wanders around the country looking into any enterprise, not just football clubs, to decide whether their managers are getting treated properly?'

It was a right and proper question to ask, and Holmes was trapped. It was impossible for him to escape. Newbon showed mercy by ending the interview, but not without suggesting that it might be better for all concerned that he 'kept his nose out of Derby County's affairs'.

I let out a huge sigh, having held my breath, and switched off the machine. The significant part of the interview was that it was now public knowledge that Clough had resigned once before. This piece of news proved beyond doubt that the story had come from Longson, or someone close to him. It would be no use challenging the interview. ATV would have ensured that their facts were correct, on legal grounds.

I was about to wheel the video machine out of the room when the phone rang. I expected it to be McGuinness. It was Clough.

'Don. Did you watch it?'

'Yes, Brian. Why the hell did Holmes get involved with us? Do you know?'

Clough paused. 'Have you got half an hour?'

We met at the Kedleston half an hour later. Clough came in with Keeling. I had their drinks waiting.

'Right.' Clough clasped his hands together and nodded at Keeling. 'Tell Don.'

Keeling cleared his throat. 'Yes. One of the directors – can't say which – told me Sam Longson hired a private detective who had you checked out. When they couldn't find any dirt on you, he went for McGuinness, to try and discredit him.'

Clough raised his eyebrows at me.

'Okay,' continued Keeling. 'He couldn't, because McGuinness has got a Rams season ticket. Holmes was ideal. Gary Newbon couldn't be blamed. He wasn't doing it on behalf of the board. It was a news scoop. But the board are celebrating, I can tell you. Longson's over the moon.'

Miserably, I nodded. 'Well, Bill didn't join the Movement to sabotage it, did he? He worked hard, especially on match days with leaflets and canvassing. We can't knock him for that, whatever his motives.'

Clough pointed a finger at me. 'It's damaged you. It'll be in all the papers. ITV will probably use it nationwide.'

I switched the conversation to the players, hoping that, with Keeling present, Clough might not mount his high horse. 'Brian, I know you don't like me talking about the players but don't you think we should—'

'Correct.' Clough interrupted me. 'Next subject?' He pointed at me again. 'You keep on putting pressure on the board. Leave the players to me.'

'But I'm only—'

He talked over me. 'Just keep at it, Don. You're nearly there. Do what you're good at. Publicity. You must keep going.'

But go where?

GEORGE EDWARDS RANG ME. It was 10 a.m. the next day. 'Don. Got some news. Archie and Toddy want to see you.'

Intrigued, knowing that Edwards was usually to be found in the Kardomah Café at lunchtime and only too glad to escape from my study, I decided to go down and see him.

I parked the car and walked towards the Corn Market, past white-coated women standing under the Market Hall arches selling 'Monks Pyclets', a type of muffin, from white barrows. They had been there as long as I could remember. And round the corner was the Kardomah Café, warm and inviting with its aroma of ground coffee beans percolating into the Corn Market, strengthening as I approached.

Edwards sat inside the main room facing the double doors. I sat down and ordered a coffee. We exchanged comments about the Holmes TV interview. I told Edwards that Clough had warned me of what was to happen, but I was more concerned with immediate matters. 'George, what do Toddy and Archie want to see me about?'

'At a guess it's about striking.' Edwards quickly looked around, conscious perhaps of speaking too loudly. He turned back to me. 'They want to see you tonight, separately.'

I was both pleased and worried. If Clough found out I was seeing any of the players I'd be in trouble. 'George, I'll see them, but we must stop Cloughie finding out.'

George scratched his ear, grimacing. 'Yeah. Difficult. He's ringing them up all the time. He's like a sheepdog with his flock. That's him. He can't help it.'

'But they don't have to tell him anything, do they?'

George gave me an ironic smile. 'Why do you think he keeps checking on them?'

I shook my head.

'I've been talking to one or two players,' Edwards said. 'The story I get is he's worried there's a couple of them who don't want to strike. It might fail because of that. What do you think?'

I agreed. I said I thought it was Clough's ego that wouldn't allow him to risk a show of disunity in the team. He'd see it as a personal affront. 'Think how he'd look if it failed; he'd be mortified.' I told Edwards about Clough's suspicions of McGuinness and the trap he'd set to see if it was justified.

Edwards chuckled. 'That's Cloughie. He has this thing about people wanting to get at him. Has he ever said anything to you about it?'

I remembered. 'Yes. He did, actually.'

'Did he say he likes to go home at night and lock the door?'

'Not you as well.' I gave a laugh.

'Yeah. There you go. I think he's paranoid. Mind you, a man like that can't go through life without making enemies. He'd probably say "I'm entitled."'

'He probably would.' I finished my coffee and thanked Edwards. I was leaving when he put up a hand.

'Don. Let me know – when you can – about your meeting tonight.'

'George, if the press is to be told you'll get it first.'

Five minutes later I found McGuinness inside his restaurant. We talked about the Holmes debacle. McGuinness was annoyed. 'If somebody had told me a Notts Forest supporter was in the Derby County Protest Movement I'd have said he was a spy, working for the board. But it was the opposite! They got him on just to make us look bloody fools!'

I told McGuinness that Todd and Gemmill wanted to see me.

He was stirred by the news. 'That's great! That means they want to strike. They'll have questions.' He threw up his arms. 'Jesus. Cloughie's their god. Why the hell can't he just come out with it! Why talk to us? He's only got to say the word and they'll strike!'

'You know, John, I'm not so sure. It could be all about Cloughie's pride. He can't stand any of those players not obeying him. I reckon he'd rather risk not getting back than be snubbed by his players.'

McGuinness asked the waitress to organise a makeshift lunch for the two of us, while we sat down in the rest room to map out the plan of action. It would begin with a full-blown strike of the playing staff at Derby County, the Movement simultaneously staging a march to the ground. Beforehand we would appeal to the 40,000 faithful to join in. At the same time the Movement committee, twelve in total, from every profession and walk of life, would write letters to the press – but not to club directors – as well as seek interviews on radio and television. All of this was to show that ours was a community protest, not a rabble led by a few pals of Cloughie. It would help dissipate the damage done by the Holmes interview.

The players' strike, we decided, would have to be carefully orchestrated. Just beforehand, each player would receive a telephone call with the code word, 'Operation Snowball', symbolising the gathering opposition to the board that would finally overwhelm them. That was McGuinness's idea.

I resisted the temptation to state wryly that a snowball starts to melt at the first spot of heat.

TODD AND GEMMILL lived opposite each other in Dean Close, Littleover, a recent development of executive-style houses situated just off the main Uttoxeter Road that led into Derby. I arrived at Todd's house at 7.30 p.m. His wife was changing baby Andy's nappy as I walked in.

Todd was his usual calm self, offering me a beer before we sat down. He said that he'd seen Holmes's 'execution' on TV. 'A load of rubbish, wasn't it.' He yawned and put a hand to his forehead. 'We've talked. Well, some of us, anyway. We want to go on strike. But we need everybody out.'

'Can't Cloughie get everybody out? Is it Cliff Lloyd?'

'Yeah. All that contract stuff. There's a couple of us. They're not as keen.'

He wouldn't tell me who they were. 'To be honest, I'm getting a bit fed up. What I want to know is, are you doing anything, the Movement?'

I told him about the march and publicity barrage we were staging. I paused while I thought of the best way to put it. 'Colin, you don't need every player to agree to strike. You can have a majority vote.' I went into the plan that McGuinness and I had hatched. 'We're calling it "Operation Snowball".'

He smiled at the name.

I emphasised how important it was that the players were seen to demonstrate their concern and to believe that *they* were Derby County. Everybody else, including the directors, were there to back *them*. I told him that the support they would get in the town would be tremendous. If there were any financial worries over loss of earnings I was certain that there were enough wealthy businessmen, Rams' fans, who would find ways of making up their shortfall. I ended with an appeal. 'Just take a majority vote. And let me know. But nobody must talk to Cloughie. That's the danger.'

'Okay. I'll go with that.' He seemed satisfied.

Encouraged, I said goodbye on the doorstep. I was just about to cross the road to Gemmill's house when Todd gave me a parting instruction. 'Tell Archie we'll barricade the Close together. Stop Dave Mackay getting at us. We'll stick some chairs and tables up.'

I laughed. Toddy was one of the most likeable men you could hope to meet. I went across the road and pressed the Gemmills' doorbell. It soon opened and the little Scot with a serious expression on his face brought me inside. We sat down in the living room. 'So what's happening?' Gemmill asked.

'I thought you might tell me,' I replied. 'I thought you were all going on strike.'

'Aye, well, we will if we can.'

'Is it because you can't all agree?'

'Aye. That's about it.'

I gave him the 'Snowball' plan of action, telling him that Toddy was right behind it.

'That's good. Aye.'

Gemmill was not a great conversationalist and I wasn't certain that he understood all that I was saying. I even sensed he was holding something back.

I touched upon the players' fear of the possible loss of earnings during a strike, but he waved it aside.

'Och, I'm not bothered. Let's get the boss back. He'll sort it out.'

I went over the plan again. I felt he was overly cautious, maybe because I was not of his world.

I heard the doorbell ring. Seconds later I heard Archie's wife speak to the caller. She sounded surprised. 'Oh. Hello.' She sounded hesitant. 'Er…come in.'

There was the clunk of a male footfall on the wooden floor of the hallway.

Clough strode in, his arm rising to target me. 'Don. You are messing about with my players. I told you I will deal with them!' He paused to allow his barb to sink in.

I said nothing, stunned by his sudden appearance.

'Mind if I sit down?' Clough grabbed an upright chair and placed it with its back facing Gemmill, about two feet away. He sat astride the chair and rested his arms on the top bar. Lowering his chin to his clasped hands, he stared into Gemmill's eyes.

'Now then, my wee laddie. How's it going?'

'Okay, boss.' Gemmill was expressionless.

They stared at each other. Although still shocked, the thought struck me. How did Clough find out I was there? Only George Edwards knew of my visit outside the team. It pointed to my suspicion being correct, that it must be a player, or a player's wife, who was keeping Clough informed.

Clough's face broke into a friendly, relaxed smile. 'Are you doing anything to get me back, Archie?'

'It's up to you, boss.' Gemmill remained expressionless.

'What's up to me?'

'If we go out on strike or no.'

Clough clasped his hands together. 'Is that what you'd do for me?' He spoke paternalistically and with affection for Gemmill, one of his favourite players. 'Archie. Would you go out on strike for me?'

Archie nodded mechanically. 'Aye, if you tell me to, boss.'

'I can't do that.' Clough was patient. 'Would you strike for me to get back as your manager?'

'Aye. If you tell me to.' Still no change in Gemmill's expression.

Clough paused for thought. 'Archie. Listen.' He spoke slowly. 'I want to get back. You know that. But I can't order you to strike. I'm no longer your boss. You see that? Do you understand?'

'Aye.'

'So. Would you – will you go on strike to get me back?'

'I would – if you tell me to.' Gemmill continued to hold Clough's stare. I couldn't decide if Archie was challenging Clough, or missing the point.

Clough sat back slowly as Archie's wife brought in mugs of tea. He took one. 'Thanks, love.'

Gemmill sipped his tea, still gazing at Clough. I loved watching the little wizard play, his work rate second to none. He buzzed all over the field, tackling, dribbling and passing with speed and precision, always difficult to dispossess. Kevin Hector once said to me, 'Archie could sometimes dish it out, but only when the other side got dirty.' I wanted him to be tough now, to tell Clough that he wanted to go on strike. But Gemmill waited for the order. And Clough waited for him to understand that he couldn't give that order as manager of another club.

I desperately willed Gemmill to say what Clough wanted to hear, or Clough to tell Gemmill what he wanted to hear. It was crazy. It was only a matter of semantics.

If Gemmill failed to understand the implications why couldn't Clough simply tell him that he *wanted* him to go out on strike but couldn't order him, the order being implicit in the statement? Blood rushed to my head as I willed one or the other to speak.

'Archie, I'm having a word with Don. Do you mind a minute?'

Gemmill nodded dutifully, got up and took his mug into the kitchen.

Clough gave a deprecating sigh. 'Archie. But I wish I'd got eleven of him.'

I seized the opportunity. 'Brian, why don't you tell Archie that you'd be happy to find out that he'd gone on strike? You hadn't ordered it. You can't be blamed.'

Clough pushed his cheek out with his tongue and gave me a dry look. 'Don, let me handle Archie.' He glanced towards the kitchen. 'Things are happening, okay? I don't want you too involved.'

I put the question, albeit tentatively. 'Can you not tell Roy Mac to start a strike? He would—'

Up came the sharp umpire's finger, signalling me out. 'Don. Let me—'

For the first time I dared to talk over him, determined to fight on. 'Brian, listen, I talked to Archie. He told me that the players will—'

'He shouldn't.' Clough stopped me dead. 'Archie shouldn't be telling you anything. It should come from Roy Mac, the captain.' He raised his hand at me, palm outwards.

I hit the buffers, nodding in defeat.

'So, what else is happening?' Clough sounded reasonable.

'To be honest, Brian, I don't know.'

Clough grinned. 'I bet you wish you'd not taken this on.'

I smiled back. 'You're right.'

And then Clough did a remarkable thing. He laughed.

It encouraged me to protest. 'What can I do, Brian? I feel my hands are tied.'

'Don, don't be disheartened. Things will happen. Keep up the good work.'

With a confident smile, he went into the kitchen to say goodbye to the Gemmills and then left the house by the back door, leaving me utterly confused, angry and disbelieving. Yet again he'd interfered. And where had it got us?

I went into town to see McGuinness and told him of my frustration. 'We've got to get that meeting with the players.'

'It's in the bag, Don. It's tomorrow night.'

'You're kidding.'

'No, I'm not.' He told me that he'd spoken with McFarland who'd assured him that most of the players would attend and the likely result would be a majority vote for strike action. The meeting would be held at the health club for utmost secrecy.

I was concerned about Clough finding out. 'One of the players must have told him I was seeing Archie and Toddy. The same thing's going to happen if we call a strike meeting. How do we stop that?'

We decided that each player would be notified of the time and place at the last possible moment to reduce the risk, but we had to assume that the informant in the camp, whoever that was, would inform Clough. Based on his recent track record it was then almost certain that he would try to disrupt the meeting. The only defence we could think of was to have a password, silly though it sounded. The challenge would be answered by the password which was intended to keep Clough out of the building long enough for a vote to be taken. If a strike was agreed upon we would telephone the media immediately, so there would be no going back. The strike would be on. For me this was the last throw of the dice. If Clough did manage to break in and ruin yet another attempt to rescue him, then that was that. I'd walk away, go home and leave it behind for ever.

McGuinness rang me the next morning. 'It's definitely tonight. Seven thirty. Here.'

I breathed a sigh of relief.

Then, at the last minute, after all the arrangements had been made, McGuinness rang me again. 'Don? You won't believe this. I've had to cancel. Cloughie knows about it.'

My heart sank. 'How do you know?'

'Keeling just rang. He said that Cloughie asked him to take him to McGuinness's health club tonight. He put two and two together.'

'Keeling?' I was disbelieving.

'Yeah. At last. He's helping the Movement for once, instead of bag carrying and driving Cloughie around. He's not stupid. He knows Cloughie better than we do.'

We decided to canvass the other ten members of the Movement committee, tell them the situation and ask them for their opinions. By early evening we'd established a consensus, which was to wait a couple of days to see if Clough came to us with a plan, hopefully for a strike. If we heard nothing then we'd go for a players' strike, minus Clough, dissident or no dissident in the camp.

I was pleased we remained patient. A new player sprang up in the game, a most unlikely one: Barbara Clough. She had arranged a meeting with the team. It was Keeling who had told McGuinness. It sounded promising.

Clough could ruin anything we organised. But how could he – or dare he – destroy his wife's attempt? For the first time in weeks I was amused.

NUMBER 28, Ferrers Way, was full of banter and laughter. Barbara was throwing a party for the players and their wives. She, herself, had made the phone calls to the wives, not to the players, an extra precaution to avoid suspicion. She wanted all the team present, so that the faint-hearted could be brought back into the fold and thus secure full backing for a strike. Barbara also intended to make it clear to everyone that the Clough family was not moving to Brighton, or any other town. Their hearts lay in Derby. If the aim of the party – to engineer a strike – failed, then Barbara hoped to get the wives to sustain the momentum for as long as possible.

The first arrivals were Mr and Mrs O'Hare. Then came Kevin Hector and wife Pat. Henry and Hazel Newton, were the last to arrive.

Everyone was in a relaxed and talkative mood. The wives had gathered at one side of the room, the men at the other. The tinkle of glass struck with a spoon brought their attention, all eyes turning to Clough, ready to address them.

'Lads and lasses. Thanks for coming. I'm just going to say that I may be at Brighton but everybody knows where I really want to be. Sorry we didn't make it to Majorca. It was a daft idea. But this isn't.'

He gestured at the players who were standing in a group. 'These reprobates enjoy being pushed around by me. You can't do without me. Bunch of masochists.'

He paused for laughter. 'Don Shaw and his mob have got another public meeting at the Pennine on Saturday. I was hoping you all came to your own decision, to unite in taking action. Barbara? It's your party. Go ahead.'

'Thank you, boss,' said Barbara. It brought laughter. 'Okay.'

She addressed the wives. 'Whatever happens we have to support the Movement. They're doing a grand job. If the players don't do anything before Wednesday then I hope you girls will join me at the Pennine for Don Shaw and his meeting. You all did a brilliant job at the Kings Hall. No reason we can't do it again.'

'Yes! We will. We'll be there.' The wives were vocal in giving their support. Pat Hector, vivacious and dark-haired, clapped loudly and gave a cheer.

'Just a minute. Sorry, boss.' It was John O'Hare. 'I support you. Course I do. I want you back. But I don't want my wife being used like that. To me that's not on. In fact, it's stupid.'

'Stupid, John?' Clough cocked his head back, mouth open, in query.

Normally such a look would quell any opposition, but O'Hare was determined to finish. 'Yeah. It is. What's my wife got to do with it? Look, boss, to be honest, if you hadn't signed for Brighton we'd all be out. But you did, you signed.' O'Hare looked around in the silence then turned to meet his wife's embarrassed look.

'Well,' said Clough. 'You'd best not be here, then. Had you, John?'

O'Hare hesitated, mumbled his apologies to Barbara, then looked to his wife to follow him out. They left the room, with everyone silent.

'Bye then, John!' shouted Clough. 'Goodbye and shut the door when you go out!'

The tension eased as they heard the front door open and close, voices quickly striking up conversation to cover the general embarrassment.

'Hang on. Look.' Clough had their attention once more. 'John was right. I shouldn't have signed for Brighton. But I did, for whatever reason. But it makes no difference to my commitment to you lot. There's most of you want to go on strike. There's some who're worried about it. But I can't be seen to lead it. It's up to you. If you want me back, it's up to you.'

It was a key moment. If the players had taken a vote at that moment to strike it would have been adopted. Like so many great moments in history, destiny can swivel on the click of a trigger or the stroke of a pen. In this instance it came in the form of a suggestion, the result being that another vital and pivotal moment in the campaign was lost, as it diverted thoughts away from Clough's positive mention of strike action. Someone said, 'While we're here why don't we write a letter? Not to the board, we've done that. Useless. But to Dave Mackay? From all of us?'

Barbara liked the idea. 'Yes. If he gets your letter I reckon he'll resign. How would you feel if you were the new manager and told by the team you're not wanted?'

'He knows that already,' said Clough.

'Hah, yes,' said Barbara. 'The beauty of this is you're implying you're not supporting him, in training, on the pitch or wherever. How can he stay in his job when he gets a formal letter like that?'

There was an awakening of enthusiasm with calls of 'Let's give it a go' and 'Nothing to lose, everything to gain.'

'I've got a typewriter,' said Barbara. 'I'll type it out.'

The letter was handed in to the Baseball Ground the next day. Mackay read it and threw it into the wastepaper basket. He didn't even bother to show it to Longson, or Webb.

A FEW DAYS later Clough rang and asked if I would like to go with him to watch Brighton play Walsall at their West Midlands stadium. 'And bring your lad, Martin, along.'

Martin sat on my knee in the back seat. It was in the days before rear seat-belt legislation. Roger Davies and Colin Boulton were squeezed in beside us. Clough was in the front passenger seat, with Keeling driving. Brighton won the game 1–0.

Afterwards we returned to the team hotel and sat down for dinner with Clough and Taylor. Clough's assistant, John Sheridan, went over to the players' table halfway through the meal and returned with a request.

'Boss. The players are asking if they can have a drink.'

'No,' Clough said abruptly.

I noticed that there was no wine or champagne glass in front of him, nor had anyone a glass in front of them around the table. I understood. It would be too hard to see the players drinking when he was trying to kick the habit.

On the return journey I exclaimed in pain as Martin's weight had stopped the blood flow in my thigh.

'What's up?' Clough asked.

I explained. Clough was scornful. 'Don. Pain's nothing if you tell yourself it's natural.'

I recalled Kevin Hector's back injury and McFarland's damaged tendon.

14

OPERATION CLOUGH

To LOSE IN a European Cup semi-final was painful enough, but to lose to cheats was traumatic. As the weeks and months passed Clough found he could not move on from that dark night in Turin and the return leg at Derby. Every inch of his being rebelled against forgetting or forgiving. He tried to rationalise, doing what the pop psychologists in their 'How to' books recommend, to treat it not as a 'step back' but as a stepping stone towards greater challenges. He tried hard to perform that life-affirming twist of mind, without being able to drive out the demons. Tormented, he repeatedly asked the question both to himself and to anyone who would listen: 'How can they sleep at night? If it's just about money I can understand that. But they want to make their fans happy, the team happy, the bloody directors happy! Happy for what? How can the bastards be happy in a lie?'

There was one spin-off from the unfortunate business and that was a temporary improvement in his relationship with Longson. The chairman sympathised with Clough, sharing his disgust and pain. But, to use footballers' parlance, 'at the end of the day' Clough was incapable of coming closer to a man for whom he had no respect. Longson's alienation from Clough was undeniably the latter's fault. He could easily have thanked Longson for his role in bringing him to Derby. But tact was not in Clough's dictionary, not when it clashed with his strongly held virtue of honesty. He had become famous for his outspokenness. It was this lack of tact that made for much of his strength but, in being associated with ego, also helped fashion his Achilles heel.

The best that can be said for Longson was that he failed to understand the nature of the genius called Brian Clough.

Clough was never logical and that, too, defeated Longson's attempt to come to terms with him. 'Be reasonable!' was Longson's anguished cry time after time, but Clough was incapable of being 'reasonable'. For him, 'reasonable' men only achieved reasonable results, well below the level he'd set himself.

Thus, the Juventus disaster only served to give the two warring parties breathing space. The European campaign had provided Clough with yet more offers of TV work and special appearances of the knockabout variety, further angering Longson. 'He's paid to work for Derby County, not bloody freak shows!'

Longson might just have tolerated Clough's television perform-ances had they been solely about football. But, in effect, they were all about Clough, the man himself. The farmer's boy had always hated 'show offs'. Clough was now the biggest and most flagrant of them all, sought by producers just to appear and say outrageous things, whatever the subject. There were other TV mimics, apart from Mike Yarwood, wagging the finger while uttering the cele-brated phrase, 'Now, young man!' Clough told the TV producers what his fee would be and they paid it willingly, as ratings soared on his appearance.

Longson especially hated away games where, it seemed, he was forever apologising to other club directors for Clough's behaviour, often for remarks he had made about *their* manager or *their* players. He deemed it a breach of contract and began to think seriously of bringing Clough before the board on that charge. But, after the success of the European campaign, it would have taken a miracle. No one in his right mind could be seen to sack Clough. Longson's frustration only served to superheat his bile.

One morning Clough arrived at the Baseball ground to find Longson brandishing copies of the *Sunday Express* and the *Sun*.

'You can't bloody well serve three masters!' Longson roared. 'You're on telly in *On The Ball* and *The Big Match*! You're on the back page and the front of these papers. I can't bloody well escape you. Here, this is what I do…' Longson tore up the newspapers and tossed them in the bin.

'Mr Chairman,' Clough was at his most dignified when shouted at. 'May I—'

'Don't Mr Chairman me!' shouted Longson. 'Do you know what you're doing, for God's sake! Have you read what you've written in the *Sun*? You're slandering directors as well as managers. You can't do that!'

'Mr Chairman.' Clough's right arm was tucked in against his chest, his right index finger raised to chin level. He spoke in his most pontifical voice. 'I'm charged here with getting results. I've got them. From what you say I should go home to bed and stay there for half a week. No, I don't do that, because I'm thinking twenty-four hours a day what to do next to take us to the very top. You ordered me to go on TV when I came. No – listen to me. One of our fans wrote to me. He'd been on holiday in Corsica. He said a waiter asked him where he came from. He said Derby. The waiter said "Brian Clough." Mr Chairman, we're going to be known from Stockholm to Sydney. We're going places you can't imagine. Why don't you enjoy the ride and let me do the work?'

'Brian. Look.' Longson's voice shook as he tried to sound rational. 'Bill Shankly goes on TV but Mike Yarwood doesn't impersonate him. So why you, eh?'

Clough smiled thinly. 'You'll have to ask him, Sam. Maybe it's because you're the chairman of Britain's best club. And who created it? Me.'

Longson turned away fuming, then stopped. He gathered himself and half turned.

'I'm sorry about your mother,' he mumbled. 'Ever since that Juventus…I'd forgotten to say that.'

'Thank you.' Clough spoke formally. There had been a split-second hesitation on his part in which he could easily have grabbed the old man's hand. But Clough did not offer Longson that olive branch. His bereavement from his beloved mam had been tough. Her death had stiffened his resolve to stay hard when others would suffer bereavement and be weakened by it.

Clough, as his hubris intensified, began to court even more controversy and, consequently, danger. He was not averse to publicly demonstrating his powers, like a man on a high wire, daring gravity. It both empowered and amused him to see the effect he had on people. Where other men would not risk being attacked or taken to court for committing slander, he could say almost anything, with apparent impunity. The thrill was in getting away with it.

I had direct experience of his compulsion to shock. As I sat in the Midland with him, enjoying a drink, he suddenly stood up and beckoned me to follow him into a corner of the bar. There sat two men, chatting quietly. They broke off as Clough stood over them, in lecture mode. 'This man, Don, works for Derby County. He's a liar and a thief. This man' – he pointed to his companion – 'works for Nottingham Forest and is a good man, honest and true. And they drink together.'

Such was Clough's unnerving brand of magic that both men smiled back at him. It was as if the slandered Derby official had been praised, so modest and humble was the smile he returned.

As we returned to our seats Clough said, 'Never let them take you on. You take them on.'

In a much greater public demonstration of risk taking, he wrote a piece for the *Sunday Times* attacking his nemesis, Don Revie, and his Leeds United team.

His loathing for them was exacerbated when Derby played a home game against Leeds, the topmost team in Division One. As the teams ran out on to the pitch the crowd's shouting became suddenly muted, stopping altogether as lungs emptied. It wasn't the Leeds first team but the reserves, which had emerged. Revie had clearly saved his best side for a European game a few days later. As it dawned on the masses, booing broke out underneath where I sat in the Ley Stand. It was taken up by the majority in the stadium. Clough fumed. He said it devalued the game and cheated all those people who'd paid good money to see a top-class match. It also robbed him of the pleasure of revenge in the inevitable home win.

Not long afterwards Clough learnt that the Yorkshire club had been found guilty of 'persistent misconduct on the field', for which they had been fined £3000, suspended for one year. Clough reached for his pen and drove it into Revie's jugular, condemning him as well as his team. He needed little urging as there was an added motivating factor. In his loathing of Juventus he could now link it with Leeds United. Although Revie's team stood halfway down Clough's personal table of villainy with Juventus on top, he was able to get rid of some of his bitterness by attacking the 'dirty' Leeds side, thus gaining revenge on Juventus by proxy. This was Clough at his most censorious. To make it worse the *Sunday Express* was a newspaper that was already anathema to Longson:

Don Revie should have been personally fined and Leeds United instantly demoted to the Second Division after being branded the dirtiest club in Britain. Instead the befuddled minds of the men who run soccer have missed a wonderful chance to clean up the game in one swoop. The trouble with the disciplinary system is that those who sit in judgement, being officials of other clubs, might well have a vested interest. I strongly feel that this tuppence-ha'penny suspended fine is the most misguided piece of woolly thinking ever perpetrated by the FA, a body hardly noted for its common sense. It's like breathalysing a drunken driver, getting a positive reading, giving him back his keys and telling him to watch it on the way back home!

Longson's mood, always sour on a Monday morning, turned vitriolic when he was met by Jack Kirkland with a cutting of the article. Longson read it and exploded. 'Jesus Christ!' He huffed and puffed his way to Clough's office, found him not there, so he picked up a pen and a sheet of notepaper. He angrily wrote: 'You are not to ring me or talk to me in person any more. I don't want to even see you.' He clipped the note to the newspaper cutting and left it on Clough's desk. Then he stormed out to ring Hardacre at the FA and apologise in a fit of anger and humiliation. His next move was to summon Webb and ask him how they could accuse Clough of breach of contract.

Webb's first reaction was that Clough could easily have breached his contract in that he regularly spent two or three days a week in London working in television when, clearly, his employment at Derby demanded a full five- or six-day working week.

'Okay.' Longson nodded. 'Right. Now I want you to compare the hours he spends here with those on TV. That includes travelling. Do it, Stuart – make it priority.'

Clough, later that day, found Longson's message on his desk. He read it and showed it to Taylor. 'The old twit doesn't want to see me. I'm a non-person.'

Taylor read it and dryly commented, 'Derrick Robins will be pleased. Sam's sent you to Coventry.'

Clough stepped outside his office and found Longson, at the far end of the corridor, staring at him. Clough put up a hand. 'Sorry, Mr Chairman. You mustn't see me!' He went to the toilet.

In the late afternoon Longson was about to get into his car when he saw Webb hurrying towards him. He had a press release in his hand. It was from Raymonds News Agency and reported that Clough had been offered a full-time job working for London Weekend Television at £18,000 a year.

Longson closed the car door. 'Is that definite? By God, if it is – let's check it. Make sure. Because if it's true Christmas has come early.' He walked quickly back into the ground.

Having talked to Raymonds as well as George Edwards, Longson put down the phone, clutching his chest. 'It's genuine. Thank God!' He reached out and took Webb's hand. 'Thank God.'

The drive through the Peak District in its winter shroud was especially beautiful, but his pleasure in arriving home was destroyed by Jack Kirkland on the telephone. 'Sam. Clough's put out a press statement. I'll read it. "I thank London Weekend for their offer but have decided to work for them part-time without any detriment to my work at Derby County."'

'He's still in breach,' Longson panted. 'He's still in breach.' Then he sighed, replaced the receiver and buried his face in his hands.

'COME ON, PETE. Let's get it done.' Clough sat down with Taylor at the Kedleston. As they drank, they drafted a letter to be sent to each director, complaining about Longson, its gist being 'He won't talk to me. What are you going to do about it?'

However, if Clough thought it would lead to Longson's sacking, he was mistaken. All it did was stoke the fires of Longson's enmity.

The war moved towards its climax.

A pre-season tour abroad had been planned and Longson turned down Clough's request for his family to accompany him. As Clough was not allowed to see him, Longson sent him a written message delivered by his secretary. 'It's too expensive and no director's taking his wife and kids so why should you?' Longson hoped the provocative wording would enrage Clough to the point of resignation. He was disappointed as Clough sent back a reply to Longson's secretary.

'This message must be a hoax as the Chairman has refused to speak or communicate with me in any way. Please inform him I am proceeding as arranged.'

Longson's hatred of Clough had to find some outlet, and Clough himself was fast approaching snapping point. Somebody or something, soon, would have to give.

It did, within forty-eight hours.

Longson suddenly collapsed and was rushed to hospital for a major operation. Clough relented sufficiently to send him a 'Get Well' card. In return an anonymous card landed on Clough's desk. In it was written: 'Happy now in what you've done?'

Clough let out a roar and set about unearthing the card sender. He discovered it was an office cleaner. She was on the books for as long as it took for her to hit the street.

With Longson absent in hospital, new director Jack Kirkland, the brother of Bob so ignominiously forced to quit the board at Longson's instigation, sought out Clough. But it was not revenge that he wished for on behalf of his brother, quite the opposite.

He wanted Clough to front a grand plan for a new stadium holding 50,000 spectators and with a sports and leisure centre attached. Kirkland's business in plant hire and construction would benefit, and his chance of replacing Longson as chairman would be high.

Clough was not impressed. 'Hang on. We need money for the team. Let's win the European Cup first.'

Kirkland was candid. 'Something as big as this project needs a good manager to give investors confidence in the future. You're famous. We need your face. You'll do well out of it – eventually.' He raised his eyebrows, significantly.

Clough nodded and said he was busy at the moment but would attend to it later. He hated business dealings with directors, even if it was to his advantage.

Again, a more cunning Clough might have shown more enthusiasm as Kirkland would have done his job for him by ousting Longson. But Clough was unsure of Jack. At some point in the future he might seek revenge for what Clough had done to brother Bob, and so Clough kept him at arm's length. In the short term it proved the right thing to do since Longson, a tough old bird, was soon recovering from his operation and back at the Baseball Ground, forcing Kirkland to shelve his plans.

On Longson's return he found something welcome on his desk. It was Webb's report specifying the comparative times that Clough spent at work with Derby County and that he spent in the service of London Weekend Television.

Longson put down his cigar and read that Clough travelled to London for a day and a half each week. On Sundays he would return to contribute comments and analyses. He also had a regular newspaper column. Longson was delighted. For him, it proved a clear breach of contract.

'Nice,' he murmured. 'I think we've got him. Yes!' His voice grew louder. 'We've got him!' He crammed one of his many daily tablets into his mouth. At the top of the report he scrawled in red ink: '*Immediate action*'.

Clough, tipped off by Keeling that Longson was summoning a

board meeting to charge him with breach of contract, asked him to produce a similar statement concerning his work hours. Keeling, who knew Clough's travel habits better than anyone, subsequently produced a report that was passed to the club solicitor, Mr Timms. Having read it, he informed Longson that it was sufficient to neutralise Webb's report.

Longson was in the hospitality suite when Webb came in to tell him the bad news. He let out a long, harsh sigh. Then he dismally told Webb the joke that was going the rounds of boardrooms nation wide: '"Longson sits at home watching Clough, reading about Clough, wondering how God could treat him as he does and then finds out – He *is* Clough."'

Webb laughed politely. 'Mr Chairman. I've come to—'

'Sam. You must call me Sam when we're on our own. Sit you down, lad.'

'Sam,' said Webb. 'I don't know what to do. Either Mr Clough goes or I go.'

'You're not going, Stuart. That's final. Bloody hell, no way!'

'I'm sorry. He's made my job impossible.'

Longson stared at him grimly. 'Stuart. Desperate times need desperate measures. Come on, let's go to my office.'

On reaching there, Longson went straight to his drinks cabinet. 'Drink, Stuart?'

'Not while I'm working, thank you, Sam.'

Longson poured himself a whisky. 'You know,' he said. 'Clough's improper. Improper people need improper kicks up the arse. What would stir him up? What's his weakness, do you think?'

Webb was non-committal, perhaps embarrassed. 'Well, maybe–'

Longson cut in. 'Isn't it his pride, Stuart? It's his ego, isn't it?' He tapped his own forehead. 'I've been thinking. What about Taylor? There's a man, his mate, always in his shadow. Don't you think he must get a bit jealous of him, sometimes? I know I would if I was him. Taylor spots the players. He's worth every penny we pay him. How about if we pay Clough his pay rise of five grand? How about if we give it him and we give Taylor nowt?'

'You mean make Taylor even more jealous?' Webb looked uneasy.

'Exactly! Drive a wedge between them! We tell Taylor that Clough's been bad-mouthing him, doesn't want him to have a rise. What would Taylor do?'

Longson took Webb's embarrassed silence as respect for his cunning. 'Clough depends on Taylor a lot. I think Clough would go too, if he went. Don't you think?'

Webb escaped his embarrassment by raising an issue that was of real concern to him and which could have affected Clough's employment with Derby County. It was the question of the manager's drinking habits.

Longson gestured at him through a cloud of cigar smoke. 'Just tell me what you mean. Go on.'

'It's a safety issue. I'm genuinely concerned for the staff.'

'Oh.' Longson was disappointed. 'Well, he's never knocked anybody over or—'

He broke off as Webb produced a pamphlet and laid it on the desk. It was a government-issued pamphlet for all employers. Webb said that the Health and Safety at Work Act, passed the previous month, required all employers to ensure their employees were safe in the workplace. There was a paragraph dealing with the misuse or abuse of alcohol.

Longson picked it up and narrowed his eyes. 'Really.'

He read the paragraph: 'Where there's danger at work to fellow employees the employer has no choice but first to warn and then dismiss the offender if that has no effect.'

Longson stood in triumph. 'Bloody hell, Stuart! Bang on the money, lad. We'll warn him and lock up his drinks cabinet. With any luck he'll resign. He can't do without it. Bloody marvellous!' He pointed at Webb. 'You're a bright lad. A very bright lad.' He thumped his desk. 'Even his solicitor can't stop that one!'

After Webb had gone Longson called in Kirkland. 'I've got a beauty,' said Longson. 'We're going to lock up Clough's drinks cabinet. He won't cope with that gone. He'll resign!'

Kirkland pretended to be pleased.

'Hold on,' said Longson suddenly. 'Let's make certain. We've got Plan B and C. Let's have plan D. Let's have it, belt and braces. Come on, Jack. Any ideas?'

Kirkland hid his lack of enthusiasm and allowed Longson to do most of the talking and thinking. The conspiratorial session ended with Plan D, which would have the board insisting that every article Clough wrote and every TV appearance he made, first had to be sanctioned by the directors. Longson was cock-a-hoop. 'That or the drinks cabinet will finish him. Just wait to hear the roar when he gets back.' He sat back and laughed. 'I'd love to see his face.'

CLOUGH STARED AT the typed message stuck across the keyhole to his drinks cabinet. 'This cabinet is not to be opened without permission of the club secretary.'

He'd just returned from a training session at Matlock and fancied a drop. He was in no mood for games. In fury he went out to march down the corridor, seeking Webb.

He was told he was closeted in the boardroom with Longson. Clough went there and knocked on the door. 'Mr Webb. Please.' There was no answer. He went back to Webb's office and stuck the offending message on his desk. It had been altered to read: 'My cabinet will only be locked by the manager without permission of the club secretary.'

Clough went on the prowl like a caged tiger, but his enemies were lying low. Later, that evening, Clough spotted Longson at the far end of the corridor.

Before he could escape Clough was bearing down on him, arm levelled.

'Mr Chairman. The secretary has locked my drinks cabinet. Can I have your permission to sack him?' His eyes riveted Longson, but the chairman held his ground and stared back. He wasn't going to be scared by the braggart.

'I know,' barked Longson. 'He's acting on my instructions. We consider your use of alcohol as excessive and likely to cause danger to our staff.'

'I want that cabinet unlocked.' Clough's fist was clenched, his face set in determination.

The two men stared at each other, the red-rimmed, watery eyes of Longson caught by the brilliance of Clough's.

Longson waved an arm. 'It's the Health and Safety at Work Act! You should read it. It's nowt to do with me. Take it up with the government.' He made to stomp off down the corridor, but stopped. 'Oh. One more thing. The board decided you can't go on television without its permission. You've to cut down the hours you spend down there. If you don't, you're out. It's all in a letter. You'll get it in the morning.'

Clough's voice shook the building. 'You bloody hypocrite! When I got invited on the TV World Cup panel you said I must do it! And you came with me. You bloody well lapped it up!'

He walked quickly away. He brought Keeling into his office.

'I want you to find two of the new directors. The three of you, get hold of Longson. Tell him you can't work with him. He's got to resign. Can you do that?'

Keeling quaked at the idea. But Clough had given him an order.

The following day he nervously gathered his two 'new to the club' directors, to stand outside Longson's office. After they had stewed a while, Longson invited them in. He didn't offer any of them a chair. Instead, he sat back, scrutinising Keeling with a faint smile of contempt.

'I know what you're here for. Your boss. You've come to tell me your boss can't work with me any more. Am I right?'

Keeling, with a sinking feeling, realised that one, or even both, of his colleagues, must have let slip their mission to at least one other director. Someone had blown the whistle. He opened his mouth to bluster his way out, but Longson forestalled him. 'If you think I'll resign instead of Clough then you've got another think coming. Now bugger off. I'm ashamed of the lot of you.'

Clough heard Keeling's report in silence. He merely nodded. So far all his bullets had been blanks. He had to find some other weapon.

TWO DAYS LATER Longson sat in the boardroom, gloomily appraising the situation with Clough. None of his plans had worked. The plot to drive a wedge between Clough and Taylor had started promisingly. On hearing that Clough had been offered – and had accepted – a pay rise, Taylor had fulfilled initial expectations by sparking a row with his long-time friend and partner, saying he was hurt. 'After all this time, you do that to me behind my back.'

But Longson had underestimated Clough's sense of fairness and the strength of their partnership.

'Pete,' said Clough. 'I wasn't thinking. You're right. You'll get your rise. I'll make sure of it.' He sent a note to Longson's secretary. 'Chairman, I'd forgotten that the assistant manager, under contract, always gets his percentage of any rise I get in pay. Please expedite.'

He hesitated and then added a further note. 'I now bring in my own drink. I may have been causing too much expenditure and the club needs every penny it can get. I wonder if any director might like to copy my idea?' After a pause he added: 'I shall not ask the board's permission every time I go on TV. It's a waste of time and energy, which we need to concentrate on what matters: winning the European Cup and the Championship. I'm sure, on reflection, you will agree.'

On reading it Longson's black despair welled up from a bottomless pit. He went outside to stand by the directors' box. Sleet and rain rattled the corrugated roof. He gazed at the Ley Stand. It represented Clough: sleek, sharp and modern, putting to shame the old wooden stands flanking it – they represented himself, old and miserable. He thought how marvellous it had been through the years of victory and celebration. Now he felt a sudden pang of remorse, a tightening of the throat. If only Clough could be taught to accept that he was not the boss but – and then he angrily ripped the intrusive idea from his head. He would not give in to his one-time wonder boy. It could be no other way. There was not a manager in England who treated his employers like— but the thought slipped in again, causing him pain.

If only Clough, even now, came to tell him how grateful he was for his part in the resurgence of Derby County, he would force him to sit down with him and— he broke off his anguished thoughts and returned to his office. He placed both hands on the boardroom table and stared into it. The shining mahogany reflected back a very old and miserable man.

The hard, inescapable fact was that Clough had to be stopped. The awful prospect of him defeating the board and putting in his own arse-lickers was unthinkable.

The storm clouds gathered.

THE DATE WAS 13 October 1973. The venue: Old Trafford, Manchester. The visiting manager of Derby County was upset to learn that the players' wives had no seating allocated to them. Clough immediately protested to the club officials.

After some confusion seats were found, but only after he'd threatened to delay the start of the game until the matter was resolved.

The match started promisingly for Derby, with Kevin Hector scoring an early goal and the Rams held their lead, even after Brian Kidd and Tony Young both hit the Derby crossbar in the seventyninth minute.

The away victory comforted Clough. It was a further feather in his cap, intensifying his sense of invulnerability. As he congratulated and joked with his players, the 'old twit' was in the United boardroom enjoying cigars and whisky with Louis Edwards, the Manchester chairman, unaware of the bombshell about to be dropped.

Edwards was urbane, and initially complimentary about Clough. 'You've got a real prize there, Sam. How long will he stay with you?'

It was a loaded question, and put with not a little irony. Clough's struggle with the Derby board was common knowledge around the First Division clubs.

'It's difficult,' said Longson. 'But...' he shook his head, not eager to discuss it.

Edwards smiled. 'I heard he was off to Barcelona and then it was Sunderland.'

'Rumours, Louis, rumours. That's all. You know how he is.'

Edwards looked around to see Matt Busby in quiet conversation with Bill Foulkes, director of youth football at United. Both men were survivors of the Munich air crash. Other Derby and United directors were chatting in small groups around the room.

Edwards judged he could speak unheard. He lowered his voice to speak in a confidential manner. 'Sam.'

Longson, whose hearing was not too good, took a step nearer and cocked his head. 'Yes, Louis?'

'He's got one problem though,' said Edwards. 'One you'll have to sort out.'

'Eh? What's that?'

Edwards dropped his voice to a whisper. 'I'm afraid he gave Matt Busby and me the V sign.'

'What!' Longson's loud voice brought the attention of everyone in the room. His face was contorted in anger. 'He did what!'

'Gave us the V sign. Because of the wives, their treatment. It was a misunderstanding. We should have saved them seats. We did apologise.'

'He did that? He gave you...' Longson stormed out of the boardroom.

Clough had since left the players and was in the hospitality suite, drinking with Taylor and one or two United officials when Longson burst in and caught his eye. Roughly, he gestured at him. Clough went across. Longson was blunt. 'Did you make a V sign at Louis Edwards and Matt Busby?'

'No.'

'Louis Edwards said you did.'

'No, I didn't.'

'I'm telling you, I'm not asking, I'm ordering you to apologise! Now!'

Conversation had fallen in the room. All eyes were fixed on Clough's confrontation with Longson.

Clough remained calm. 'I've told you. I've got nothing to apologise about.'

'You can't do this! Matt Busby's a friend of mine!'

'Eh.' Clough said sharply. 'You're playing for Derby, not United. Let's sort this out, shall we?'

Clough stalked off, bound for the boardroom, towing Taylor behind him, Longson following, puffing, red in the face. Clough entered the boardroom, diminishing the chatter by marching up to Edwards. 'Mr Chairman, have I offended you today?'

The boardroom fell silent.

Edwards cleared his throat. 'I don't think we should be talking about that now, do you?'

Clough looked round, catching Matt Busby's eye. He nodded at him. 'I cried for you after the Munich crash. I cried when you got to the Cup Final with the reserves. But I'm not crying in apology for something I didn't do.'

He turned to see Longson entering. 'Mr Chairman. We're off.'

The journey back to Derby by coach seemed a long one. Normally in victory the players would be ebullient and full of chatter, some playing cards, only the odd one asleep. Now, on hearing the news of their boss's latest encounter, they sat still and quiet, thoughtfully gazing out of the window as the lights of the city faded behind them.

Longson made the journey home in his Rolls, leaving the driving to Kirkland.

THE LOUNGE BAR of the Midland Hotel in Derby was a damp, sweaty, smoky and noisy place, packed with Rams supporters and club hangers-on as well as the press. It was two and a half hours after the end of the United game. The main centre of interest was a spot by the window that looked out on to the train station. There, Clough and Taylor sat in leather armchairs, holding court. Surrounding them were Gerald Mortimer and George Edwards of the *Derby Evening Telegraph*, Neil Hallam of both local and national papers and Mike Ingham of Radio Derby, the latter a little out of breath after racing back from being match commentator at Old Trafford.

Keeling, as chief disciple of Clough, had created another focal point across the other side of the room where he was being entertained by a small group of businessmen eager to be invited on to the Derby board. They saw, in Keeling, their main backer.

It was George Edwards, sitting directly opposite Clough, who dared raise the topic that was on everybody's mind. 'So what happened then, Brian? About Louis Edwards accusing you like that?'

Clough shook his head. 'Look. I would never have given the V sign. What for? The wives' seats? That was just a cock-up.' He grinned, pushed his head forward at George Edwards. 'George. Come to think of it, that's what stand seats are, aren't they, cock-ups?'

The reporters laughed politely. Clough's puns and jokes were often witty, but occasionally forced.

'Louis Edwards was just stirring it,' Clough continued. 'He knows about Longson and me. And we'd won the game fair and square. He wanted some revenge. Simple as that.'

The hotel receptionist approached him. 'Telephone call, Mr Clough.'

Clough followed her back towards the phone cubicle. When he returned he spoke to Taylor. The manner in which he spoke, at the side of Taylor's ear, was picked up by the reporters.

They sensed trouble brewing.

15

OPERATION SNOWBALL

It was 4.30 p.m. and the idea of the long, cold November night ahead had me by the fireside, watching television. Liz reminded me I hadn't taken Butch for his walk. I had just picked up his lead when the telephone rang. It was McGuinness. 'It's on. Operation Snowball. Tonight. My place.'

'This is definite.'

'Definite.'

'What time?'

'We'd best meet before they come. Can you make half past six?'

'Half past six. Okay.'

'Now listen. The front door of the restaurant's locked, so go round to the side, up some steps and you'll find the service door. Ring the bell. It's lit up, you can't miss it. Remember the password. I'll let you in. The players are coming between seven and half past. I've staggered them so they won't be noticed. You okay with that?'

'And BC?' He's not in the loop this time?'

'Don.' McGuinness took a deep breath. 'Even if he was tipped off, he won't get in. It doesn't even matter if Cloughie knows the password because I know his voice. We all know his voice.' He laughed. 'The whole nation knows his bloody voice!'

I chuckled. 'Okay. Operation Snowball.' Then I added, unable to resist it. 'Let's hope it doesn't melt.'

'Don. It won't. Next week we'll have the gaffer back where he belongs.'

A DRIZZLE OF rain drifted across the headlights as I drove into McGuinness's parking bay. I stepped out of the car and looked around the deserted square. Opposite, Victor Buckland's music shop was lit up in white fluorescence, the other shops around it shrouded in darkness. I climbed the steps and rang the doorbell.

'Password.' It was McGuinness's voice.

I gave it. The door was unlocked and I stepped inside. McGuinness, grinning, wore a blue tracksuit and white trainers, his rectangular face beaming. 'Don. Come in.' He beckoned me to follow him. 'We'll have a coffee.'

We went into the rest area adjacent to the gym. 'Sit you down, Don.' McGuinness limped to the coffee machine. 'Tonight's the night, eh?'

'Let's hope so.' I stretched out my legs, relaxing. 'I feel as though I've been doing this for years.'

McGuinness pulled the cappuccinos. 'I worked out I've spent at least three hundred hours talking on the blower, meeting people – my phone bill's going through the roof.'

'And me. I spent two hours last night talking to Neil Hallam and Mike Ingham.'

McGuinness sprinkled chocolate on to the cappuccinos. 'But, it'll be worth it.' He brought over the two foaming cups. 'Eh – we know what the rest of Britain doesn't. Tomorrow the board will collapse. And we'll have done it. What's it feel like to be head of a conspiracy, eh?'

McGuinness said that he'd already talked to his business contacts about the possibility of raising a fighting fund for the players and their families. His feedback, he told me, was positive.

'Good.' But first things first. I produced a slip of paper with the telephone numbers of all the local media, plus that of Raymonds News Agency. Once strike action and its timing was decided upon we would ask Roy McFarland to make the appropriate calls to the media. He would make no mention of McGuinness and myself. If it was known that we had actively roused the players into taking strike action, then the board would be able to blow the whistle, call 'Foul', and sympathy might conceivably switch back to Longson.

I looked at my watch. It had just turned 7.30. The first players should have arrived by now. I felt a warm rush of apprehension.

The side doorbell rang. I sat upright, instinctively.

McGuinness went into the passageway. I heard the mumble of voices and then the sound of the door being unlocked. The first of the players had arrived.

I could see the headlines: 'CLOUGH BACK. BOARD FALLS.'

SAM LONGSON HAD looked forward to his visit to Manchester United with the excitement he'd felt as a lad on his first trip to Blackpool. Living in the north of Derbyshire he had always felt an affinity for United, just over the hills. At one time it had been a toss-up whether he became a fan of United or a Rams supporter. Even when he became a director of Derby County, for him the Mecca of football was still Old Trafford.

On his way home, the humiliation he'd suffered in those hallowed halls, and observed by legends of the game, brought him tears of misery. He tried to wrestle with his emotion, force his mind to work on ways of getting rid of Clough. But his age, the recent operation, the travelling and the stress he'd suffered, all combined to throw a blanket of cold weariness over his mind. Nevertheless his determination to rid himself of Clough remained fixed. He decided that, the next morning, he would devote himself to the task, to plan revenge on the man who had blighted what years he had left. He lowered his head, tried to sleep and failed.

He had been right to defer his planning. As he woke the next day he remembered the danger posed by Jack Kirkland whose own aim, financing the expansion of the Baseball Ground, was largely dependent on the use of Clough, the publicist's dream.

Should Kirkland succeed he would demand no less than the chairmanship of the board as reward for his enterprise. Longson knew he had to act fast. His first step would be to call an emergency board meeting, which would result in Clough's immediate removal for the disaster at Old Trafford. He hoped that a complaint to the FA would bring Clough before them on a charge of bringing the game into disrepute. He wrote down the names of a few who could easily be persuaded to make that complaint.

Just then Webb came to his office with news from Old Trafford. 'I...er... spoke to the United secretary. Apparently Clough may not have made the V sign. You know how he's always gesturing with his fingers.'

'Oh.' Longson paused and then said, 'But it's not definite. Louis Edwards was definite.' He shook his head grimly. 'All right. We'll give him the benefit of the doubt.' He made a rough gesture. 'It makes no bloody difference. I want him out.' A thought slipped in. 'What if...?' He took out his wallet. 'Derrick Robins. I won't ring him at the ground. Hang on.' He sifted through his wallet looking for the card bearing the Coventry Chairman's home number. As he did so a few other cards and one or two photographs fell on to his desk. 'I know Robins wants him. Well, he can have him. So long as he pays him enough. Clough can name his price. I don't give a monkey's...' He broke off as his gaze fell on one of the photographs. It showed Clough with his family nestled around a lit Christmas tree. On it was written in bold black handwriting, 'To Sam, Christmas '67, Brian.'

He let out a sob and sat down heavily, clutching his face.

'You all right?' Webb frowned.

Longson shook his head then took a deep, shaky but determined breath. He stood up. 'I'm going to give it one last try,' he said, his mouth quivering.

'How do you mean?'

'I'll accept he didn't give the V sign. And let's face it, he's one hell of a manager. I...I try to think what I can say that can...can change him.' Longson's hands bunched tight, his teeth clamped. He made pounding motions with his fists. He ground out the words. 'But how can we get rid of him? The fans, the players – the whole world will think we're bloody mad! We have, we've got a team here that can beat the bloody world. And he's done that. He has bloody well done it. But...I...I can't get him to understand. That's what it is. He can't understand that we're a club. We have to be run like a club. Why can't he get that! Why can't...'

Webb, the professional administrator, trapped between an unpredictable maverick of a football manager and an embittered old man, his employer, dearly longed for an easier life. But he felt he had no choice but to give an ultimatum. Either Clough left the club – or he did.

Longson had his face in his hands, his voice muffled. 'I'm giving it one last go. I've never had it out with him. Not properly. I'll get him to see that you have your job and he has his. We've got to see if there's any way we can keep him without us all going potty. If we can't then, well, he'll have to go. Somehow.'

'Who would we replace him with? Have you thought?'

'Eh? I've been thinking about nothing else. Bobby Robson. He'll jump at it. Decent man. Everybody likes him. Why can't Clough be a bit like him!'

CLOUGH WAS AT the training ground when he heard that the chairman wanted to see him. 'Oh aye. Does he. I thought he said he wouldn't talk to me any more. Well, I don't want to talk to him in that case.' He turned to see a yellow-vested Hinton hit the crossbar from out on the wing. 'I don't pay you to do that, you clown!' Clough bellowed. 'Not from that bloody angle! You're the best crosser in the league, so cross!'

IN THE LATE afternoon Clough arrived at the ground and parked his car. He got out to open the boot. As he rummaged inside he paused and then turned round. Longson was staring at him from twenty yards away. 'I've an apology to make,' he said flatly. 'I'm told you might not have made that V sign.'

Clough turned away to continue fiddling in the car boot.

'I want to talk to you, Brian.' Longson's voice seemed to cross a void.

'You said you didn't.' Clough slammed the boot lid shut. 'You said never again. You put a note on my desk. You didn't even want to see me.'

Longson shook his head. 'Bloody hell, Brian. This club's in a hell of a mess.'

'Is it? I thought we were doing pretty well.'

'I'm talking about the admin and the accounts. Webb tells me we're illegal. Can you not...' Longson broke off and sighed.

'I'll talk.' Clough spoke lightly. 'If you want me to.'

Longson looked hopefully at Clough. 'Now?'

'Yes. I'm not letting you accuse me when it's been you not talk-ing to me.'

They left the car park for the boardroom. Longson entered, going instinctively to the drinks cabinet. Remembering who his guest was, he diverted away to sit at the table, gesturing. 'Sit you down. I'm not offering you a drink because you've got a problem.' He clenched his hands together and looked earnestly at Clough. 'Brian. Be honest. It's causing us worry here. Do you accept that?'

Clough sat down and faced Longson. 'Have I ever been drunk at work?'

'No, but you've been close.'

'Incapacitated?'

'No. But seriously, Brian. Have you seen anybody about it? There's…'

'Eh.' Clough cut in. 'I can't go to Alcoholics Anonymous because every bugger knows who I am!'

Longson chuckled. Then his face crumbled. 'Oh, Christ.' He silently practised an opening sentence, failed and tried again. 'Brian. I'll be straight with you. If you'd just – for all these years you've been here – if you'd just showed me a bit of respect. Who was it who brought you here? Me. Don't I deserve just a simple thank you?'

'No, because it wasn't you who got me here, it was Shack. And you know what you gave him as a thank you? A box of chocolates and a tin of biscuits. You're a mean man, Sam. So I couldn't do it.'

'Mean!' Longson was shocked. 'What did I give you and Barbara when we won the Second Division? And all those toys for the kiddies?'

'That was because I was a success. That was fair. But it wasn't fair you giving Shack a box of chocolates. For getting you the best manager in England? I believe in fairness. I believe in what's right.'

'Brian.' Longson put his arms on the table and leaned forward in emphasis. 'Are you telling me all this time we've been at logger-heads because of a box of chocolates? The way you've treated me is because of Shack? He just phoned me up one day. He said he knew of a brilliant young manager. You. That's all he said. It was me who had to…to drive up to the end of the world to see a Fourth Division manager! Have you forgotten that my board didn't want you? I had to fight to get you? I drove up to bloody Scotch Corner for you. Took the entire board up to you I did. Jesus Christ! I think that deserves some thanks, doesn't it?'

'No. You wanted me to do a job. I've worked my socks off to get you and the rest of the board sitting in posh boardrooms, supping brandy and showing off. That's all you ever wanted from me, wasn't it? I've given you what you yearned for. It should be you thanking me. Eh, I'll tell you something else. You've put no money of your own into this club and you fancy a place on the League Management committee and you think I've cost you your place. In my book that doesn't beg respect.'

'You're right. You have cost me my place. By the way you've carried on. You're notorious, Brian. You get results but…but…' Longson paused and swallowed hard, fighting back the tears. He waved his arm roughly and stood up. 'I know why it is. It's all this class bloody warfare stuff. I'm a rich, posh director! Well I came up from a farm labourer!' He jabbed his finger at Clough. 'I'm the same as you. I made it to the top, the same as you! We're the same, Brian, you and me! So why can't I have an ambition as well? Yes, I wanted to get on the League Management and you stopped me. Right. I'm on the other side to you. So what! You've got ambition to win games. I…I…'

'And you haven't.' Clough's eyes were bright as coals.

'Oh for f—' Longson broke off, his expression grim and hard. 'Eh. Don't you ever say that to me again.'

'I won't.' Clough nodded. 'Course you want to win games. Yes, I can apologise if it's needed or due.'

Longson stared at Clough. 'Brian. You mean that? You're sorry?'

'I just said so. Fair do.'

Longson's lower lip trembled. He stood up and went to the window to look down at the ground. 'I've never told you this, but

I was once thinking of leaving you a lot of money.' He turned to look at Clough. 'You didn't know that. There. Now I've told you. I wanted…I wanted to…' Unable to finish, he ran a wavering hand over his mouth.

Clough was silent a moment, then spoke quietly, in a matter-of-fact tone. 'The trouble is, Sam, I know of only one way of doing things. It might be different to what you want but I get results. I produce the goods. But you want more than that. You want me subservient.'

'No, I bloody well don't!' Longson angrily came back to the table. 'Remember there's other people than players who work for this club. If you're the boss you don't upset or attack people. You railroad, upset everybody. You don't do that! You have to motivate people!'

Clough chuckled dryly. 'Funny that. Everybody in the game says I'm the best motivator.'

'You know what I mean. I'm not on about players.' Longson eagerly spread out his hands on the table. 'You don't just boss the players, you boss everybody else as well. No problem if you can keep your hands off the staff and concentrate on football and not go poncing off on the telly every other day! Can't you do that? Please? For the fans, for the club?'

As Clough opened his mouth to speak Longson cut in. 'Brian, please listen. Look. The basic fact is you interfere right down the line. You create chaos. But you're not the company manager! Webb's in charge of the bloody admin, not you!'

Clough paused. 'Right, okay. Here's how it is. If I interfere, as you call it, it's to get results – on the pitch. I don't barge in anywhere unless it's to do with getting results. I don't care what I have to do to get results. Wins. Championships. FA Cup. European Cup. And you don't get them without talent. My talent. As manager of this club doing things the way I have to do them. To take us to the top and stay there.' Clough stared at Longson, keeping his face and body still. 'That's it.'

Longson stared back in silence, then turned and went to the

cabinet and poured himself a drink. Clough stared at the glass of whisky as it was brought back to the table.

Longson sat down. He spoke without emotion. 'I'm going to be straight. I wanted to talk to you so you won't get the sack.'

Clough smiled. 'Oh aye. Really? And when will that be?' He stood up. 'Well, I'd best clear out the desk ready, hadn't I?'

Longson was on his feet. 'Brian. For God's sake! You know how they feel about you on the board!'

'I don't think that's true, Sam. I've got my own ears on that matter.'

'Oh yes. Your mate, Mike Keeling?' Longson put on an ironic expression.

Clough pointed at Longson. 'I'm going to be straight with you now. You went on about Matt Busby and Louis Edwards when you wouldn't even have been anywhere near Old Trafford if it hadn't been for me. You'd have been in the boardroom at bloody Accrington Stanley or Scunthorpe or Crewe Alexandra. This club was a gonna till I came along and saved it. And now you want to sack me. You talk of thanks. What kind of thanks is that for me taking a no-hope club to the very top?'

'Makes no difference. The board want you out. I'm trying to get you to understand I'll support you. But you've got to agree to ways of going on.' Longson tapped the table top with his knuckles. 'Give me something I can go back to the board with. This television stuff. The board want you to cut it down.' His face suddenly screwed up in pleading. 'Please. Can't you do that? I ask you again – if not for me, for the fans, for the club?'

Clough shook his head slowly with a tired expression. 'Sam. We've had all this before. Is it damaging us? Are we losing matches because I'm on the telly? You know what I reckon it is?'

'What?'

'Jealousy.'

Longson slugged back the remains of the whisky, slammed down the glass and paced the room. 'Yes! Yes! I'm bloody jealous because your face is splashed everywhere. On the telly, on newspapers, everywhere. You haunt me with your face, in my own living room! I deserve some of that. I get absolutely nothing!'

'And why do you think that is?' Clough looked at him calmly.

Longson made frustrated gestures, panted and sighed. 'Look. Can we get back to what's at the root of it? You know what? Even if you didn't put up those two fingers at Manchester, you created enough stink the way you complained. It was just somebody forgetting to get the seats. I wanted to crawl away out of bloody sight at you ranting on. That was shit awful and you know it. It's your *behaviour*, Brian!'

'I did not put up two fingers.' Clough's voice was flat and deadly. 'I did not. And I complained. Rightly. We wouldn't forget their wives' seats if they came here!'

Longson panted heavily. 'Shall I tell you how I see it? I see you as a dictator at this club. And I might as well not be here. Nor anybody else except a typist and a bloody bookkeeper!'

'Not a bad idea, Sam. I could just about work with them.'

'Yeah? Well you don't. There are people here who matter to Derby County—'

'Eh,' Clough cut him off, speaking rapidly. 'Don't you tell me about people who matter when Pete and me have done all that mattered and we've had to beg for all our pay rises and we're one of the top teams in Europe. Especially when all that matters to you is going to boardrooms and drinking their whisky and chinwagging with Matt Busby and Louis bloody Edwards! It's you who's got your priorities wrong, Mr Chairman, not me!'

'Right. You've done it now. I'm having a board meeting and I'm going to make sure that you're sacked.'

'Don't bother.' Clough stood up. 'I'm done. I've finished here.'

'Eh?'

'I'm resigning!'

Longson paused. 'Do you mean that?'

'I just said so. I don't need this. I can get a job anywhere with anybody.'

'Right. Put it down in writing and we'll have a board meeting tomorrow morning. All right?'

'Fine. Nice talking to you, Mr Chairman.' Clough reached the door. 'Oh.' He stopped and turned. 'At your board meeting do tell them that if I leave you'll go back down where you came from. Third Division. Oh and…er…I never told you. Barcelona, Sunderland, Coventry and Everton were after me. I might go to Real Madrid though. They like winners there.'

Clough went out.

Longson went to the drinks cabinet, then sat down, putting his fresh glass of whisky on the table, and, not for the first time that day, buried his face in his hands.

A dry racking sob escaped him. Then another.

16

CLOAK AND DAGGER

SOMEWHERE A CLOCK had just chimed the half hour as I heard the service doorbell ring.

This time the warm rush I felt wasn't apprehension but relief. At least one of the players had arrived. Surely the rest couldn't be far behind. It was John McGovern who now entered the room, followed by McGuinness.

'Sit down, John. Coffee?'

'Yes, please.' McGovern, hardly giving me a glance, sat down on one of the chairs arranged to form three sides of a square. He was smaller than he'd appeared on the pitch, trim and neat in his sweater and fawn trousers. He looked straight ahead with a tense expression, as if in a dentist's waiting room.

Two minutes later Kevin Hector and David Nish arrived. They, too, sat down without a word. Hector was also smaller than I'd imagined. The next players to arrive were Archie Gemmill and Colin Todd, followed shortly afterwards by the tall figure of Roger Davies. The last to enter, perhaps as befitting a captain, was Roy McFarland. No one spoke.

McGuinness served coffee, which helped break the tension. I was surprised by the players' quietness and politeness. To me, as a fan, they were giants on the pitch, each with a personality that was reflected in the combative, but cultured, way in which they performed. Now, in this quiet place, sitting upright and silent, they had been transformed into, well, schoolboys, almost. And then it dawned. Wasn't this the type of personality that Clough always sought?

McGuinness, as host, began. 'Okay, lads, we all know why we're here and thanks for coming. Don and me, well, we're just a couple of fans who want to keep Clough as much as you do. We've had a few ups and downs in the Movement so far, and we don't want to fail at this hurdle. It's important. Time isn't with us. Mackay is getting his feet further under the table. We've got to act quickly. Don?'

I backed up what McGuinness had said. 'So we're really upset about how you've been treated. You're Derby County, not the board. It doesn't exist outside you, the team.'

I said that none of them was likely to lose their player licence for not 'reporting for training' – that was to be the key phrase, rather than use the word 'strike'. I said it was an internal matter, between the limited company that was Derby County and its employees, the team. It had nothing to do with the Football Association or the Football League. The PFA, their trade union, had no option but to accept the right for them to withhold their labour. How could it be otherwise?

'The miners have decided to strike because of pay,' I reminded them. 'You're deciding to hold back your labour for another reason, but it all amounts to the same thing. It's about your livelihood. Under Clough you're going places. You'll win the European Cup as well as the championship again. That's money for you as well as putting up your value on the transfer market. Without him you've every chance of losing all that.'

'Don's right.' It was McFarland who spoke. 'We've come here, Don, to show our support. We have to do that before we strike – sorry – I mean before we don't report for training and—' He broke off to chuckle with the others. 'What we'd like to do is time our action with the Movement staging a march to the ground.'

'We can fix that,' McGuinness said. 'We've got the BBC and ITV lined up. They know things are happening. It'll be a big story. Longson will have to resign and then—'

The door leading to the darkened restaurant flew open, the sudden draught sweeping cold air into the room. Striding through came Clough, his camel-coloured raincoat wide open, his loaded rifle of a right arm pointing directly at me.

'Don, I'll kidnap your children.' His voice was deadly. The rigid arm swivelled rapidly to McGuinness. 'John, I'll burn down your restaurant if you harm any of these players' careers!'

In the absolute silence that followed, which seemed like an eternity, I noticed that the shoulders of Clough's raincoat were partly wet. This was surprising because it was dry when we had entered and there had been no forecast of rain. I also noted that he carried a bulky brown bag in his left hand. A clinking noise came from it as he took a step forward into the room. The arm now made a left to right theatrical sweeping movement, pointing finally at the service passageway.

'Out. Out, all of you. Back to your bairns and your wives! Off. Off. Out. Now!' Clough's parade ground voice brooked no argument.

The players, as one, rose to their feet and filed out. David Nish, at the end of the line, paused and turned as if to say something.

Up went the Clough arm, raised like a Nazi salute. 'David! No! Off! That would have been a ten-pound fine a month ago!'

As Nish turned and slunk out I sat back in my chair and glanced at McGuinness. His face wore a vacant look, but then, I must have looked similar.

The players had gone. Clough dragged a round table towards us, dumping the brown bag on top, producing more clinking noises. He brought out three bottles of brown ale, each bearing a red Marston's label, followed by three chunky glasses.

'I've brought my own drink. I'm not going to be beholden to you, John. I've also brought my own bottle opener. Think ahead for all eventualities.'

He quickly prised off the metal caps and began to fill the glasses with foaming beer. 'Nor, John, shall I beg thee for cake. If I invade I do not plunder.' He tipped the dregs of the last bottle to be emptied until the dripping ceased. 'I'm not a great lover of this stuff but it will do for our purpose.'

He dragged up a chair to join us. 'Right. Now.' He grinned at McGuinness. 'I bet you thought I was the Inland Revenue, John.'

I tried hard to think, but I was still numbed, similar to how I'd felt following a car accident.

'Derby County.' Clough raised his glass.

Oh, God. I picked up my glass.

'Now, then. Where are we? What do you want me to do?' Clough carried on, still in a matter-of-fact manner, as if nothing had happened, as if we had agreed to a meeting without any of the players having been there. Then the first thought penetrated my mental fog. Clough could only have entered the building by the front door to the restaurant, except that McGuinness had assured me it would be kept locked.

Going through the motions of the bizarre toast, my thoughts ended in the inescapable conclusion that he must have lent the key to a third party, from whom Clough would have received it.

Clough took a drink, put down his glass and rubbed his hands together. 'Now, then. Don't worry about the players. Don. Go on. Tell me I've ruined your party.'

'Brian.' McGuinness spoke. 'I think you—'

'I'll come to you next, John,' cut in Clough. 'Don? Tell me what you think. Then we'll listen to John and decide what to do.'

'Brian.' I found it difficult to form words. 'The players had just agreed to go out on strike – for you.'

There was a pause. Clough stood up abruptly. 'Half a mo. Make sure they've all gone.' He went out through the service passageway.

McGuinness, after a hesitation, got up to follow him.

I tried to make sense of what had happened. Clough had originally suspected McGuinness of working for the board, but had then cleared him. Now McGuinness was back on trial – for doing what? Letting the real traitor in, Clough himself. He'd ruined his best chance of returning to Derby County. The game was up. The final whistle had gone. Without the players going on strike we had nothing left but protest. The board could sit it out until we got tired or bored and forgot about the whole silly business. That was how I felt now. Tired of the whole silly business.

Most depressing was knowing that if I'd harboured any doubt as to Clough not being his own worst enemy then he'd removed it in one lightning and dramatic stroke. My first suspicions, aroused when he'd warned me off the players at the Kedleston hotel, had been confirmed. What had he said? 'Don. Don't get involved. We're all doing our best for you.' Then he'd burst in on my tête-à-tête with Archie Gemmill. He would not, could not, allow anyone to manipulate *his* players. The fact that he was now manager of another club made no difference. It was *his team* that had sat in the health club, not Mackay's. And the players themselves had shown they were still captive to his command, witness the speed with which they had obeyed him. 'Don Shaw is messing about with my property' was the notion that had over-ridden his pressing desire to return as manager. The mysterious powers that possessed and drove him to fame had got their wires seriously crossed in the matter of our campaign.

Imperiously, with head tilted slightly to one side, he re-entered the rest room with McGuinness and sat down, pulling his chair round to face me directly, exactly as he had with Archie Gemmill. He looked at me, a faint smile playing on his lips. 'Don,' he said. 'I don't need you to get the players out on strike. I can do that. Any time.'

'I thought you'd tried and failed, Brian.' My comment came out flat and dull, reflecting my mood.

He leant forward, speaking quietly. 'Don. I can get those players out at any time I like. Do you want me to do that?'

'Yes, of course.'

'So far I've let you handle it. The reason I've stopped you is because I worry about those players.'

'But Brian, you want them to go on strike. You said so.' I stuck to my guns.

He nodded, slowly stood up and moved towards the window, mouth tight, and looked out over the lights of Derby. Then he returned and sat to stare at me. He said nothing.

I sat in the same pool of light, darkness beyond. The tension rose. I found it hard to breathe. Then he flicked out a finger. 'What's happened with the team since I left?'

'Sorry?' My throat was dry.

'Have we won any matches?'

'They've not played well. Is that what you mean?'

'We've lost to Sunderland, Ipswich, QPR and Sheffield since I left. Why do you think that is?'

'They are throwing games after all?' I was tentative.

In response Clough allowed himself an ironic curl of the lip. He took out a pen and picked up a leaflet lying on the coffee table. He began to write on it. 'John? Do you mind? I want to keep this as private as possible.' He glanced up to see McGuinness's forehead furrow. 'John. This is a case of "need to know". It's no aspersion on you.'

McGuinness abruptly went to leave the room, then suddenly stopped and turned, as had Nish.

'Brian. This is bloody ridiculous.'

'No. Not ridiculous, John.' Clough came back instantaneously, his voice sharp. 'Everything will turn out well. Grateful for all you've done. I said, no aspersions.'

McGuinness, hard faced, turned and went into the gym.

I was thinking more clearly now. Obviously, by his voice and actions, McGuinness would never have conspired to wreck the meeting for which he'd worked so hard. It stretched the bounds of credulity. Maybe someone had smuggled the key away for half an hour and had a copy made at a nearby key-cutting shop. Mystified, I plucked up courage to try and find an answer.

'Brian. How did you get in here? The front door was locked.'

Clough hesitated, then carefully folded the leaflet. 'My business,' he said shortly.

He handed me the leaflet, folded, his eyes on mine.

'This is the name and address of a player. He can solve all our problems. Now, listen. This is what I want you to do.'

17

DOWNFALL

WHEN CLOUGH'S BATTLE with Longson had ended with his snap resignation, he went outside and found Taylor inspecting the pitch.

'Fancy a couple of days in Majorca?' With deliberate irony, Clough had used Taylor's ritual of a question whenever they lost a game, which was rare. If they won they celebrated with champagne. It cost them nothing. Clough had flagons of the bubbly, prizes for winning 'Manager of the Month' on a regular basis.

'Why, what have we lost?' Taylor glanced towards the offices.

'I think we've lost this joint. To be honest.'

'Oh. Right.' Taylor stuck his tongue in his cheek and looked around the mist shrouded stadium. 'Bad as that.'

'Yep. I've had enough.'

'Let's go in. We'll have a beer instead.'

Taylor always had a calming effect on Clough. He never spoke rashly or unadvisedly. With narrowed eyes and the tip of his tongue pressed against his upper lip, he sat in Clough's office, listening to the account of his row with Longson.

When Taylor spoke it was with care. 'You didn't resign *me*, Brian. And *you* haven't resigned unless you put it in writing. So let's step back a bit and think about it before we do anything we'll regret.'

Clough was dismissive. 'The old twit's out to sack me. He wants a board meeting. We should demand one. Get our punch in first.'

Taylor was silent a moment. 'Actually, I think I've got more cause to resign than you, after what's just happened.'

'What's that?'

'When I got in this morning Kirkland stopped me, asked me what my job was here.'

'He what!' Clough sat bolt upright, his beer glass in danger of fracturing from the strength of his grip.

'Said he's doing an economy drive. Slim the management down. I might be superfluous to requirements.'

Clough stood, slamming the glass down on his desk, spilling the beer. 'He said that?'

'Yeah.'

'The bastard!' Clough calmed himself down. 'Hang on. I know why. Do you?'

'Yeah, I think so. If he gets rid of me he gets rid of you. You'll resign.'

'No.' Clough shook his head. 'No. Kirkland wants me and he wants a new stadium. His economy drive is to show he means it. To show willing. To save money on wages to help pay for it. It's a stunt to impress backers. Right. Showdown at the OK Corral. We'll have that board meeting tonight. And I'll tell them how we won the League championship while fighting them and how we actually won the European Cup except that we were cheated. Economy drive? After we've brought them bloody El Dorado? I could pick up that phone and be manager of Barcelona next Monday. This lot would-n't recognise the bloody Crown Jewels if you gave them to them. That's it. That's me done.' He sat down. 'We need a letter doing.'

'I can't write.'

'Neither can I.'

'Let's go to the pictures.'

Clough laughed. Taylor was the perfect foil for his intensity.

Taylor refused to be rushed. 'What if the meeting backfires on Longson? What if they kick him out, not us? Are we still quitting then?'

Clough thought about it. 'No. I'd stay – but there's Webb. He's got to go.'

Taylor mused, his head held back. 'If Longson and Webb go, we could run that board. We could shore up Keeling. He'll be our man in there. He'll recruit directors who'll work for us.'

'And the moon's made of candy.' Clough was scathing. 'What we need's our own club.'

'Yeah, "Taylor" made.'

Clough smiled, acknowledging the pun.

Taylor scoffed at him. 'You'll never go to Barcelona. With your kids happy at school here? Barbara's happy, isn't she?'

'Yeah.' Clough reflected. 'Sometimes I wish I was back at Hartlepool.' His gall rose again. 'A board meeting? To sack us? No, Mr Chairman. We're out to sack you.'

He went to ferret out Longson, only to be told he'd left for home an hour ago. Clough popped his head into Webb's office. 'Has the chairman summoned a board meeting for tomorrow morning?'

'No,' said Webb. Clough lingered a moment. Webb looked away from Clough's stare.

Clough re-entered his office. 'He's not there.'

Taylor refilled their glasses.

Clough sat down and looked at a photograph that stood on his desk. It was a family picture. He was immensely proud of Simon, Nigel and Libby. Nigel might, he believed, make the grade as a top footballer. He loved them all and was forever grateful to Barbara for her patience and her loyalty. He didn't want to uproot them. It was so tempting to succumb to Longson, apologise and knuckle down. And go for the easy life? Impossible. He had to follow his instinct. He looked at his watch, then dialled Longson's number.

'Hello?' It was Longson's voice.

'Mr Chairman. Brian. We'd like you to get a board meeting for tonight. Because we're walking out of it. We're done.'

There was a pause. 'You're definitely resigning.'

'I've just said so.'

'Right. Put it down in writing. I'm not driving all that way back tonight. Have it on my desk by nine o'clock tomorrow morning.'

Clough heard the phone go dead. He called in his secretary and dictated a letter. It was then placed on Longson's desk.

That night, in the cool, quiet aftermath of the day's skirmishing, Clough and Taylor sat in the Kedleston, staring at each other.

Clough broke the silence. 'You want me to do something? You want me to ring somebody?'

'Yes. Funny enough. Yes, give Philip Whitehead a ring. He's a mate. He's got contacts and he's got a brain. And he supports Derby. See what he advises.'

Whitehead was the Labour MP for Derby North and an acclaimed television producer, currently known for his work on the ITV documentary series, *World at War*.

'Okay.' Clough went into the hotel lobby to use the public telephone. He was lucky. Whitehead answered. A mild-mannered man, he had a deep sincerity and a self-effacing charm. He allowed Clough to talk without butting in. When he did speak he was calm and measured in his tone.

'Brian. My advice is not to knock them any more. You've made your point so many times. I'd stay calm and don't give the board a chance to sack you. If you do want to tell them where they've gone wrong, do it logically.'

Clough was silent as he digested the advice.

A keen Rams fan, Whitehead took the opportunity to press home his advantage. 'You've got all the cards, Brian. You *are* Derby County. They're just the guardians. I really beg you not to resign unless you're absolutely certain you don't want the job any more. And it will be a big sacrifice. And where would you go? You'd have to start all over again when you've got a superb team here. Why jeopardise all that? I heard you'd promised one of the players that if he signed on you'd never leave Derby? Is that true?'

Clough admitted it was the case, but didn't name the player.

Whitehead was silent for a moment and then said. 'Brian. Do you know the Derby president, Sir Robertson King, well? Are you friendly with him?'

'Yes. Nice man. He's okay.'

'Why not speak to him tonight? Get him on your side. Make sure he'll vote against Longson in a no-confidence motion.'

Clough thanked Whitehead and came back to inform Taylor of Whitehead's advice.

'What do you think? King a nice bloke but at the end of the day he's another director. He'll be with them at the death.'

Taylor was less doubtful. 'No. I'd do it. Ring him. We've nothing to lose. We can't go back now. We're committed.'

Clough gritted his teeth. 'Yes. Sod it. Let's turf the old twit out.'

An hour later Clough and Taylor met King in a small private room at the Nag's Head pub in Borrowash, a village between Derby and Nottingham.

Clough told his story, calmly and without rancour and King, for his part, listened thoughtfully.

'Brian. I only ask one question. Are you absolutely certain you want to resign?'

'No. That's why I'm here. I'm asking you to be at the board meeting tomorrow morning. Tell them that I'll stay if Longson goes. Would you do that? For the sake of the club. For the fans? For Pete and me?'

THE NEXT MORNING, 16 October 1973, the antagonists gathered, grim-faced, around the boardroom table. This was where Clough's war would be won or lost. The boardroom, so often the scene of animated conversation liberated by alcohol, had taken on a formal look, with an atmosphere more like that of a military tribunal. The drinks cabinet was locked and carafes of water stood on the long mahogany table, scratchpads and pencils laid neatly at each place. The directors filed in quietly and took their seats. Sir Robertson King headed the table, Longson at his left-hand side. All the directors were dressed in dark suits, as for a funeral.

Mike Keeling had been briefed by Clough and told to deliver the speech of his life, when called upon by Sir Robertson King. Unfortunately, when the moment came, Keeling's voice sounded taut and, peculiarly, had taken on a Clough-like monotone. 'We all know the trouble we're in and because Mr Clough is the best manager we can find I can only see one way out and that is if the chairman resigns.'

He glanced quickly and nervously at Longson, whose face was turning redder with each word he spoke. Hastily, Keeling added. 'I'm not asking the chairman to quit the board, just to stand down so we can get back on an even keel.'

'Keel or Keeling?' Longson spoke bluntly. 'You're just a spokes-man for Clough. You don't have a regard for the board.'

'Of course I do. But I'm more concerned about the future of this club.'

Longson snorted his contempt.

Keeling made one last appeal. 'All I can say is the manager will withdraw his resignation if the chairman steps down.'

All eyes turned to Longson.

WHILE THE DRAMA was building in the boardroom, Clough was out and about in the town performing his duties as a celebrity. By 10.30 a.m. he had cut the ribbon across the doorway of a shop and then went to the Manor Hospital to visit geriatric patients with whom he was attentive and sympathetic. No one would imagine that his job was on the line.

Then, news of the board meeting and what it signified leaked out of the Baseball Ground, raced into the town and jumped into the news editor's lap at Northcliffe House, slap bang in the middle of the morning's editorial conference. The front page was held, a reporter sent to the ground and another to hunt down Clough.

Radio Derby despatched its radio car to the Baseball Ground and Raymonds News Agency held back its national feeds until the board had made its decision.

The news ripped through the factories and offices. At Rolls-Royce a union convenor and passionate Rams supporter rang the club to appeal to save Clough, on behalf of its workforce.

A large crowd soon gathered outside the Derby County offices and – to make the occasion a major news story – TV news units were already in their estate cars travelling along the A52 and M1 respectively, hoping to be in at the death.

At noon the newspaper seller at the corner of St James Street and Victoria Street waited for the van which would deliver him copies of the midday edition. It was delayed, pending the outcome of the drama. Two placards had been made out in readiness for the result: 'CLOUGH STAYS' and 'CLOUGH QUITS'.

The subject of all the commotion, seemingly unaware of all the fuss, said goodbye to the headmaster of a junior school, his last visit of the day, and then turned to the matter in hand.

At 12.10 p.m. Clough drove the car through a mass of fans and reporters to come to a stop at the Baseball Ground. He got out, ignoring shouted questions from the press and the cries of the fans, the latter eager to touch him with their affection. Their raucous chant was heard in the boardroom. 'CLOUGH IN. BOARD OUT.'

Clough went immediately to the boardroom ante-chamber, where he found Taylor waiting, while listening to the chanting of supporters out in the street.

Clough sat down beside him. 'What's the score?'

Taylor shrugged his shoulders. 'Nil nil. Nobody's been sent off yet.'

Clough leant forward, his impatience coiled. Nothing stirred him more than the prospect of a fight. Thoughts about the morrow, even less of the future, were forgotten. This was his opportunity to put it on the record. This day he would give them hell.

Suddenly the door into the boardroom opened and Longson appeared.

'Right, you two,' he said brusquely. 'Let's have you in.'

Clough said grittily. 'Eh, mister. We're not numbers, not convicts. Not yet.'

He stalked past Longson into the boardroom followed by Taylor.

Sir Robertson King waited until they were seated.

'All right, gentlemen. The board has discussed your written resignations of last night linked to your response to the conditions laid down a week ago, which included your television appearances, Mr Clough, as well as other matters which have caused the board some concern. Now—' He broke off as Clough raised a hand.

'Sorry, Sir Robertson, I know what you're going to say, but can we get on with it?' Clough was in no mood for long-winded preliminaries. 'My response is that everything I've done has been for the benefit of Derby County. Everything.' He tapped the table top. 'I've no apologies to make to anybody.'

He gave a deliberate glance at Longson. 'My record—' He broke off to indicate Taylor, sitting next to him. '*Our* record has been the best since this club opened its doors light years ago. I stand accused of going on television too much when every time it's benefited this club with publicity that your chairman asked me to get in the first place. So I'm not being told by him what I can say or write and what I can't. If this board withdraws its ultimatum and gets rid of Mr Longson we can withdraw our resignations and get on with the business of winning the championship again and next time defeat the cheating Italians for the European Cup.'

Clough paused for effect. His voice took on a softer tone. 'Now that's a good deal. You're getting all that at the expense of one man who's put nowt in the club and wants everything I can give him. And remember. You've got to answer to the fans if we go. Now you have your vote and we'll go outside and wait for the outcome. Thank you for listening, gentlemen.'

Clough smartly marched out of the room, followed by Taylor. There was a moment of silence. Keeling put up a hand, nervously. 'I propose a vote of no confidence in the chairman.'

'Any seconder?' Robertson King looked around the table. 'If there aren't any I will second the motion. The motion is that Mr Longson be asked to stand down as chairman of the board. All those in favour, please show?'

Hands were raised. Innes was considering whether to join them or not when he caught Longson's hard stare. He kept his hand down.

'Those against?'

The majority responded. King nodded his head in acceptance. 'The motion is defeated. We now have to vote on whether we accept the resignations. Those in favour?'

It was carried. Longson clasped his hands together, placed his elbows heavily on the table, hunched in deep pleasure.

It was Kirkland who opened the door to the ante-chamber. Rather than face Clough he addressed Taylor. 'Would you please come back in.'

It had the semblance of a court martial, the judges seated, watching Clough and Taylor enter to stand before them.

Longson got up slowly, smiling smugly. He would cherish the moment and re-live it for the rest of his days. 'The president has taken the vote. I stay as chairman and we've accepted your resignations.'

'With reluctance,' piped up Innes, looking sheepish.

Longson ignored Innes's remark. 'Now if Mr Clough and Mr Taylor would please put their car keys on the table and go and clear out their desks. We'd like you off the premises as soon as possible. If you don't mind.'

'I do mind. I'm driving home.' Clough scanned the faces. 'You bunch of cowards. I'm ashamed. The whole of Derbyshire will be ashamed. Not one of you has got the guts to stand up for the fans just because you're pals of his.' He jabbed a finger at Longson then turned to walk out.

'Leave your car keys. I said leave your car keys! You're finished here,' shouted Longson, but Clough disappeared. Longson waved a dismissive hand at him. 'Good riddance.'

KEELING, ANXIOUS TO show his mettle, having made a poor show in defence of Clough, was proud to announce that he was also resigning, in protest. Thus, the one man who would have channelled the weight of the Protest Movement to its target, the board, had ended that possibility, giving Longson an added bonus.

Longson wanted to celebrate with whisky but was summoned to the executive lounge where TV crews had set up their lighting.

When he arrived he found Clough, who was used to the paraphernalia of a TV set up, already answering questions. He spoke without emotion, in a matter-of-fact, business-like voice. 'I've done everything for this club and this is what they do. There's no accounting for some people. They want you to work for them and when you do it, well, they tell you to stop doing it. What a way to run a club.'

Longson, flustered by Clough's proximity, was then ushered in front of the bright lighting. Blinking hard he tried to respond to the opening question. 'Well, we've…er…accepted the resignations… with…with…sadness…we accepted them…er…well, we didn't want to but we felt we had to…with sadness, as I say, but he was going on television and we'd asked him not to…well…it got too much. There's only…well, what do you say when that…er – I'm sorry – it's these lights. I can't see!' Longson, eyes closed, waved a hand at them. 'Can we stop a minute?'

The camera swung to Clough who seized the moment. 'You see what I've been up against? I feel deeply embarrassed for the chairman. And deeply ashamed for Derby County that he can't put two words together.'

'Eh? It's these bloody lights!' Longson roared, making the sound recordist swing his boom, nearly hitting Kirkland as he hurried to snatch Longson's arm.

'Come on, Sam. Come on.' He hurried Longson back to the boardroom, the chairman looking back over his shoulder, bearing a smile of victory.

'You'll be looking like that when the fans get to you!' called out Clough.

'Brian? Can you give us one last—?' The appeal from the unit producer was ignored as Clough's eye fell upon a large jug of water. He picked it up and strode aggressively towards the boardroom. Taylor, realising what was intended, raced after him to bar his path.

'For God's sake. Time to go, Brian. They know. They know. It's over. Come on, give it me. It's over. Come on.'

Clough breathing heavily, allowed Taylor to take the jug from his hand and return it to the executive lounge.

A FEW MINUTES LATER they threaded their way through members of the staff, who had been attracted by the upstairs commotion, and went out to the car park. 'The bastard tried to get me to catch the bus home! After seven years!' ground out Clough as he wrenched the car door open. 'Seven bloody years.' He fumbled for his car keys.

'Hang on.' Taylor had his hand out. 'You're in no fit state. Let me drive.'

Clough paused, took a deep breath and composed himself. 'I'm okay.' Calmly he got into the car.

Seconds later, they drove past the front offices of the Baseball

Ground for the last time, leaving behind a trail of anguished fans. The photographers took their last shots as the Radio Derby reporter, who had tried but failed to get an interview with Clough, described the scene.

'Well, there he goes. A man who's worked miracles at Derby County. He resigned but effectively he was sacked. There are a lot of fans here who're very upset. I'm going to talk to one or two of them.'

The Mercedes turned at the end of the street. As it did so a small boy, heading a tennis ball, recognised the car and waved excitedly at its driver.

It was the end of seven years of history making at the Baseball Ground.

It was the start of the Protest Movement

18

TRAITOR

Still dazed by Clough's bombing of the players' meeting, I sat watching him scribble the name and address on the back of the leaflet.

'This will solve all our problems.' He spoke like a traffic cop handing out a speeding ticket. 'This is what I want you to do. You've got the name and address of a reserve. His name's Tommy Mason. Good lad. Won't ever make the first team. But he's the right stuff. Go there, speak to his landlady. Don't go before training has started. Go around eleven o'clock. Tell her to go to the ground and find Tommy. Tell her to tell him there's an important message waiting for him. When he arrives you tell him to take the reserves out on strike. Tell him when he's done that Toddy and the rest of the first team will follow. Tell him that it's from me. But tell him to keep it absolutely secret. He will not tell anybody. Not a soul. Even McGuinness. Understood?'

He made me repeat his instructions. The address he'd written down was one of the terraced houses close to the ground, first built to house factory workers. Satisfied with my grasp of his plan, Clough went into the gym to seek out McGuinness.

I stared at the leaflet, hardly able to comprehend what had happened. A kamikaze pilot, in killing himself, at least had the satisfaction of having destroyed his enemies. Clough had contrived not only to destroy his chances of returning to Derby County but also the hopes of his allies, the players, as well as the fans.

He returned with McGuinness. 'Got a nice place here, John,' he said. 'I wouldn't have liked to have burnt it down.' He turned to me. 'And your Martin's a good lad, Don. He can kick a ball. Look after him.'

After he'd gone, McGuinness looked grimly at me. 'What did he ask you to do?'

'He wants me to make contact with a player. I've got to keep it secret.'

'Oh yes?' McGuinness broke away. 'Well, you're welcome. He's mad. You know that? He's stark raving bonkers. Why should I go to all this bloody trouble!' He slammed a cup down by the coffee machine, almost breaking it. 'We've worked our socks off! What for? So he can barge in and destroy the thing he wants most! He's fucking insane!'

I wasn't listening, but thinking, seeing it from Clough's viewpoint. He would have disrupted the meeting because one or two players were suspect in his eyes. He would be impelled to have all his players out on strike, or none at all. He would not, could not, countenance any lack of unity, which would reflect badly on him. His return to Derby County had to be in triumph, born on the shields of all his warriors, anything less would have been a failure. How would that unity be achieved? By ensuring the reserves went on strike first. The first team players, who had shown uncertainty, would then be morally obliged to join in. If reserves earning half their wages could fight on their behalf then they would be honour bound to support them.

It was a brilliant idea. Clough had to destroy the meeting and then hand me his substitute plan. The 'Mason' plan was a sure-fire, copper-bottomed replacement. It would surely succeed.

Confident in what I had to do, I could now set my mind to the puzzle of Clough's entry. 'John? How did he manage to get in? The front door was locked, wasn't it?'

'Yes, it was. I've no idea.' McGuinness was still smarting from the Clough assault.

'Somebody must have given him a key, then.'

McGuinness shook his head in irritation, tapping his chest repeatedly. 'No idea. But it's my property. He barges in. Into *my* property. And buggers up everything we've done for him.' He sat down and pressed both hands to his face. 'Bloody hell. He is. He's mad.'

'John, I don't want to upset you, but did he break in? Don't you think you should check? For security?'

He stood up, the blue vein at the side of his head palpitating again. 'Oh, to hell with it.' Angry with himself, he limped quickly through the door by which Clough had entered and returned a minute later. 'The door was unlocked. It was locked before you came. And all the keys are where they should be.'

'Somebody had a copy made. Gave it him?' I said.

McGuinness shook his head. 'I'll ask Debbie. She's the waitress. She's the only one who could have done it. She hates football. She doesn't know any directors. No idea. Christ.' He carried on with his tidying up. 'All I know is that he's treated me like dog shit. If I wasn't a fan I'd be suing him for my wages, all the time I've worked for him.'

I COULD NOT sleep that night. McGuinness was clearly innocent. The mole had to be someone who knew Clough intimately, someone who knew that anyone manipulating *his* team would be given short shrift, irrespective of their good intentions.

I got up to make myself a mug of hot milk. I then sat down to think. What if it wasn't somebody working for the board? What if it was somebody who had their own private reasons for not wanting Clough back? Alan Hinton, who had been terrified by him?

Never. Clough had turned his life around, brought him rewards he would never have gained at Nottingham Forest. He regarded Clough, as did Gemmill, as a man you couldn't love, even be afraid of, but someone who brought you good fortune.

Was it John O'Hare, who had walked out of Barbara's party? No. O'Hare was a man of principle, a player who was proud of his independent thinking. He would never stoop so low.

What if it wasn't a player but…

Taylor. Oh my God.

Taylor.

I almost forgot to turn the gas off as the milk began to froth in the saucepan. I was back at the Kings Hall noting the concerned look on Taylor's face, even alarm, at Clough's display of emotion. Taylor had robbed him of the microphone.

In telling us all to 'cool it' he had not been addressing the mass audience, but *Clough*. Until now, I had never looked at the situation from the assistant manager's viewpoint. A reserved man, with a dry sense of humour and a practical approach to life, Taylor had every reason to want the Movement to fail. He didn't want to return to Derby, as would have been expected had Clough been reinstated at the Baseball Ground.

Clough had told me that Taylor wanted to retire at Brighton with its grand seafront attractions and when Chairman Bamber had shown them photographs of houses for sale, 'Pete lapped it all up. He'd have moved in one the next day.'

Taylor wanted to stay at Brighton. The jigsaw pieces began to fit together. Taylor would need Clough's expertise in building a good, new team at Brighton. That would take two years. Clearly, he had a motive for sabotaging Clough's early return to Derby. And Taylor, possessing all the home phone numbers of the players, was chatty with all of them.

He would have extracted the information in the normal course of conversation, the players totally at ease, unaware that their destiny was in his hands. As far as they knew Taylor was on their side, fighting for Clough's return, wasn't he? He was the perfect mole, beyond suspicion. It might not have been Longson who had passed on information about Holmes to ATV Sport, but Taylor. He knew those contacts better than anyone, bar Clough. He had featured many times in their weekly sports programme. And Taylor, the shrewd observer of human nature, the ace selector of football talent, knew Clough intimately, in some ways better than Clough himself. He would know what Clough's reaction would be to anyone conspiring with *his* players.

The kitchen clock struck 1 a.m. I had sat there for half an hour, working it out to my satisfaction. But then doubts began to surface. I considered Taylor's loyalty to Clough. Was he really capable of behaving so treacherously towards a man who'd been his best friend and colleague since their playing days with Middlesbrough?

Taylor was, in his own way, as proud of his achievements as was Clough and shared his values. Disloyalty was not one of them. And there was another strong possibility that would have deterred Taylor from being a traitor. Preventing Clough returning to Derby was one thing, but the likelihood was that a First Division club would have tempted Clough away from Brighton within a few months, well before he'd had chance to build a successful squad on which Taylor could have thrived. And it was odds on that Taylor would have gone with him.

These troubled thoughts would have bothered me not a jot – would have become irrelevant – had I known that, following Clough's disruption of the meeting, the players had not gone home to their 'bairns and wives' as Clough had instructed, but to Todd's house where they had sat down to groan and moan, their enthusiasm for striking diminished by the very man they were trying to save.

Now the future of Derby County lay entirely in the hands of an unknown young, reserve player called Tommy Mason.

IT WAS A fog-shrouded, miserable pig of a morning as I drove towards the Baseball Ground. I passed through streets I had walked as a boy. With my pals we would arrive by trolley bus and walk between the terraced houses at late dinner time to the smell of burning coal and boiled cabbage, eager to secure a good spot in the boys' corner.

Notices stuck on house doors advertised safe parking for bicycles, price sixpence. The bike would be wheeled up the entry and stored in the backyard leaning against the outside lavatory, to be picked up after the match.

I parked in Mason's street and got out of the car.

A mongrel dog eyed me suspiciously. Otherwise there was no sign of life. I found the house after a short walk, less than three hundred yards from the ground, and knocked on the door.

The landlady, a friendly small woman, opened it.

'Sorry to bother you,' I said. 'I've got an important message for Tommy Mason. Is it possible to get him here? Just for a couple of minutes?'

The landlady hesitated. 'What's it about? I'll have to tell him summat.'

Caught by indecision I found myself telling her that it was to 'do with Brian Clough', but stressed that if she had to mention his name she must whisper it, in case somebody overheard.

Assuring me that she would be the soul of discretion, she insisted that I waited inside the house. The small chubby lady, wearing a floral-decorated pinafore, bustled off towards the ground. I could have been the best conman in the world. But then, as I looked around, I saw there was very little worth stealing: an old black-and-white TV, a few pieces of imitation brass and copper and two pottery dogs facing each other on the tiled fireplace.

Ten minutes later I heard the sharp clatter of football boots on the blue tiled pavement. It was Tommy Mason running with excitement. He braked hard outside the door, whipped off his boots and entered, a short, pimply teenager in his player's kit, showing muddy knees. 'Does Mr Clough want me at Brighton?' he panted eagerly, not waiting for any formalities of introduction.

'Tommy,' I held out my hand. 'I'm Don Shaw. I'm running the Protest Movement. Brian told me to come and see you—'

'Does he want me at Brighton?'

In his continuing excitement and outstretched hope I suddenly felt ashamed.

'No, he doesn't, Tommy. Sorry.'

'Oh.' Tommy's face fell to stare at a square of worn carpet on the linoleum covered floor.

'What he wants is for you to go back to the ground and tell the reserves that you're all going on strike. If you do that Colin Todd and the first team will follow.'

'Oh,' he said again, cast down.

'Sorry, Tommy.'

He nodded unenthusiastically, his dream dashed.

The landlady came in from the street. She caught Tommy's hang-dog expression, his lowered head and drooping shoulders. She put out a hand to him, concerned. 'You all right, duck?'

He nodded. 'The boss wants me to take the reserves out on strike.'

The landlady pulled a face. 'He's got a bloody cheek, hasn't he? Eh, want a cuppa tea?'

'No. I'd better get back.'

'What a carry on.' She went into the kitchen.

'Tommy.' I spoke earnestly. 'If Brian gets back here he won't forget what you'll have done, I can promise. You'll get some reward.'

At this he perked up and a bright smile lit his face. 'Great.'

'But don't forget. Only tell the reserves. And strike tomorrow. Okay?'

I watched him jog back to the ground. This was a world away from the inspirational and glorious launch of the Protest Movement.

MY WORLD COLLAPSED that afternoon. It began to crumble when McFarland rang me half an hour after I got home. 'Don. We heard about Tommy Mason. A bit late because we'd already decided not to go on strike. We had a meeting last night and took a vote. We still want Cloughie back. But it's up to you now.' He said that the momentum for a strike was at its greatest just at the moment when Clough had taken the wind out of their sails by joining Brighton. The latest incident had left them sadly disillusioned.

After the call I slumped in an armchair, stricken in the knowledge that the mission had been doomed before I'd even embarked upon it.

The next phone call came within five minutes and was worse. It was George Edwards. 'Don, you've created a right old stink with Tommy Mason.'

The mention of the name stabbed me with fear. 'What happened, George?'

'He came into the ground – the reserves were jogging round – and he just bellowed out, "Mr Clough wants us all out on strike!"'

I felt a wave pass through my body, leaving me shaky, my hands and forehead hot and clammy. What had I done?

Longson, on hearing the news, had gone to find Webb in his

office, rubbing his hands together. 'Bloody wonderful! We've got him. We've got him! Stuart, call the club solicitor and tell him to get over here. We want Mason's exact words recorded. Brilliant. Bloody brilliant!'

Half an hour layer Mason sat in Webb's office being interrogated by the club solicitor, Mr Timms, Longson and Webb looking on. After ten minutes Mason was dismissed and the solicitor finished his note-taking.

'What's the verdict, then?' asked Longson anxiously.

The solicitor spoke carefully. 'Mason said that Shaw definitely told him that it was Clough who told him to do it. If it can be proved that Shaw, through Clough, has incited an employee of a company to breach his contract with that company, as it seems, then that's an offence.'

'Can we sue him for it – and Clough?' Longson was eager for the reply.

'We'll have to submit for an opinion. I can't say if you'd be successful. But I think it looks like you have a case.'

Longson, convinced of victory, went to Mackay's office to toast him as the undisputed manager of Derby County. He was surprised to find that Mackay seemed unenthusiastic, perhaps even a shade embarrassed.

'What's up, Dave? You realise this means he won't trouble us any more?' Longson went to the drinks cabinet. 'Come on. Let's celebrate.'

'I dinna like kicking the man when he's down.' Mackay sounded flat. He tossed a paper he was reading on to his desktop. 'He's a fantastic manager.'

'Dave.' Longson frowned. 'You've nothing to feel guilty about. Look. Shaw's lucky we didn't do him for inciting the players to chuck matches. Let me tell you something. Clough made my life a hell. No club in the country can take his kind of bloody interference. I told Alan Hardacre how he treated us. When he gets this news Cloughie won't manage another club again. Alan will celebrate. The FA committee will celebrate. By God they will, after all the stick he's given them.'

He broke off as he saw Mackay still looking unhappy. 'Eh, don't you worry, Dave. You'll be a better manager than him. I know managerial talent when I see it.'

While Longson thanked his lucky stars at the Baseball Ground, I was talking to Peter Scragg, my solicitor, in Burton upon Trent. He listened carefully to the whole story. After a pause he said I had probably committed an offence under the Law of Torts. And I could be sued for damages. I didn't like his sympathetic tone of voice. I rang off, only to pick up the phone again and dial Clough's number. My finger hesitated on the final digit and stayed there until it pulled back in finality. I lacked the courage. His situation was dire. Subverting a club, while managing another, had to be the most serious of crimes in the FA book.

I sat down to kill time by watching the television midday news, but World War Three could have been proclaimed and I would have been oblivious. I switched off the set and waited in a slough of despair, Clough's silence tolling like a funeral bell.

The phone rang. A harsh, jangling noise. I dashed into the hall.

'Hello?' I was out of breath.

'Don.' It was McGuinness. 'After the players left here last night they decided they weren't going on strike. They'd had enough.'

'I know. Roy Mac told me that as well.'

His call, though irrelevant, had me thinking once again on the phenomenon that was Clough. I'd been worrying unnecessarily about the possibility of him conspiring with the players, keeping me in the dark. But, if anything, he'd kept them at a distance, unable to get involved in conspiracy because that would have implied he was at one with them. The only time Clough had come down to the players' level was during that dotty and nostalgic evening at Newton Solney, when a trip to Majorca had been mooted. I should have realised that he was incapable of plotting with anybody. He would always have to be in control. Trapped in his own hubris he had lurched from one fiasco to another.

As Longson celebrated the day with champagne, I contacted Keeling who promised to ferret around and let me know the state of play through his contacts at the Baseball Ground. He rang back an hour later.

His news was devastating. The club solicitor, at that moment, 'was talking to counsel with a view to suing Brian Clough and Don Shaw for inciting employees of a company to take strike action, thus damaging and undermining that company's operations'.

I felt sick.

19

AMBUSHED

WIND-DRIVEN RAIN swept against the front door. I sat in the dim light of the hallway, thinking desperately, hoping that Clough would ring. The man who could defy the world must surely be afraid, for once in his life. The failure of his latest 'plan' could see him facing expulsion from the game in which he had so majestically starred.

I had a question that needed an answer, but one I was scared to ask lest it be one I didn't want to hear. If I refused to testify against Clough – which I would certainly do if the chips were down – what weight and kind of evidence from Tommy Mason would be required for a 'guilty' verdict?

I rang Peter Scragg, but he was out for the evening. I began to telephone as many supporters and friends as I could, searching for any crumb of comfort. After a few calls, none of which amounted to more than tokens of sympathy, I rang George Edwards, hoping he might have better news from his sources at the Baseball Ground. He had nothing beyond what he'd already told me.

By 8.30 p.m. I had given up hearing from Clough. When the phone rang I was startled at his voice, even more amazed at his casual manner of speech. 'Don. Sorry I've not rung. I've been repairing trains with the boys. Pop round, we'll have a chat.'

'But haven't you heard?'

'Heard what? You mean Tommy Mason? Oh, don't worry about that. Come over.'

Startled and nervous, I drove to Ferrers Way to find Clough still in the same light-hearted mood. Barbara was out at a meeting. The children were in bed. He offered me a drink, which I accepted.

'Don't worry,' he repeated, pouring out a beer. 'They won't sue.' He then spoke in a mocking tone, spacing out each statement. 'Mason told the lawyer – that I told you – to tell him – to tell Toddy – to tell the reserves – to go on strike,' he scoffed. 'If a pig was sold from country to country round the world it'd come back a bloody cow! And remember, the players are on record as wanting to strike. That would be thrown back at them if the board sue us. I hope they do. Give 'em hell, eh?'

Was it all fearlessness? Yes, I could see him now in his boast, flying a Spitfire taking on an armada of German aircraft.

He chuckled at my – still – anxious expression. 'You don't need your worry beads. I'm suing them after all, for what they said about me. My solicitor now says we have a good chance. I can always say I'll withdraw my lawsuit if they withdraw theirs.' He grinned. 'More than one way to skin a cat.'

We sat down by the fire. He continued. 'The message you gave Tommy Mason could have been the time of the next train. It's only his word against yours. There's no written evidence. You could have made it up or dreamt it. Where's the evidence linking it with me?' But then remembering, he said, 'What did you do with that leaflet with Mason's name and address on it?'

'I burnt it.'

Clough relaxed. 'Good. That might have made things a bit tricky.'

I still felt nervous. 'Brian, you're okay, but what about me? The landlady knows I was there. She heard what I said. She got Tommy out of the ground, told him it was a message from you.'

Clough blew out his cheeks with a dismissive sound. 'Don, if they bring any action against you I'll be on to them like a ton of bricks. My lawsuit's bigger than theirs, I can tell you.' He paused, then looked quickly at me. 'You don't think I'd drop you in it to save my own skin, do you?'

'Course not.' He looked so offended. He would stay loyal to his friends. It was important I knew that. I added. 'Thanks, Brian.'

Inwardly I breathed a sigh of relief. Working with Cloughie was a roller coaster of emotions. Fear, followed by relief, followed by fear, again and again. Yes, he would drop you in it but then he'd snatch you out of the stuff of his own making.

'Brian.' I found it difficult. 'I have to tell you that the players are not going on strike. They had a meeting after you came to the gym and sent them home. They took a vote.' I watched for his response.

He merely pursed his lips, nodded a few times and paused before speaking. 'Fine. They're entitled. I've got a plan in case that happened.' He grinned at my drop-jawed expression. 'This one's no chance of going belly up. This is what you should do.'

Dear God, he was sitting round to face me again, positioning himself to instruct me in another crazy plan. I sat bolt upright, this time determined not to look at him. I would listen, take note, take it away and consider what he'd said in calm repose. I stared fixedly into the fire. However, his insistent voice had the effect of turning my head automatically towards him.

'Go to the House of Commons and see the Minister of Sport, Denis Howell. He was a bloody good referee,' intoned Clough. 'Wanted me to stand as a Labour candidate – till I told him I'd have to take over the Labour Party. First see Philip Whitehead. He's a mate of yours. He'll fix it. Just go along, see Howell and tell him what's happened and…'

As his insistent voice droned on I knew I would obey.

It was some time before he spoke again and when he did it was with a deep sincerity. 'I love that team. I love it.'

For a moment I thought he would weep, but quick as a flash came the sharp eye, bright in the firelight. 'You've got to believe in yourself. Whatever happens, Don, believe in yourself and it will happen'

I decided it was time to go. As I went through the door he gave me a wry smile. 'You'll be able to tell your grandchildren one day how you saved Derby County.'

Did he mean it? I saw the prospect as remote. This time I wasn't filled with an unthinking compliance. I had doubts and would not have obeyed had it not been a simple and risk free task. I would enjoy meeting Philip Whitehead again, an old friend, and a trip to the House of Commons was always interesting.

On my way home my first thought was that his 'I'll drop my lawsuit if you drop yours' notion had probably come from his solicitor, which robbed him of some kudos. But he'd made no mention of the FA. The accusation that he'd attempted to subvert Derby County while manager of Brighton, need not go into a court of law. Tommy Mason's evidence would count. Their disciplinary committee could still boot him out of the game. Did he know that? Was he hiding his fear? Surely, knowing he still ran the risk would take away at least some of his self-confidence.

I told Liz I was going to London to see the Minister of Sport. She said I was insane and likened my situation to that of a secret agent dropped into enemy territory by my controller, the dangers all too obvious. 'Haven't you learnt already? He's using you.'

'I know he's using me. He wants me to get him back at Derby.'

'You've been a wreck over Tommy Mason. Why can't he get somebody else do it?'

'He asked me to do it. You know how he is,' I said defensively.

I MANAGED TO speak to Whitehead after he'd returned from a late sitting at the Commons. Yes, he would introduce me to Denis Howell, the Minister. He suggested I caught the 10 a.m. train from Derby to St Pancras the following day, where he would be waiting. I sighed in relief. Nothing could go wrong with this mission. For the first time in weeks I could relax. I promised myself I would even enjoy the trip.

Then McGuinness rang. Had I spoken to Clough? I told him of Clough's sanguinity. He was unimpressed. 'Don. The club might not go for him over Mason, but the FA could, couldn't they? I bet he's got you doing something else now, eh? Equally barmy?'

Sheepishly, I told him that he'd guessed right but I couldn't talk about it, not until I got back from London.

He replied as I expected, with a heavy sarcasm. 'Brilliant. What will it be this time? You never learn. I wouldn't do a damned thing he says. I think he's dangerous. Well, he is to you, isn't he?'

'He has been. But this should be straightforward. I've got to give it a try. What else is left? Another march? Another leaflet drop? We're getting nowhere.'

As I STEPPED off the train on to the platform at St Pancras my eye fell, as it always did, on the base of one of the huge metal arches built by a Derbyshire foundry in Victorian times. Still discernible was the date of manufacture as if it were constructed yesterday. As I went through the barrier, Whitehead, bald and bearded, smiled happily in greeting. On the way by taxi to the House of Commons he agreed with me that Clough created his own problems by the sweep of his convictions and naked ambition, the two characteristics that had also made him great. Whitehead would not stick on Clough the label 'genius'. Not yet. I told him that it was that belief which had motivated me to try and save him for Derby County. What other manager could compare?*

I was introduced to Denis Howell in the Lobby at the Commons.

At one time a top League referee himself, he came across as a chubby-faced affable man with a love of the game unrivalled in Westminster. He shook my hand warmly. There was no need for me to explain. Already briefed by Whitehead, he had no hesitation in voicing his opinion.

'Clough's an amazing man,' he said. 'I know there's been jealousy and falling out, but they should realise he's a treasure. How can they be allowed to toss away a multi-million-pound investment on a personality issue?'

'Brilliant man. Fantastic,' Howell continued over lunch in the small Members' canteen, not the restaurant, where the prices were much higher. 'The trouble with these businessmen is they don't understand the game. Or, should I say, they don't *appreciate* the spirit of the game. What you should do is be totally bold. Philip tells me you write for a local paper each week.'

---

* *Years later, after Clough's success at Nottingham Forest, he agreed with me. He even topped it with: 'The greatest football manager in the world.'*

'Yes, I do.' Whitehead was an excellent MP, missing nothing in the local press, always on top of any problem.

'Right. Devote it to a rallying call. Ask the public not to go to the next match. Ask for a general strike of supporters. Just one game. Empty terraces speak louder than full ones.'

I thought it very neat, said it was a saying Clough would have used. He laughed.

I thanked him, but not as 'Minister'. He urged, 'Call me Denis.'

On my return home there was a message from McGuinness asking me to call him.

'Hello, Don. Trip to London okay?'

'Very good. Philip Whitehead introduced me to Denis Howell, Minister of Sport. He's behind us. Thinks I should call the fans out on strike, not the players.'

McGuinness grunted. 'Well, at least it's better than that Mason business. That was an absolute cock-up.'

'I know. I can't believe I did it.'

'Good.' There was a pause and McGuinness's voice changed. 'Don, I've not told you before, but I've had one or two phone calls I don't like. I wondered if you'd had any.'

'How do you mean?' I said, tautly.

'I had a threatening phone call – I've had two phone calls. The same man. He said he was out to get me if I didn't stop the Clough thing. That's exactly what he said.'

I froze.

'Have you had any calls like that?'

'No.'

McGuinness sounded bitter. 'It's not how it started, is it. Not how it was meant to be. I'm a bit pissed off, if you'd like to know. Cloughie's sabotaged everything we've tried to do.' He hesitated. 'I can handle myself man-to-man but this guy sounded as if he might have something more than a fist. Look. Let's meet up. Well away from here. You never know. They've got these bug things now.'

'Okay. Where shall we meet?'

IT WAS FOGGY and bitterly cold as I drove into Markeaton Park, this time parking well away from the gay 'cottage', under a lamp that cast a yellow glow on the mist surrounding the car. I killed the engine and pressed the central locking button, waiting for McGuinness's blue Mercedes to appear. Traffic on the nearby A38 swished and rumbled past as I thought about the events of the past few days.

I was still struggling in my mind over Taylor. Whichever way my mind turned there was no full stop. Short of asking each player what they knew or what they felt, there was no way I could resolve my doubts.

Then I dismissed the irritating thoughts and switched to the threat against McGuinness. I tried to recall our conversation. He had first mentioned Tommy Mason, then – at that point I stopped. Mason... 'that Mason business...' *Mason.*

I was breathing hard, the palms of my hands suddenly warm and prickly. I'd not mentioned the player's name to McGuinness so how did he know? Then I suddenly relaxed, letting out a big sigh of relief. Of course he would have heard about it. Mason had blurted it out to all and sundry at the Baseball Ground. Everyone there knew of it, as did George Edwards at the *Telegraph*.

Nevertheless, I checked that the car doors were all locked. I sat back and drew a deep breath. If I continued like this I'd end up a nervous wreck. I looked at my watch. I'd been there ten minutes. McGuinness was either late or – I was suddenly dazzled by headlights. A car approached and then slowed down to creep alongside. The driver, in semi-darkness, was looking at me. I had the impression of a big man. And it wasn't a saloon, but an estate car. A Volvo. It passed by. I watched its red tail lights in the wing mirror slowly fading into the gloom. I switched on the engine – just in case. The Volvo was turning to come back. Sheer terror had me clamping my foot down, spinning wheels in a burn of rubber before catapulting towards the park exit.

I got back on to the A38, breathing hard, continually checking the mirror to see if the Volvo was following me. It wasn't.

Finally, in relief I relaxed my grip on the steering wheel and drove home safely.

As I entered the house the phone rang. I hesitated and then picked it up warily. 'Hello?'

It was McGuinness, thoroughly apologetic. His car had broken down, he said. He wanted to meet me the next day.

I hesitated. 'I can't, John. I've got to pick up my TV work again. They've ditched my Hollywood film *Wingate* because of the Israeli war.'

There was a pause. 'You sound as if it's the end, Don. Is it?'

I paused. 'No. It's just I'm tired. But I'm banking on this *Derby Trader* piece I'm doing.' I told him that my appeal for the fans to boycott the next home game would be in the next edition. I would impress upon them that, if they wanted Clough back, they had it in their hands. 'Whatever happens, we'll keep the Movement going. We know he wants to come back. We've got to be ready,' I said.

'True. I'm still with you. Despite Cloughie, eh?' McGuinness laughed. 'We never had this trouble with Glentoran. Look after yourself.'

I went into my study and sat in the swivel chair, surveying the pile of correspondence I'd ignored in the long battle. I let out a sigh. I'd been scout, messenger, saboteur and spear carrier for Clough, all of them hazardous jobs. Now I could get back to dealing with conflict that was drama, not real-life threats. I could dream again.

I had hardly settled myself at the keyboard when I reflected upon the fact that only 800 of the 30,000 plus Derby fans had actually joined the Movement, the vast majority sitting back to watch our antics in hope. Well, they could continue in their slough of lethargy and win by merely staying at home on the next match day. How I wished that the players had shown more unity and militancy and that Clough had not spiked their every move. Clough was right when he told me that there were no revolutionaries in the Derby workforce. And his players were noted for their placid temperament.

In my *Trader* article I had written that I looked forward to a 'mass frontal attack on the board by an invisible army'. Then I urged the call to arms, Shakespearean style: 'And gentlemen in Derby now abed, shall think themselves accursed they did not stay away on Saturday!' Well, stick a bit of humour in. Football was supposed to be fun. Wasn't it?

I STOOD OUTSIDE the Baseball Ground with McGuinness and the rest of the Movement committee. It was half an hour to kick off. Our appeal for the fans to boycott the game had so far fallen on deaf ears. A number of fans recognising me, deliberately looked away, anxious that I didn't catch their eye. With fifteen minutes to go the ground was almost full. Only a small percentage of fans had stayed away. I walked back to my car, shutting out the noise from the stadium.

But if I thought I could settle back in peaceful domestic harmony I was in for another shock. When I got home Liz told me that Philip Whitehead had telephoned, wanted to speak to me, urgently. I rang him back immediately.

'Don,' he sounded hurt. 'What have you done? I don't believe it.' He went on to question my sanity. 'That was barmy. You've reported a government minister as saying he advocated strike action.'

Apparently someone, probably at Longson's prompting, had anonymously sent Howell a cutting of my article. Whitehead said that Howell had spoken to the editor of the *Trader* insisting that he had not urged me to seek a strike by the general public.

Don Shaw had 'told lies', he said, and demanded that the *Trader* gave his statement prominence in the next edition. He was contacting his solicitor with a view to taking action against the *Derby Trader* and Don Shaw.

Whitehead ended the call with a promise that he would explain to Howell that I was under great pressure and hadn't thought of the consequences. He would convey my apology for the mistake if I admitted my error in my next article. I was only too eager to agree.

As Whitehead rang off I sat back, my forehead hot and moist. Driven once more by a Clough command I had, once again, incredibly, stupidly, allowed myself to obey, totally blind to the consequences. Was there anything that Clough did that was not crazy? After my experience of him in action any rational person would have stood back before committing themselves to another dangerous farce.

The phone rang. Pray let it be Clough.

'Don.'

'Brian. I was going to ring you.'

'I know. I've heard all about it. Eh, you're breathing hard. Is that running or worrying? Philip Whitehead tells me you made a balls-up. No need to worry. Come over to the Kedleston. Eh.' He slowed down in heavy emphasis. 'And on the way just think why you don't need to worry. Okay?'

I did think. I thought hard. I thought laterally. And then I thought how the hell did Clough manage to come up trumps every time he had a bad hand?

When I arrived at the Kedleston he was already ensconced in his usual place, glass in hand. When he saw me he stood up, ready to go to the bar, his eyebrows raised in a dry smile. 'Well, did you think? Did you get it?'

I shook my head. 'No. Tell me.'

'Don, Howell won't sue. Philip Whitehead was there. He was a witness. And you know him. He'd never lie. Never. He heard Howell tell you what to do. They're mates. It wouldn't happen.' He went to the bar, still grinning. 'A pint for my friend, Don,' he said to the barman.

I sat down. And marvelled. It could not be luck alone that had given Clough a Houdini-like skill in escaping the ropes and shackles of fate.

I watched him chatting to the barman. Danger man, yes, but not lucky. He was unlucky in his pride. It was the source of his strength but also his weakness.

He came back with my pint. I had to ask him. 'Are you worried about the FA going for you over Mason?'

'Come on. Tommy Mason's one of my lads. Would he give evidence against me? I'd be there at the hearing, looking at him. He'd look at me.' Clough gave me a sardonic smile. 'Never in a million years.'

I nodded in relief. Anxious to change the subject I asked him about his job at Brighton.

'How's it going?' I said.

'It's going.' He sat down, took a drink, placed the glass carefully on the table and put a hand to his face, the fingers spreading out over his cheek as he seemed to muse.

I studied him. I knew that Brighton was only a whistle stop on his great journey. I knew that he would get to the end of the rainbow and find his crock of gold. You can't be in the presence of a man like Clough – for there was no man like Clough – without realising he was bound for greater things. He would not rest, like other mortals, when glory incessantly beckoned.

'You know what sticks in my gut?' He was frowning to himself. 'Schools where they give a prize to every kid win or lose. Don't they realise that learning how to lose is as important as winning? What matters is trying. And you learn to win as well. I'm going to ask the FA. Let's have a rule of conduct. After the game the winners line up, like in rugby, shaking the losers' hands. You tell 'em if they played well. Better luck next time. That's how you get trained for life.'

He took a deep breath. I noticed a small reddish patch on his cheek. Many years later his face would be coloured by numerous marks from the ravages of drink.

He looked at me suddenly. 'Right. It's going to take longer than we thought. But we've not lost. We're on the back burner. That's all. We're on hold.'

He put out his hand. 'Don. Many thanks for all you've done. I mean that.'

I took his hand, too full to say anything, blinking a few times to clear my eyes.

He brooded for a moment, then stuck a finger in the air. 'Not done yet.'

20

NEVER SAY DIE

On 31 July 1974 the news placard at the corner of St James St bellowed 'CLOUGH JOINS LEEDS'. I bought the paper in utter disbelief. I had understood Clough's reasons for joining lowly Brighton, but what possible reason could there be for him taking over a team whose standards he abhorred, despite them being League champions? What kind of career move was that? What kind of hypocrisy was he showing the world, given his public denouncement of Revie and his players? I had my opportunity to find an answer when, within a fortnight, Clough invited Liz and me to join his family at Wembley where Leeds, as champions, faced FA Cup holders Liverpool in the Charity Shield match.

The night before, we stayed as his guests at the Royal Garden Hotel, Kensington. As Liz and I waited for the lift, Billy Bremner, the fiery Leeds captain, joined us. Noticing Clough approaching, he ducked away and took the stairs, his head down. Intrigued, I waited until I had a chance to speak to Clough. Luckily, I encountered him in the lobby just before dinner.

He appeared in a mellow mood so I dared ask. 'Why become their manager? You don't like them. They don't like you.'

Clough looked me in the eye. 'Don. I'm entitled. I'm a professional football manager. The job came up. Top of the First Division. End of story.' He quickly put up a hand to disarm me. 'And you're entitled to question.' He took a quick glance around to see he wasn't overheard. 'They're nothing like Derby. I can't get one of the buggers to turn and look at me in the dug-out.' He laughed, but I detected a hollow ring to it.

The game the following day was distinguished by Bremner having a spat with Keegan of Liverpool. Bremner was sent off and threw down his shirt in disgust.

Shortly afterwards he was summoned to appear at FA headquarters charged with bringing the game into disrepute. By chance my visit to the BBC TV Centre coincided with Clough's journey to represent Bremner at the disciplinary hearing. We travelled together. Although he had a first-class ticket he would not sit in the coach designated. 'Bound to be some bloody football director who'll come up to me.' The train staff knew of his aversion and had provided him with a table tucked in a recess, next to the dining car. As we drank champagne I asked him how things were going at Leeds.

He gave me a wry grimace. 'I played the missionary, Don as you would going into the jungle. I laid into them on day one. I told them what I wanted: decent, sporting football, Hunter first. "Hunter," I said, "why does everybody call you 'Bite yer legs?" He just grinned at me. I thought I'd wind him up. I said, "How many friends have you got in the game?" He said, "I don't give a f—"' Clough broke off as he spotted a female dining-car attendant hovering nearby. He continued. 'If they'd been my Derby team they'd have hanged Longson from the crossbar and I'd have been back.' He perked up with a big grin. 'Eh, how's that for a morality tale?' Shaking his head at the foibles of fate he gazed out at the autumnal countryside speeding past.

I sat in wonderment. How could he rule the enemy, let alone associate with them? How long would he last?

Clough leant towards me and spoke quietly. 'Besides being dirty, they cheat. Don Revie taught them. They picked it up in Europe, learnt it off the Italians. They remind me of Juventus. I'll never forget that night. Never, ever, till I'm pushing up daisies.'

He quickly changed the subject to dispel the pain. He talked about trees. He was in love with them. Strong, true trees. Colourful trees. The day before the Ali–Frazier title fight he'd gone out into the nearest woods.

'It was so peaceful. I know nowt about poetry, but that

Wordsworth. I read one of his. And I got it. Bang on the nail.' He recited the verse in his lecturing tone. '"One impulse from a vernal wood, may teach you more of man, of moral evil and of good, than all the sages can."' He paused. 'Now Nixon's gone I'd stick that President Ford and Chairman Brezhnev in a wood and I'd tell them to feel and smell and they'd come to realise that this world is too bloody precious to blow up.'

As the train rolled slowly past the St Pancras gas holder he made one last remark, foreseeing his inevitable departure from Elland Road. 'I've got talent. I'll be back.'

Clough departed from Leeds eleven days later with a substantial pay-off, ousted it was said by 'player power', a complete reversal of the situation at Derby. He told me that the players had failed him.

THE PROTEST MOVEMENT rumbled on in the form of letters to the local press and many, many phone calls that achieved little. The annual get-togethers, which Clough always attended, were like those of an elite regiment, now disbanded, with tales of heroes and villains and much laughing and lamenting. Then, on 19 September 1974, the Movement threw a party for Clough at the Pennine Hotel. Clough, I observed, had stopped drinking. He looked fit, cracked jokes and spent a long time in earnest and sympathetic conversation with an octogenarian supporter who had seen the great Steve Bloomer play for Derby before the First World War. Liz said 'I wish my mother could have been here.'

Clough made a speech. Thanking everybody, he said how bad he felt after all our hard work had come to nought. He then made an astounding announcement.

He was handing all his shares in Derby County – apparently an early gift from Longson – to Mike Keeling who would sell to each of us one share for one pound, the money to go to charity. There was a proviso: 'You promise to go to the Annual General Meeting of Derby County and kick up a stink. You never know, you might get me back!' He grinned hugely as he was cheered mightily.

The AGM of Derby County FC was held on 13 December.

It was packed with our supporters. I sat on the front row, ready to stand up and denounce the chairman and the board for their stupidity in getting rid of its greatest manager. The chairman was first to speak and then, in one physical action, defused our protest in an instant. Sam Longson took the microphone and placed it carefully in his ear, as though talking on the telephone.

The room was hushed in pity and embarrassment as he began his opening statement: 'The respect I hold as Chairman is something I cherish above all. I've no intention of talking about Brian Clough. On three occasions I've sacked him and told him to bugger off.'

When the first of the Movement supporters tried to speak, he said, 'I've got four men here who'll pick you up, carry you downstairs and kick you out into the street.' I then stood and tried to ask a question but was told by Longson to 'shut up.'

There was no point protesting. After the meeting we gathered together outside the ground. It felt like the aftermath of a funeral service, we the mourners standing outside the crematorium wondering what to say and how to say it when all we wanted to do was break away and go home.

Clough, on hearing of the incident, was philosophical. 'Well, it comes to us all. Don, never say die. You get me the right deal and I'll be back.'

THE LONG WAR between the Movement and the board at Derby County, which had long been at a standstill, suddenly gave off its first whiff of grape shot since the heady days of '73-'74. It came from an unexpected quarter after Longson, still bravely fighting to keep his position as chairman, had been deposed by George Hardy, a scrap-metal millionaire.

Taylor was still at Brighton, still enjoying the seaside life, when Clough became manager of Nottingham Forest in 1975 – it would be another year before he rejoined his old mate. At 9.10 a.m. on 15 February 1977, I took a phone call from McGuinness. Hardy, he said, was intent on wresting Clough away from Forest and restoring him as Derby manager. Apparently Hardy had spoken to

Clough by telephone and had received a cautious but encouraging reply. In the meantime McGuinness conveyed Hardy's hope that I would sound out Clough's sincerity, given his reputation for 'playing around with directors'.

Hardy, McGuinness stressed, saw Nottingham Forest rising rapidly in the Second Division and it would only be a matter of time before they rejoined the elite. It would then prove much harder to entice Clough back to Derby. He felt he had to act now – which meant I had to put my skates on.

I rang Clough. Within an hour we were sitting in the Kedleston, Keeling having dropped him off so that we were alone. Dispirited, I saw that he had fallen off the wagon. He had ordered what looked like water, but was in fact a tall vodka.

'I never told you I was sorry about Leeds.' I said.

'I wasn't. I made a packet.' He said he'd been entitled to make a mistake in taking on Leeds. 'Like Hitler trying to take Moscow,' he grinned. 'I was frozen out.'

I laughed. In each case a city too far.

He stopped smiling, pursed his mouth, looking down at the table top. 'A nightmare, Leeds. I was so low I rang Pete Taylor down at Brighton. It was the night after the Wembley game. I cried down the phone. I told him I'd made a terrible mistake, but could he join me. At least we'd have a laugh.' He checked himself and looked at me. 'Funny, me telling you all that,' he said, surprised at himself. He brushed his weakness aside. 'So, what does Hardy want to know before we meet?'

I was nervous. 'He wants to know if you really mean it.'

Clough stared at me.

'You know. Your stringing along boards? Having fun with directors?'

Clough put his glass down, leant forward and spoke intently. 'Do you know just how much I miss Derby?'

Of course I knew.

The next day the placard at the corner of St James St and Victoria St declared 'CLOUGH BACK'. If there was not hysteria in the streets it can be said that it roused the town – was there ever such a fizz! But it had the reverse effect of a winning side bringing home trophies. Production, instead of rising, actually fell as everyone stopped working to talk about it. The buzz transmitted itself electronically. I gave my views to the press and Radio Derby. What could I say other than I was amazed and delighted?

Unfortunately, there was a problem. Hardy had not yet offered Clough a salary. When the offer came it amounted to £17,000. Clough asked for an increase of £5,000. And he insisted that Taylor received £11,000, now that he had joined him again. Webb was present at the meeting, which took place at the Riverside Hotel in Branston. Clough told me, later, that he never once looked at him during the three hours they were together.

Nevertheless, hands were joined and a deal agreed.

Clough, foreseeing the next game against Liverpool, left Hardy saying, 'I'll be sitting alongside you next week, Mr Chairman, at Anfield.' He promised that he would be at the Baseball Ground the next day by 12.30 p.m. for lunch with the board.

Clough went home, played with his children, read a bedtime story to Libby and went to sleep, on his own admission, in a blissful state of intoxication.

He woke up the next morning with a hangover. It persisted all of the grey winter's morning. In the cold light of day and with a clearing head, the emotional pull to return was strong, but logic told him to be wary. He loved Derby, loved the people. But, overshadowing his strong desire were the spectres of Longson and Webb. Hardy had told him that he could not promise to deliver either head on a plate. And there was another depressing thought, equally daunting. Confronting him, yet again, was the enormous challenge of scrapping a team in order to build a new one. It would be his third rescue mission. He had already gone through the long labour pains of giving birth to a winning team at Nottingham Forest, which would be promoted the following season, he believed. Why should he fight old battles with Longson and Webb still in office when he was on the verge of producing another European Cup winning side? His decision was the more painful because he knew he was letting down the Movement, which had fought for his return over five years.

At the Baseball Ground, Hardy sat alone in the boardroom, nervously biting his fingernails and fiddling with his watch. Clough was now an hour overdue. Hardy could not eat lunch, conscious of the hovering TV cameras and reporters and the air of tension that had gripped the staff.

At 1.35 p.m. Clough got up from his settee in the living room and went out into the cold, damp garden. It lay in a pall of drabness, every plant and bush in mourning, echoing the melancholy in his soul. He remained there for some minutes and then went into the house to telephone Keeling with the instruction to take him to the Baseball Ground.

Clough saw the bevy of reporters and TV crews waiting for him. Even before the car had stopped he was besieged.

Grim-faced he stepped out to pointed cameras, boom microphones and a cacophony of shouted questions. He had to push his way through the crowd.

Inside the Baseball Ground there was Hardy, exhaling in deep relief, his hands held aloft. 'Thank God. I rang you fifteen minutes ago. I wondered if something had happened to you.'

'It has,' Clough said abruptly.

Hardy hesitated, his heart sinking.

'Let's go in your office,' Clough said. 'I've got some explaining to do.'

Hardy listened to Clough's caveat about Longson and Webb, his face grey and cold with anger. 'You bastard,' he said. 'You said nothing yesterday about them. We shook hands on it.'

'It wasn't me who shook hands. I was pissed.'

Hardy stared at him in incredulity.

'Here's how it is,' said Clough bluntly. 'You get rid of Longson and Webb. If you get rid of them I'm back.'

Hardy couldn't promise that. In desperation he made some phone calls and came back half an hour later with another offer: £30,000 a year for Clough and £20,000 for Taylor. Clough said he would go home and think about it, but he knew in his heart that no kind of monetary reward could give him what he wanted, a club he could run without having to cope with Longson still on board.

At 3 p.m. I took his telephone call. He thanked me for all I'd done and said he was turning down Hardy's offer. He said that, having toyed with the directors of Aston Villa, Sunderland, Barcelona and Teheran, he could not do the same with Derby. He could not string Hardy along any more, nor could he keep the fans in suspense.

'Sorry, Don. But I can't do it.'

I felt a pain in my throat. 'Okay,' was all I could manage. 'I understand.'

LIZ FELT WE owed Clough and family a meal. It was late October 1977 when they arrived for lunch on a bright day. After the meal Nigel, Simon and Martin played football, while Clough and I strolled to the top of the garden and looked out over the landscape towards Burnaston village, the ploughed fields reddish brown, with rooks circling over a solitary tree. It seemed like the end of a journey. He must have felt it too, by his silence. Then, divining my thoughts, he turned to me. 'Don, most fans aren't bloody maniacs like you are. They've got wives and bairns and they support the team, but they won't die for it. Anyway, you ought to know by now that no bugger goes out on strike in Derby. It's not Liverpool or the Yorkshire coalfield.'

He put up the collar of his overcoat against the cold easterly. Then he looked at me, sensing my mood. 'Eh.' He spoke gently. 'The game's not over till the whistle blows.'

I must have looked miserable because, gazing at me, he spoke softly, but firmly. 'Don't be downhearted. There's no point. Do what you can. Achieve what you can. But never be downhearted. Because you've tried. I've given players hell who've come off having scored a goal or two. Because they didn't try. They got lucky. But you have. You've bloody well tried. That's all that matters in this life.'

21

REQUIEM

THE THEME OF Greek tragedy is the danger of uncontrolled power corrupting the hero.

His weakness is called 'hamartia', a tragic flaw, demonstrated as an 'error of judgement'. This is seen as hubris or arrogance. He is a man who believes himself superior to most of his audience. He believes he can ignore, or outwit, fate. It leads to catastrophe.

Was Clough a true fallen hero, akin to that of classical tragedy? No, because he did not, in the end, meet with disaster. His life was more of a roller-coaster ride to the stars, his Achilles heel more like occasional attacks of tendonitis, en route. But he was truly heroic – and in more ways than one.

First, 'Old Big 'ead' was the people's hero. There are few today. Health and Safety and the well-meant but deeply flawed Human Rights Act – Clough said it should have been the Human Responsibilities Act – has produced a society in which the outspoken and the risk taker are viewed with caution.

I saw Clough leap up one day, spinning into orbit on reading that a council in the north of England had destroyed a line of fine horse chestnut trees because a boy had fallen from one, breaking his arm.

Clough reminded me of a multiplicity of heroic, as well as anti-heroic characters. There was something of Arthur Seaton about him, the abrasive and rebellious young working man in *Saturday Night and Sunday Morning*. He was also the embodiment of the 'Cheeky Chappie,' the brash Max Miller, of the music hall. He had the physical magnetism of Steve McQueen, and he could have been any one of the tough, intelligent and alert screen heroes of the war film and the Western. He 'talked the talk; and he 'walked the walk' of Robert Mitchum and John Wayne.

When we talk of the greatness of men, like Churchill, it is their vision at which we bow. Clough caught the imagination of people everywhere. The Greek waiter in Glyfada who mentioned his name did so with a knowing smile and a shake of the head. The director from Barcelona, black-bearded, balls of steel, a rich and hearty man, toasted Clough as he might a young bullfighter. '*Hombre Valiente*!'

Wherever Clough went he attracted a crowd. On the occasions I travelled with him to London he would open up conversations with people in the carriage as if he'd known them all his life. And when we stepped on to the platform at St Pancras he had a flock of worshippers swaggering with him to the barrier, Clough their unalloyed hero.

The man in the Midland Hotel, who had been slandered by Clough, swallowed his pride just to be able to recount the tale. And the FA committee listened, without protest, to Clough condemning them in their search for a diplomat instead of an England manager committed to winning matches, such as himself. For years the FA bosses dined out on the story, not realising that what they were really doing was boasting that they had interviewed 'Old Big 'ead'.

I was initially puzzled as to his motives in sending me out on risky ventures. There is a gene known as the 'fearless' one. When this combines with a 'master' gene the result is somebody filled with the desire and ruthlessness to get to the top on their own terms. Clough was masterful and fearless in everything he did. This combination created hubris in him beyond compare. It gave him tremendous strength as a football manager, but also led to him destroying his chances of being reunited with the team he loved. Each time he ruined a golden opportunity he felt obliged to offer a plan in its place, irrespective of whether it endangered him or not. Brian Clough, by any standard, was irrevocably, and helplessly, cast at birth as a control freak, but with a conscience.

Clough felt invulnerable because he knew that the world held him in awe. That is why he could launch his slanderous attacks and suffer no consequences. The man in the Midland Hotel was reduced by Clough to a grinning shambles. There was no anger shown and no demand for an apology. And it was clear from Clough's smile of satisfaction, as he turned away, that the act had been performed for my delectation, as a stage magician might charm his audience. Lesser mortals doing the same, might have expected a smack in the face. Not Clough. He knew that the pedestal on which he stood was high enough to be out of the range of brickbats.

AS ENGLISHMEN WERE eager to tell of how they'd touched the cloak or hand of Lord Nelson – and spoke of it with pride – so do men today talk of their encounters with Clough. He was not just the 'People's Hero' but had jumped from the world of English football across the bounds of nationality. '*Hombre Valiente*! *Hero Ulysses*! *Vive Napoléon*!'

I never think of Clough as suffering from megalomania, but its dividing line from self-aggrandisement is very close. His reference to Generals Wingate, on the British side, and Patton, on the American, was significant in that their insistence on self-belief, allied to their strong feeling of destiny, was central to their military philosophy, as it was in his approach to football management. His courage was unquestionable. His statement, 'If I'd been a Spitfire pilot I'd have taken on a squadron of Messerschmitts,' could easily be dismissed as 'Old Big 'ead' bragging. But to have been in his presence when he spoke those words was not to induce intense scepticism, but to accept it, such was the matter-of-fact way in which he made the claim. His oft quoted remark 'I like to go home at night, lock the door and take the phone off the hook' did not indicate paranoia. It was the remark of a man who ruffled feathers as a daily occurrence and was aware of his many critics. He would put the phone back on the hook in the morning and go out just as he always did, his arrogance and brutal honesty melding together, ruffling even more feathers.

Clough's war was an unavoidable conflict between a man obsessed with great ambition and the directors of a limited company with necessary rules and codes of behaviour that constrained him. It could not have been otherwise. The only way forward would have been by the board succumbing to become a mere cipher. It was by some sort of miracle that Clough lasted seven years as manager of Derby County. There was only one English club that Clough could have led without friction – Nottingham Forest, run by a committee. The supreme irony was that no one, least Clough, was to know that Forest would become the place where he would flourish simply because the committee, without a powerful chairman, were afraid of him to the point of obeying his every command.

Brian Clough was supreme in man management where it mattered, with the team. His extraordinary feat in wielding a Derby squad of only thirteen players to seize the Championship will, almost certainly, never be repeated. The young players, vulnerable to Clough's powers – some of which he claimed as mystic – played as a superb team because he told them they were the best. All they had to do was respond accordingly, filled to the brim as they were with his amazing and unfailing self-belief. He may not have been a hypnotist in the true meaning of the word, but when he talked and eyeballed his players he gripped them to the point of complete surrender. I know, because I was gripped, too.

On grounds of statistics alone his achievements cannot be attributed to luck or seen as 'winged' in a haphazard manner. He took a mediocre Derby team in the Second Division to the League championship, a team which would have seized the European Cup had they not been cheated.

Then, to prove his genius, he went on to take an equally mediocre side, Nottingham Forest, also into the First Division and then on to win two European Cups in successive seasons. No other manager, either in Britain or Europe, has achieved that amazing feat. His other achievement, in exposing cheats and condemning 'dirty' play, should earn him in posterity the gratitude of fans everywhere.

I am prey to emotion at witnessing any great sporting achievement. Bob Champion, riding Aldiniti to the finishing post in the 1981 Grand National, he having fought a deadly cancer, had me gushing tears. Tony Jacklin winning the American Open had me sniffing. The run of Manchester United's scratch side in the FA Cup following the Munich air crash had me fervently willing them on. Clough, winning the First Division Championship with Derby, had me joining a cavalcade in the street hooting my car horn, my eyes prickling in joy. And when Nottingham Forest won their first European Cup a lump came to my throat, not for Clough and his team, but for what could have been at Derby.

As he managed Nottingham Forest, complete lord of all he surveyed, I noticed a change in him over the years. He looked increasingly depressed. His natural wit had deserted him. In November 1982 Taylor had left him for retirement, and gone with him was the fun which had come from Taylor's droll observations, the kind that had kept Clough so amused, even in stitches. Footballers enjoy a good laugh, but the Forest team laughed little as they caught his depression. It made for irony.

The arsenal of weapons by which he motivated his Derby players was now reduced to one: fear. It still worked, bringing the results he wanted, but he was not enjoying life, as he had at Derby.

I was surprised when he told me this. 'What about all the conflicts with Webb and Longson? That wasn't fun.'

'I'm talking about the team and me,' he replied. 'When I was with them I forgot those people. They were a fabulous bunch of players. I'll never forget them.'

In the world of football the chance of another Clough arising is nil. The ubiquitous and all powerful player's agent of today would have prevented him from hypnotising or press-ganging any player into signing. Today, the top teams with their foreign legion of players, awash with riches, would not have had the club structure so favourable to Clough as at Nottingham Forest. The power base of any Premiership club may not even lie in England, rather in some tax haven such as Panama.

As Mike Hawthorn, the first British world champion in Grand Prix motor racing, was the last of the great amateur drivers, so Clough was the last great football manager who, literally, did it 'his way'.

The alcoholism which accelerated Clough's physical and mental decline, started around the time when Liz, Martin and I were invited for breakfast in October '73. His love for champagne became an addiction, not helped by him winning flagons of the stuff as Manager of the Month. Typical of alcoholics, he refused to admit it. He cited George Best in his defence. 'Why is he always called an alcoholic when we should regard him as the genius he is?'

Kevin Lloyd, well known for his character as Tosh in the TV series, *The Bill,* told me a story, which Clough later repeated to me not knowing that I'd heard it originally from Lloyd. Although outwardly the same, both stories demonstrate how alcoholics will deceive themselves and others.

It was a Sunday evening at Derby Playhouse and Lloyd was to introduce Clough to a paying audience for a Question and Answer session. Lloyd said that Clough had entered his dressing room with a bottle, drawn the curtains, locked the door and poured out two tumblers of whisky. 'He couldn't face an audience without it,' Lloyd said. 'He forced me to drink with him.'

Clough's version was that Lloyd had entered *his* dressing room with a bottle, drawn the curtains, locked the door and forced *him* to drink. The tragic irony becomes even sadder. Unbeknown to each other, both men had spent time in rehab at the Dove Clinic in Rolleston on Dove. Lloyd died of asphyxia due to alcoholic poisoning. Clough's excessive drinking probably contributed to his death from stomach cancer.

In my last meeting with him, his face worn and scarred by years of drinking, he said he knew why fans became obsessed by football. But he could never have been one, he told me. 'I couldn't stand players living off my hard-earned wages and them not giving a hundred per cent.' And how was it, he asked, that I used to support Derby in the abysmal Third Division North, standing in the snow on Boxing Day watching the Rams play the likes of Crewe Alexandra?

I told him that a lot of the fun was in being part of a down-trodden army that lived on its humour, listening to wags on the terraces, cracking jokes.

'I don't get it,' he said. 'I'd stay at home. Keep warm.'

I persisted. 'It was a kind of a club on the terraces. There were only a few round you. You knew everybody and you enjoyed the laughs.'

At that he nodded in understanding and a hint of sadness. 'The laughs. Yes, that would have been worth it. Yes. Worth a lot.'

A year before he died, Wenda Williams, a mutual friend, was in the Quarndon village stores and encountered him following his recovery from a liver transplant. Remembering that she was a close friend of my wife Liz, he asked how she was. He grabbed a large box of chocolates off the shelf, paid for it and handed it to Wenda. 'Give it to Liz with my love.' Wenda was going out of the shop when he turned and pointed at her severely. 'Eh. And don't pinch one.'

Clough sought money as the key to security, having been born into a working-class family in the latter years of the Great Depression. He could easily have become miserly. He was the opposite.

On the car journey to the Walsall football ground he had stopped the car and got out to accost a small boy, standing by a lamp-post, pale and shivering. Clough opened his wallet and stuffed paper money into the boy's hand. 'Take it home. Go on. And get warm. Eh. And get some chips. Warm you up.'

He did not always cosset his pride, especially where women were concerned. Once, in a restaurant, his voice annoyed a customer so much that she picked out a lobster from the water tank and placed it in his lap. He replaced it in the tank, kissed the woman on the cheek and said he'd never been so grabbed by a lady. She laughed as much as anyone. He gave her an apology and thereafter lowered his voice.

I am left with an abiding sense of loss in terms of what Derby County would have been had he not resigned, a decision he regretted for the rest of his life. The mistakes – to echo his favourite Sinatra song, he 'made a few' – regardless of motive, depress me whenever I think about them. The simple act of him walking around the perimeter track, for example, at the home game against Leicester would have changed things, I'm sure. His restaurant invasion and dismissal of a team about to strike, was a sad fiasco. The 'Tommy

Mason' debacle and the Brighton phone call still twinge inside me whenever I think of them. But, the cause was Clough, himself.

I'm sure that if a fiery Billy Bremner had been Derby's captain the players would have gone on strike and their power would have brought him back, the same power that saw him dismissed at Leeds. Ironically, it was that very decency and obedience to authority that Clough insisted upon in his players that prevented them from coming to his aid.

The Derby fans could have done more to save him. We only had 800 signed-up members of the Protest Movement. Maybe the majority were too concerned with their own lives to take up the cudgels on behalf of a football manager. Maybe they did not care enough, or failed to realise his genius.

CLOUGH WAS A great man. He was true to things that mattered, that were basic to human decency. His entertainment value was immense, his sense of values impeccable.

He will live on in sporting folklore. His legend, to echo Michael Parkinson, is that of a 'pickle of a man', exciting, annoying, frustrating, inspiring, fiery, egotistical, hectoring, intuitive, emotional, perceptive and charismatic. So complex, that explaining him fully is ultimately impossible. Hadn't Barbara Clough once said that even she didn't know where his soul resided?

Ranging from the ruthless and the cavalier to a purveyor of good deeds and with a massive generosity of spirit, he left his mark on the game of football as no man before him. Allied to this spirit was an instinct that gave him both insight and foresight, as well as an unnerving self-confidence. The word 'clairvoyant' means clear sighted. That, too, was part of the magical mix, a symbiosis beyond the reach of any analysis or divination. You can't bottle genius.

On his retirement from the game Clough said, 'I want no epitaphs of profound history and that type of thing. Just that I contributed.'

A statue of him now stands in the City of Nottingham. A similar statue is planned for Derby.

On his death a bright local luminary, ruminating on how best to commemorate him as bringer of success to both cities, suggested that a major dual carriageway should provide a living epitaph. It would be seen daily by thousands, many of them Nottingham Forest and Derby County fans. It was fitting that the A52 was chosen as that memorial. As you leave either place bound for the other the sign clearly states that you are travelling on the Brian Clough Way. It's a route he travelled every working day from Derby to Nottingham for eighteen years and back again in the evening. It would have given him great pleasure to see that sign. Old Big 'ead's head would have got bigger and Peter Taylor would have been very jealous and ribbed him mercilessly about it.

IN 1975, when Clough became manager of Nottingham Forest, he invited me, Liz and Martin to see his first game in charge. It was the Nottinghamshire Cup Final against Notts County. Forest lost 0–1. Afterwards I said, 'Brian, you've got a hell of a job on here.' He replied. 'It's not a job. It's a major civil engineering contract.'

On 25 September 1982 the Baseball Ground presented a dismal scene, a cold and wet day. Derby County was bottom of the Second Division with only eight points from thirteen matches. There were fewer than 9,000 spectators as the Rams lost to Blackburn Rovers 1–2. The players seemed tired as they came off. Looking on was Longson who was still at the helm, his grumpy, shrivelled face reflecting the general mood. Even in the dark days of Third Division North in the fifties the manager, Harry Storer, taught his team to play football as it should be played, with quick accurate passing, wing play and sharp breaks at goal. It seemed now that nobody cared. Longson went back to the boardroom to suggest they enticed Peter Taylor back as manager. 'He was the brains behind Clough, wasn't he? Clough was all puff. Taylor did more than Clough,' Longson continued. 'He sourced the players.'

On 17 November 1982 Peter Taylor returned to Derby County as manager.

On 8 January 1983 Clough brought his Forest team to Derby

to compete in the FA Cup. This dream draw was billed as 'Clough v Taylor'. It was a classic. Gemmill, of Derby, shot home a free kick from outside the penalty area and Andy Hill raced on to a through-ball from Mike Brolly to give the Rams an epic victory. Clough accused his centre half of having taken a bribe from Peter Taylor. It is not known if it was meant as a joke, a la the Juventus incident.

I never found out the identity of the mole. I still harbour a suspicion that it was Taylor, but without proof I choose to exonerate him. I'm grateful for the six years he spent at Derby.

Peter Taylor resigned as manager of Derby County in April 1984, with Derby third from the bottom of the Second Division.

He died six years later at the age of sixty-two in 1990 while on holiday in Majorca.

In 2009, Nigel, the little boy who fed the rabbits with Martin, became manager of Derby County.

On 20 September 2004 Brian Clough died.

There are many amusing epitaphs for the greatest manager of them all.

I prefer to quote him:

*'Derby played perfect football on a perfect pitch,
all in the Arsenal half'*

Brian Clough. R.I.P

acknowledgements

I would like to thank all the fans of Derby County, especially Kalwinder Singh Dhindsa, who were more than helpful in contributing anecdotes featuring their legendary hero.

I was much encouraged by my sons Andy and Martin as well as daughter Jane for their enthusiasm ahead of the project, in particularly Martin, whose childhood memories of Clough remain crystal clear, so much so that he corrected me in one important detail, as did my friend, Ken Goodwin. My thanks to my wife Liz, too, for reminding me of a vital episode in the story.

I owe a special debt of gratitude to the sports writer Neil Hallam and commentator Mike Ingham. I also thank numerous sports writers who helped me in various ways, including Gerald Mortimer, George Edwards, Barry Ecclestone and Mike Carey. They kept me informed of details of the Clough–board conflict as it took place, or in its aftermath.

Thanks must go posthumously to Lionel Pickering, who helped me in the Protest Movement while owner of the *Derby Trader*, and for the information he supplied while chairman, later, of Derby County FC – and to Innes Lloyd, the famed BBC TV producer, who has a place in my heart for his battle to bring my screenplay about Clough, *Boss,* to the BBC screen, but who died from cancer while attempting it. He too, indirectly, played a part in bringing this book to fruition.

My gratitude also goes to John Newman, manager of Derby County in 1982. I am, too, grateful to Roy McFarland who followed him as manager in 1993. I wish him well in his projected autobiography.

Finally, but most importantly, I owe a debt of gratitude to Andrew Goodfellow at Ebury Publishing for his immediate grasp of how the book should 'look' and for his ongoing encouragement and support.